# Diary of a Kidnapped Colombian Governor

# Diary of a Kidnapped Colombian Governor

A JOURNEY TOWARD NONVIOLENT TRANSFORMATION

Guillermo Gaviria Correa

*Translated from the Spanish by*
**Hugo Zorrilla and Norma Zorrilla**

*Edited by*
**James F. S. Amstutz** *with*
Assistant Editors Andres Zorrilla and Rebecca Thatcher Murcia

*Foreword by*
**William Ospina**

**DreamSeeker Books**
TELFORD, PENNSYLVANIA

*an imprint of*
Cascadia Publishing House

*Copublished with*
Herald Press
Scottdale, Pennsylvania *and*
Center for Global Nonkilling
Honolulu, Hawaii

Cascadia Publishing House orders, information, reprint permissions:
contact@CascadiaPublishingHouse.com
1-215-723-9125
126 Klingerman Road, Telford PA 18969
www.CascadiaPublishingHouse.com

*Diary of a Kidnapped Colombian Governor*
Copyright © 2010 by Yolanda Pinto de Gaviria
This English edition is based on a translation of the Spanish edition, also Copyright © 2005 by Yolanda Pinto de Gaviria and Revista Numero Ediciones
DreamSeeker Books is an imprint of Cascadia Publishing House
Copublished with Herald Press and Center for Global Nonkilling
Library of Congress Catalog Number: 2009053840
**ISBN 13:** 978-1-931038-72-0; **ISBN 10:** 1-931038-72-4
Book design by Cascadia Publishing House
Cover design by Merrill R. Miller

The paper used in this publication is recycled and meets the minimum requirements of American National Standard for Information Sciences—Permanence of Paper for Printed Library Materials, ANSI Z39.48-1984.1984

All Bible quotations are translations from the Spanish.

**Library of Congress Cataloguing-in-Publication Data**

Gaviria Correa, Guillermo, 1962-2003.
 [Diario de un gobernador secuestrado. English]
 Diary of a kidnapped Colombian governor : a journey toward nonviolent transformation / Guillermo Gaviria Correa ; translated from the Spanish by Hugo Zorrilla and Norma Zorrilla ; edited by by James F.S. Amstutz with assistant editors Andres Zorrilla and Rebecca Thatcher Murcia ; foreword by William Ospina.
 p. cm.
 Summary: "Guillermo Gaviria Correa was governor of Colombia's state of Antioquia until he was taken hostage in 2002 and killed in 2003. This is his diary recording daily events and thoughts on nonviolence while in captivity." [summary]--Provided by publisher.
 ISBN-13: 978-1-931038-72-0 (6 x 9" trade pbk. : alk. paper)
 ISBN-10: 1-931038-72-4 (6 x 9" trade pbk. : alk. paper)
 1. Gaviria Correa, Guillermo, 1962-2003--Kidnapping, 2002. 2. Gaviria Correa, Guillermo, 1962-2003--Diaries. 3. Kidnapping victims--Colombia--Diaries. 4. Governors--Colombia--Antioquia (Dept.)--Diaries. 5. Kidnapping--Colombia. 6. Political violence--Colombia. I. Title.
 HV6604.C72G3813 2010
 364.15'4092--dc22
 [B]
                    2009053840

16 15 14 13 12 11 10     10 9 8 7 6 5 4 3 2 1

*To Senator Yolanda Pinto de Gaviria*

# CONTENTS

*Foreword by William Ospina* 9
*Editor's Preface* 11
*Introduction by Yolanda Pinto de Gaviria* 13

### Part I • 19
Delivered to Yolanda Pinto de Gaviria by the FARC by way of the Office of the Defender of the People of Antioquia on December 12, 2002.

### Part II • 95
Recovered by the Authorities and given by the Attorney General of Human Rights to Yolanda Pinto de Gaviria, widow of Guillermo Gaviria Correa in March 2005

### Part III • 109
Retrieved by the Army on the day of the death of Guillermo Gaviria Correa and given to his wife by the Public Prosecutor of Antioquia, one week after the failed rescue attempt.

### Part IV • 163
Recovered in the rescue operation by the Attorney General's office and given to Yolanda Pinto de Gaviria on May 3, 2003, by the Director of Fiscal Affairs of Antioquia.

### Part V • 225
Letters to Family and Friends.

*The Editor* 281
*The Author* 282

# FOREWORD: THE MALAISE OF COLOMBIA

This book—intense, sincere, painful, and deeply human—is full of malaise. A disposition that goes beyond the circumstances of him who writes it; a malaise infecting the beautiful nature through which it flows, filling with anxiety the silvery waters under the moon; filling with unrest the vision of the mountains under the sun; making every act of life as discreet and imperceptible as it might be, a dramatic act.

This malaise is captivity, the loss of liberty. If it were not for that, this would be a pleasant book of adventures: the daily fishing of shad in the rivers, evening horse rides, the coming of fireflies in the camps, the leaping of the monkeys in the branches, the sinuous advance of the snakes, the rain on the forests, the dialogue of some men in the night, their readings in the nature's neighborhood. All these elements of paradise are saturated with horror, however; a horror at times un-confessed but always implied. This paradise cannot be a paradise under the threat of guns, under the vigilance of the captors.

Nothing like the diary of someone kidnapped moves us closer to the way we Colombians live this splendid nature. A long time ago our country lost the sweetness that today is only fully enjoyed in the poems and old songs. A fear, a deep anxiety controls things; a helplessness fills the forests and ravines; a human discord has established its reign in the heart of this world.

The fact that he who suffers captivity and describes it is a governor, one of the most noble and committed persons we have had in these lands, only gives a tint to this fundamental fact. It makes us face a tragedy that the lands of one who dreamed of being governor are gradually converted into his prison and into his gallows. But his drama is, in the first place, the drama of thousands of persons pulled from their families and their routine, converted into expiatory symbols of social discord; and his drama is in depth the drama experienced by thousands of prisoners piled in jails, by thousands of displaced persons carrying their signs at stoplights, by millions of hungry beings who shiver in city slums.

This book is a living and vibrant testimony of that malaise Colombia suffers, where the opulence of a few each time is less able to be hidden from the helplessness and uncertainty of millions, and where the lack of responsibility and of commitment by the ruling class, infinitely inferior to their historic duties, corrupted by arrogance and insensitivity, throws some sectors into helplessness, some into criminality, and others into a cold and blind resentment.

Governor Guillermo Gaviria Correa, committed to the point of heroism with his generous ideal of nonviolence, was a victim of one side and the other. Of the arrogance and indifference of his own social class; of the indolence of those who govern and ordered a rescue operation knowing the immense risk being taken; of the violence of the guerillas toward those who did not seem to be persons with their own face and thoughts, with their will and their convictions, but only defenseless pieces of an implacable game of chess.

Each one of those who made him a victim will accuse the other side, and will deny his own responsibility of this fact. But Colombia will only find its way when we realize that what kills so many Colombians is this shared incapacity to build a country. A society where there is space for more persons, more ideas, and more hues than what has been to date.

Estanislao Zuleta often repeated that "Perversion is a country's lack of desire, crime is a country's lack of action, and insanity is a country's lack of imagination." As long as we do not build this country, generous and directed by desire; able to open legal opportunities for initiatives which otherwise end up being derailed; and able to offer the imagination of a horizon different from the current delirium and the insanity, we will continue living in the anxiety in each tree, the fear in each solitary traveler, and the ghost in each night that falls over the mountains.

War, jail, and asylum, which in other countries are the answer to extreme cases, among us tend to devour society because they are seen as vast and definitive solutions. War, jail, and asylum cannot be the programs of the government: they are the answer of those who have no solutions.

Governor Gaviria: I see you reading the *Divine Comedy* with lucidity and with admiration in the painful hours of your captivity. I see you accompanied by that noble and valiant man, Gilberto Echeverri, bravely and firmly facing this hell that we have woven, paradoxically with the rivers, trees, and stars of paradise. I see both of you as the characters of that book descending the staircase of that hell and trying to imagine, while doing so, how to build stairs that will lead to light and peace.

You could not have known that in the end light and liberty and the warmth of love were not awaiting you but the hour of blindness and violence, that the unresolved discord in Colombia would forcefully break your lives and would put out another light on our way.

"Like that captain of Purgatory/ who fleeing on foot and bloodying the plain/ was surrounded and knocked down by death/ where an obscure river loses its name"—thus you both fell, victims of the incapacity of Colombia to respect itself.

May the generosity of your example accompany us. May beyond this horizon of spiteful wars (this is a prayer) that beyond this insane idea that violence can be a solution, one day we will remember both of you and all those who die dreaming of a better country, and to all those who suffered the malaise of our history, and with relief tell them, as the verse from Pablo Neruda: "Light came despite the daggers."

—*William Ospina*
 *Colombian poet and essayist*

# EDITOR'S PREFACE

In *Nonkilling Global Political Science* (Xlibris, 2002; CGNK, 2009), Dr. Glenn Paige keeps asking, "Is a nonkilling global society possible?" In many parts of the world, some are answering "Yes." One of those brave souls was Governor Guillermo Gaviria Correa in the Department of Antioquia, Colombia. Not many of his political stature have been willing to take the risk of embracing nonviolence as a political strategy. Inspired by Jesus, Gandhi, and Martin Luther King Jr., Governor Gaviria incarnated the nonkilling spirit.

The first Global Nonkilling Leadership Forum was held November 1-4, 2007, in Honolulu, Hawaii, and hosted by Dr. Paige. There I had the privilege of meeting Senator Yolanda Pinto de Gaviria, the late governor's widow. Firsthand accounts were given of the five day march for nonviolence in Antioquia, the governor's capture by the FARC, and his year-long saga in the jungles of Colombia. These stories were a sobering reminder of the risks involved when moving from nonviolent theory to praxis.

Gaviria's death during a failed rescue attempt brought an untimely end to his efforts of nonviolent transformation. Many in Colombia said this proved it would not work as a political strategy. Dr. Bernard LaFayette Jr., a colleague of Martin Luther King Jr., and a foremost trainer and scholar of nonviolence, accompanied Governor Gaviria on the march. He too was captured by the FARC but released within eight hours. He articulated the radical transcendence of those committed to nonviolence when faced with their own mortality, "The biggest concern is, will the work continue?" The ultimate goal of nonviolence is to end the killing, not self-preservation.

The Anabaptist-Mennonite theological stream in which I live and work finds many points of convergence and affinity in the governor's story and sacrifice. Thanks to the generosity of Akron Mennonite Church and the excellent translating abilities of two members of our congregation, Dr. Hugo and Norma Zorrilla, we were able to move ahead with the project. Michael A. King at Cascadia Publishing House LLC also caught the vision of how compelling this story is. He not only helped bring it to light but also provided valuable coaching as we wrestled with the inevitable translation and editing nuances involve with such a project. These included a tendency to edit more lightly than we otherwise might have plus allowing some latitude for the English syntax to maintain its Spanish tendencies, given the governor's inability to respond; and the decision throughout the diary to render in Spanish the frequent term of endearment *mi vida*, which fits Spanish usage well but is less familiar to an English reader when translated as "my life." We also often chose "fighters" instead of "guerillas" to distinguish between the individuals who guarded the governor and the FARC organization.

*Diary of a Kidnapped Colombian Governor* invites the reader to dwell in the liminality of captivity. Through the governor's eyes we see the day to day existence of the disappeared. Through his ears we hear the lament of fellow captives and the deep longing for words of hope. Through his words we speak an abiding faith of one committed to a higher calling and purpose. Through his suffering and death we count the cost of our convictions to strive for a nonkilling global society. *Will the work continue?*

—*James F. S. Amstutz, D.Min. Akron, Pennsylvania*
*Pastor, Akron Mennonite Church and Author,* Threatened with Resurrection

# INTRODUCTION:
# THE DIARY OF MY HUSBAND

This book contains the diary and some of the letters written by my husband Guillermo Gaviria Correa during the long year and fifteen days of his kidnapping, while he was the State Governor of Antioquia, Colombia.

Guillermo Gaviria Correa was kidnapped by Front 34 of the guerrilla group of the FARC on April 21, 2002, on the fifth day of the march for nonviolence and solidarity with the municipality of Caicedo, which he planned and led. He was sacrificed by his captors in a failed rescue operation by the military forces of Colombia on May 5, 2003. Also kidnapped with him were Dr. Gilberto Echeverri Mejía, Peace Commissioner of Antioquia; Lieutenants Alejandro Ledesma Ortiz, and Wagner Tapias Torres; Sergeants Pedro J. Guarnizo, Héctor Lucuara S., Heriberto Aranguren, Franscisco Manuel Negrete, Yercinio Navarrete S., and Samuel Ernesto Cote Cote; Corporals Agenor E. Viellard, Mario Alberto Marín, and José Gregorio Peña. Of them only the sub-officials Pedro J. Guarnizo, Heriberto Aranguren, and Agenor E. Viellard survived.

I have wanted to publish and share with you the diary and some letters because, as Guillermo writes: "To try to alleviate this absence I daily write a little summary that I'm sending to you with topics that are conveyed through the news, the reflections and some scattered thoughts that I've had."

I trust that this document may offer us a good opportunity to reflect about kidnapping, the need to work to combat it, and the urgency to find ways of understanding that permit us to obtain the liberty of all those kidnapped.

This book is published thanks to the selfless help of a group of professionals and very special and loving personal friends of my husband. They contributed in selfless ways with economic support for its publication. I appreciate it infinitely.

The writer William Ospina accepted the responsibility of writing the foreword because of the friendship that united him with Guillermo and the knowledge he has of Guillermo's convictions about nonviolence. Thank you, William, thank you so much.

I thank the magazine *Número*, Guillermo González Uribe, and Ana Cristina Mejía for the enthusiasm they had from the first moment they had in their hands the original manuscript and the sentiment with which they worked to attain these results.

The originals of these writings rest in my power and in the hands of each one of the recipients of the different letters, to whom I am indebted for authorizing their publication.

—*Yolanda Pinto de Gaviria*

# NOTE FROM THE TRANSLATION/EDITING TEAM

Dr. Hugo (PhD) and Norma Zorrilla (MA, TESOL) translated the book from Spanish to English. Hugo is a native of Colombia and brings years of translating experience to this labor of love. Together with Norma, a native of the U.S. and teacher of English as a second language, they sought a balance between the original wording and syntax and the spirit intended. Their son Andrés Zorrilla (MA, Theology) provided a valuable bicultural perspective to the English text. Andres taught Spanish at Fresno Pacific University and currently does freelance Spanish interpreting. Rev. Dr. James F. S. Amstutz (DMin) had the privilege of meeting Yolanda Pinto de Gaviria at the first Global Nonkilling Leadership Forum in Honolulu, Hawaii in 2007, and added his editing skills to the effort. Rebecca Thatcher Murcia, an author and widow of Colombian Mennonite Saul Murcia, assisted with editing Part IV.

Our thanks to Akron Mennonite Church, Akron, Pennsylvania, and to the Center For Global Nonkilling for underwriting some of the expenses. We take responsibility for any wording or interpretation that may miss the mark. It was a privilege to play a small part in bringing this witness to the way of nonviolence to English readers.

# PART I
## DELIVERED TO YOLANDA PINTO DE GAVIRIA BY THE FARC BY WAY OF THE OFFICE OF THE DEFENDER OF THE PEOPLE OF ANTIOQUIA ON DECEMBER 12, 2002

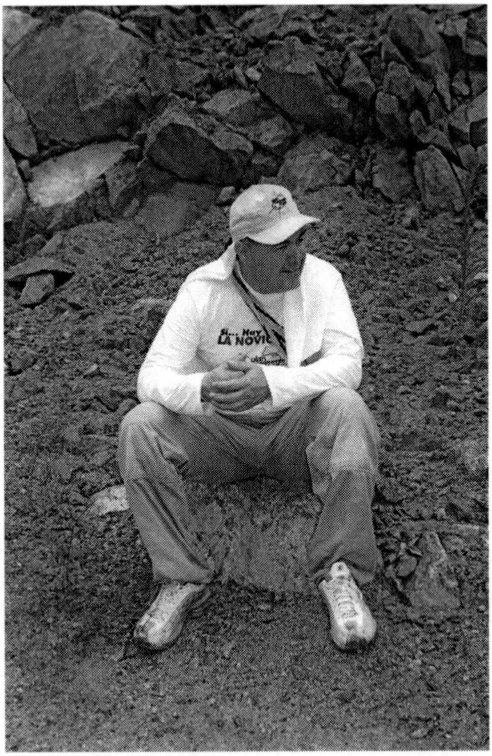

# 2002

**Monday, April 22:** The noise on the radio woke us up with the news about the kidnapping and the reactions of different people. I confess that I see the good will of those who cry out for our liberation, but sadly they do it in ways that do not put into practice nonviolence. I would have been very pleased to hear the language begin to be transformed; this should be the first step. Nevertheless, I am greatly comforted to hear the voice of Father Yépez; he indeed shares my message, and he lets that be seen in his words.

Yesterday I recited the rosary. It helped me a great deal. I had a long conversation with the young fighters about nonviolence. I hope I can repeat it with their leaders here in this region and with the secretariat. I'm sorry I did not give instructions to Father Yépez before he was separated, but everything was so quick and the hard journey of the night did not permit it, just as the overwhelming situation that produced our present circumstances. I'm sad that I could not write my adorable Yolanda. I suffer for her pain and anxiety, although I know that her strength will impel her to continue the struggle. Today's rosary also strengthens and comforts me.

Also, I am reading the Word of God. I see how true the words of Father Yépez are. The Lord our God acts in mysterious ways. I am eager to hear your message: speak to me, Lord. I will be your servant; I want to be your servant. I began in the fifth chapter of Matthew, the Beatitudes, verse 38, "eye for an eye," it explains the new justice, and it calls for turning of the other cheek, the essence of nonviolence.

Gilberto [Echeverri Mejía] is the ideal person for this journey, but it saddens me to know that he is here because of me and his family, especially Martha Inés, suffers because of his captivity. He has not lost, not even for a second, his composure and his sense of humor. He already baptized one of the men "Rascal," the name he chose with clairvoyance.

We have listened to the stories of some of the fighters, their difficulties, and how finally some of them came to the fighters. I think of the coffee crisis and how the hard circumstances of the rural areas are contributing to the fact that they find no other solution. Then routine and the status quo are making it so that violence, with its vicious circle, diminishes them with more force, and every day gives them more reasons to favor violence. With more conviction I see that only the will of God and nonviolence can help, so together we can build a way of reconciliation and peace.

My heart fills with sadness imagining the suffering of my loved ones. That is the only time sadness overcomes me. I weep imagining my mother, Daniel, Matthew [sons of Guillermo Gaviria Correa], and Yolanda [wife of Guillermo Gaviria Correa]. I know that my brothers and my father know best how to manage this absence.

**Saturday, April 27**: We have moved from camp 1 and have traveled on the back of a mule for ten hours without stopping. The distance seems a lot like the descriptions that Humboldt[1] and other foreign travelers made of their journeys. In the morning we arrived at a clearing to shortly go into the jungle, which seemed it would be our permanent place. The fighters prepared with great skill a "cove" for Gilberto and me and built a kitchen; the second day they cleared the place and each one built their own cove.

**Sunday, April 28**: We completed eight days of being retained. We think intensely of our families. We talk about issues of the province and of the country. We emphasize the need for a profound reform in the system of education. I believe such reform is urgent and must be grounded in an appropriate educational system. We hear on the news how violence is increasing, as well as Montoya's second-place finish in the Formula One race in Barcelona.

The statements of Yolanda fill us with emotions, especially me; they make me very proud. The chief of the squad is not here, we anxiously await his return. Each time he leaves, he returns with a decision. We hope the possibility to speak with the commanders may be open. We listen to Diana Uribe speak about the influence of the

French revolution on the kingdom of Spain, the naming of the brother of Napoleón in Spain, and the defeat at the hands of the English at Waterloo, and how Goya, in his paintings, showed the violence suffered by the Spanish people.

We are doing physical exercises daily, and today there's the possibility of fishing, and now with fish hooks. Little by little we are learning to manage and put up with this jungle, despite the permanent monotony of the rain.

**Monday, April 29**: Today is a happy day. We listened to messages from Lina and Camila [daughter and granddaughter of Guillermo Echeverri] and my loving Yolanda. They made us weep, but with joy. We hope this is repeated. Each time, Yolanda makes me feel more proud.

I have some blotches where my wedding ring goes, so I have changed it to the left hand. I hope I get over them soon.

**Tuesday, April 30**: Today, very early, we listened to a beautiful message for Gilberto; Yolanda did not send a message, or if she sent one, we did not hear it. It has been raining constantly. We have asked if we could carry the message of nonviolence to the commanders, but the request has been unsuccessful.

We have already learned of my being named president of a worldwide movement of nonviolence; however we do not know for certain what it is and neither does it appear to signify anything to the FARC [Revolutionary Armed Forces of Colombia].

The commander returned and today four fighters left—the couple and a female fighter who appears to have malaria, accompanied by a male fighter. It seems to me a grave error of the FARC to have us here rather than to listen to our ideas. What we want to communicate does not come from our situation of captivity; on the contrary, our desire to take this message has us in this situation. I fear that all our effort and the capacity of the government that I desire to put in the service of social transformation will be lost if the FARC does not listen to us. Time passes so slowly and the rain does not permit us to do anything.

I think of my dear brothers and sisters; of Matthew, Daniel, and of Yolanda all the time. I hope my absence has not caused too much anxiety for my mother and my father. So much sadness and pain only can be justified if we succeed in making the message of nonviolence effective. A miracle is necessary. Father Yépez should help.

We do not believe it is possible that the national government would be interested in us. The help should come from the nonviolent demonstrations of the people. We have asked that they let us send a cassette tape to our families and a letter, at least, to the headquarters of the FARC.

We have heard many flights, some of helicopters; it seems to be that of PAS [Air Program of Health] which have been coming to take care of the emergency of Murrí.

**Thursday, May 2**: We were building a bench and a little table; today I'm using them for the first time to write these lines. Today we heard the messages of Martha Inés [wife of Gilberto Echeverri], Lina and Yolanda; those are truly happy moments. Thanks for informing us and maintaining our enthusiasm.

Gilberto asks about Mono [son of Gilberto Echeverri] and I ask about Matthew. My mother should now be returning. How is she doing.... We heard on the radio that fifteen European countries declared the AUC [United Self-Defense Forces of Colombia] to be terrorists, but these countries do not agree to treat them the same as the FARC; this indicates what they think about this guerrilla group. Also we heard that the governors of the country have made an appeal to the FARC, but the communication was not read.

Today we have not heard any flights. I ask myself how the emergency at Vigía del Fuerte is been taking care of. Also we heard about the Arboletes volcano. We are both pleased that they are concentrating (in the government offices) on the Comprehensive and Nonviolent Peace Plan, but I hope they do not fail to take care of infant malnutrition, low income housing, and reforestation.

**Friday, May 3:** Today we both received marvelous messages from our loved ones: Gilberto from Martha Inés, Lina, and Camila; and me from Yolanda and Aníbal [Guillermo Gaviria Correa's brother]. I'm pleased that they remember us in their prayers and ask God for our return and to allow the FARC to understand our message of nonviolence.

Everything seems to indicate that the authorization of letters and conversations with the commanders is going to be delayed. Today on the news we heard of clashes between the FARC and the AUC in the State of Chocó, near Vigía del Fuerte (Antioquia). Today the news was a little clearer about the pronouncement of the European Union concerning the FARC.

My perception continues being that Pastrana [president of Colombia] never opened a real possibility for dialogue and accord, and once those conversations in Stockholm were frustrated, he lost even more interest in the demilitarized zone and the dialogues with the FARC. If the president was never willing to listen to governors and mayors and the Colombian society, I ask myself how much he really listened to the FARC.

Coincidently, Anibal read the gospel text of the Sunday we were detained. I have it with my documents. Really, it is a text that fits perfectly like a ring on a finger. Fortunately I brought with me Father Yépez's *Four Gospels*. I think it is important to look for autonomy and hope that Lucía González and Carlos Wolff intensely work on it.

**Saturday, May 11:** My love: In previous days, Gilberto and I wrote letters to both of you, celebrating Mother's Day. We have traveled a lot; yesterday we arrived at a place after two journeys: one in the morning and the other in the evening. Amid the whole process, I have been able to take a little time to fish.

Yesterday we fished in a very lovely river and caught some shad. I thought of our fishing trip and how much you would enjoy it here. The difference is that it's like fishing trout in a river. One has to walk and get wet. I fished with blackberries. I dream someday I can fish in all the rivers of the country and that all can live in peace. The boys among the guerrillas behave well and are surprised that I enjoy fishing so much. Gilberto does not dare to fish, but he enjoys the taste.

Today we had breakfast of fried plantains with burned cheese; it was delicious. I miss you so much.

The long marches have the advantage that sometimes we have the opportunity of seeing sunsets and daybreaks, and they are really spectacular. We have had two sunsets, toward the Pacific, absolutely marvelous, like they can't see in Medellín.

Another advantage is to be able to see the stars. The nights, when it doesn't rain, are also beautiful. On the back of a mule and looking at the stars, I've had some pretty good episodes of dizziness.

It appears that we are going to have a change of group; we both feel it, since they have treated us very well, with great professionalism. We also have great hope so that, on the part of the commander, he will listen to us.

My love: tomorrow will be your day and what saddens me most is to be separated from you. I hope you have a very special day, accompanied by your children. Forget all the bad and enjoy the day to the fullest. I will be thinking of you all and sending all my love. You have been really marvelous in your messages and you have touched me and made me proud.

**Sunday, May 12 (Mother's Day)**: My love: Today our minds and soul are with you all, your message resounds in my mind and, even being separated, I continue feeling that we are closely united. We will be very expectant about the program that is advanced with the prisoners of Bellavista. We await a good report Monday.

Today is the last day in this "little paradise"; it seems that now we will go to the mountains again. The sky is completely blue and the sun helps us to dry the humid, damp clothes. I have thought of two programs for when I return. The first has to do with bettering the rural housing, helping the farmers to better their homes with materials and technical assistance, above all in sanitation.

The second for oral hygiene, brushes, toothpaste, and fluoride. The rural families have different priorities, and it's hard for them to get brushes and toothpaste for their little ones.

I suppose that today you are in Bogotá with your children. I spoke with the lady of the house about her needs: electricity, roads, television, seeds, medicine. The Sectional Health Service of Antioquia (SSSA) comes twice a year.

**Monday, May 13**: My sweet love: Today is the feast of the Ascension of the Lord and I suppose that you have gone to Bogotá. I hope that they have celebrated the day for you, as you deserve, and I hope that next year we can celebrate it together. I ask myself how my mother is; also I would like to hear from her.

The journey of moving yesterday was hard and difficult, we did it walking and we are in the jungle again, sleeping in what they call a cove. We have been able to listen to *La Luciérnaga* (The Firefly). It's a radio show at different times, and I greatly remember how much you liked it.

On May 13 the visit of the Virgin in Cova de Iría is celebrated also, which originated the devotion to the Virgin of Fátima, which you mentioned that her image has stayed in the house.

Okay, love, the light is almost gone. I will go to think of you and of my children. A kiss. Good night.

**Tuesday, May 14**: Love: Today I heard you twice: once very briefly on Todelar Radio, about 7:00 a.m., then on *How Medellín Woke Up*. You were marvelous, I'm so happy to know that you are spending Mother's Day with Papa. We get the impression that you did not know about the death of Doña Anita [Gilberto's mother-in-law], it seems that you had not returned to Medellín yet.

Gilberto took it very hard, and it affects me greatly to see him so sad. He has dedicated his life and all his abilities to serve Colombia with honesty and it's not fair that this is happening. I would like it a lot if you would talk to and accompany Martha Inés. I would like to hear you tell it in your messages.

Concerning Yolandita [daughter who Guillermo and Yolanda wanted to conceive], we should wait and see what the Lord has, it's not clear from your words if you have decided to have her. It's possible that I will return very changed from this experience and you might not want to continue with me. If at least this process could answer some of the questions I ask myself.

The secretary of the government of Medellín spoke of a decrease in crime this Mother's Day—about half. Everything indicates that the campaign was successful, and yes the number of deaths can be reduced, if we will all put forth the effort.

**Wednesday, May 15**: Love: It seems like you listened to my request, because in your dispatch today, you mentioned Doña Anita and offered your solidarity to Gilberto. Also you read something from the gospel. I'm reading St. Luke, which he was, among other things, an Antioquenian,[2] so you can see how far this land has served.

We've run out of coffee and soap is just about gone. We don't know what is happening, but the visitor we've been waiting for has delayed. I was thinking about the topic of education. I believe it is necessary to pay a lot of attention to the renovation of teaching and visit the schools of distant regions, trying to exercise a control in transfers and carry out a good campaign of learning to read and write in the rural areas.

Also I have thought of a very didactic reading book on nutrition, how to fortify PAS. I hope to return soon so that we can put all this in practice. We have listened to news about expanding term limits and reelection possibilities. We shall see.

**Friday, May 17**: Love: Today I did not hear your message and the truth is I've felt very bad all morning. Gilberto, who noted it, encouraged me that we do exercises, which we have stopped doing since we came from the Villa Nonviolence. Exercises and bathing helped me. Later we listened to a message from the consul body and another from the governors.

The thing from the archbishop seemed to me to be important and timely. We suppose you are in Bogota. Let me tell you that I am preparing a gift.

**Saturday, May 18**: Love: Today I listened to Gustavo Álvarez Gardeazábal[3] and want you to know that I support you completely; I believe you are managing this situation better than anyone could do. I hope that you persevere and don't let him bother you. I am very proud of you and of your struggle to convert nonviolence into an alternative for the Antioquenian.

The choice of Bishop Alberto Giraldo also is more than adequate. It seems to me that the criticism that Gardeazábal makes of the Antioquenian people, and very concretely its political and private leadership, is valid.

**Sunday, May 19**: Today we have been very active: We cleared an area of the jungle by the stream to make it into a gymnasium, which we decided to call "Paradise Gym." The place is really quiet and now sunny, when the sun comes out. Today we exercised and I thought a lot about you.

**Monday, May 20**: Yesterday we completed four weeks of our separation. Today we heard that the working day in Betania turned out well. I congratulate you and I'm pleased. Because it means that you do not let yourself be influenced by the mistaken words of

Gardeazábal. I did not hear you on the radio and I really miss that so much. The day was very varied: sun and rain.

**Tuesday, May 21**: Today we completed a month of our separation; I think of you so much, and to listen to you again today; it was like being born again. I'm concerned that all of you are anxious because you have heard nothing from us, but I know very well that these silences are part of the strategy of the FARC to soften those held and their families.

Most important is not to lose faith, alive or dead; this is the bond. Also, I think of Aníbal and I hope he is maintaining his strength as always. Your news about the advance of nonviolence pleases me greatly—that justifies our suffering.

Yesterday I had a long conversation with Gilberto. We talked about the economic history of Antioquia, about the middle class and bureaucracy, and we mulled over our Bandera projects[4] and the dinner with Gonzalo Restrepo. I have been thinking a great deal about what terrorism signifies, and inevitably I ended thinking of Pastrana and the way he has managed the country and how unwisely he conducted the process of peace; while the more I complain, the more I convince myself that he never really thought of Colombia nor of peace; I believe that he only thought of himself.

I have to remember this and always keep this in mind. In these jungles there is great potential, there is corkwood and *macana* palm which I believe should be considered to produce in a semi-industrial way. Sure, there are many other species that constitute the "ecological capital" of which I speak.

To write to you is like feeling you very close. I love you. I hear news that saddens me about the confrontations in the metropolitan area. The conflict in the cities is being announced already.

**Wednesday, May 22**: Love: Good morning. Today we listened to you and also Martha Inés, Lina, and Camila. Your words and the passages from the Bible were very beautiful, thanks so much. Both Gilberto and I feel very good about your message, although it seemed to us that toward the end you were breaking down a bit.

Love, I know that being in captivity is very hard, but to always be in your place would be much harder. Every day I listen to you and I hear news about Antioquia. Everything indicates that our state has been chosen for escalated violence which always accompanies elections and especially presidential elections.

I have been thinking and talking with Gilberto about using the radio as a means for massive literacy teaching. I want to try a pilot program in Antioquia and, if necessary, take a census and give radios to the schools and rural homes in the distant regions.

Another topic that is very interesting is solar energy, which I believe we should complement with the briquettes. I have been eating cheese, the kind we like. I think also of a system for commercializing agricultural products, helped with a decision by the state and the citizens of the metropolitan area, something that would put into motion the concept of "peacemaker capital."

I have thought of terrorism versus centralism. Both are violent forms of imposing beliefs that are more or less equivalent, right? We listened to your information about Peque; it comforted us greatly. I believe that the most important is the voice of the countrymen.

The rising river destroyed our little gymnasium but the swimming place was improved, so we decided to rename it "Paradise Swimming Pool." We heard some contributions of your talk on Todelar Radio, but it is not clear if it's going to be broadcast or already was; your words are very appropriate, I congratulate you, I would have liked to hear the whole thing.

**Thursday, May 23**: My sweet love: Today I listened to your marvelous message (also of MI, L, C), I'm happy about your convictions and the impulse of nonviolence. Let me tell you that today the fighters killed a spotted *paca* (large rodent) and tonight we'll eat well. We believe that your messages reveal advances in the efforts of the bishop (Alberto Giraldo) and Anders Kompass; I hope we're not mistaken.

I'm very sorry I cannot go with you this weekend.

**Friday, May 24**: Love: Thank you for your marvelous message. Today I will say a rosary to Mary the Helper. We hear good news from the ELN [National Liberation Army]. I hope that nonviolence is sifting through the same to the FARC and society. Also nonviolence has to be sold to the AUC.

Today we again ate the fried shad one of the fighters fished. Everything indicates that this, from today to tomorrow, will be the second full moon of being separated; I will be thinking of you. Your news about the progress of the government work calms me. I wish you would talk more about this.

**Saturday, May 25**: Love: Today I woke up with a cold. Already two of the fighters have had it, and I was sure that it would not escape me. Last night I thought a lot about you and thought about not thinking about it too much. I decided that I had better take care of myself, since the cold and the humidity can make it pneumonia.

Also a couple days ago we heard a very beautiful message from the people of Caicedo.

**Sunday, May 26**: Adored wife: I'm writing as I listen to the election returns. Now it is clear that Álvaro Uribe won in the first return; I'm very sorry Serpa did not have his opportunity.

I tell you that the weather today is the best we've had in all this captivity. I have thought a lot about you; since last night you have not left me. Today was the worst day of the cold; I hope now it begins to improve.

We don't know which direction our lives will take and how it will influence this election; we have tried to have them listen to our statements concerning nonviolence, but everything has been in vain; we only talk about it here with the fighters. This topic has to be discussed with their leaders or all will have been in vain.

**Monday, May 27**: Love: I listened to your beautiful message today; I want you to know that I listen to all your messages. Also, I would like you to know that from here I help you with decisions in your efforts and wish telepathy would allow me to reach you so I could make you feel my encouragement.

Gilberto sends you the following message in regard to Horacio Serpa's defeat: "This is another proof of the wholeness that you have shown during this difficult time, from which you will come out morally and intellectually strengthened. Being in politics makes a person do things well and know how to face challenges. Each time one gets out of a difficult situation, one grows, matures, and is enriched intellectually. Afterward one looks at it with a certain smile."

I was so happy with the news of your children; I hope that these difficulties help them to advance in this respect. I would like you to promote the view of Anders Kompass and the archbishop; nonviolence is an excellent way.

Remind me to read *When Colombia Burned,* by Henderson, and *The Making of Modern Colombia: A Nation Despite Itself,* by a North American writer, David Bushnell.

It seems that the full moon brought a change in the day; with this, two days of sun. To my cold I have applied the guerrilla remedy: a bath in cold water, but they do it at 5:00 a.m. and me at 10:00 a.m. but now I feel better; I am following your advice about not overindulging it so much. It seems that tomorrow we move from this place.

The more I think, the more I'm convinced that the way is nonviolence. Amid the euphoria that the country shows in the radio for the election of Uribe, I continue believing that the way of nonviolence has to be introduced—a way which allows us to transform Colombian life without killing each other. I do not see it as a magic solution; it is more an attitude that permits us to work together.

Today is the thirty-ninth anniversary of the founding of the FARC, after what happened at Marquetalia.[5]

**Tuesday, May 28**: Love: How I miss you, how much I feel your absence; it seems that you are all I need to live happily. I have been thinking a lot about nonviolence. I believe we should again schedule the march to Caicedo. To commemorate a year of the kidnapping, next April 21 [2003], I think we should renew this initiative.

Also I want to move ahead with the Global Center of Nonviolence and the "pedagogy of the marginalized," which has to do with the crystallization of the concept of small paradises and with a metamorphosis of education. We need to teach people to see the opportunities, perhaps with appropriate models, as a prototype for all to visualize, so that from there ideas can be brought out to better their environment, homes, education.

**Wednesday, May 29—Saturday, June 1**: Love: I could not write earlier, but I have thought of you every minute of the four hikes which I'm going to sum up for you. The first three were at night and the last during the day. All were very hard but beautiful and inspiring, at times accompanied by the moon, at times by the stars, and almost always with rain.

The first was very dangerous: one mule died and two more ran away. The one that carried our baggage was lost for more than twelve hours. The best of all is that the Paisa[6] told me that he talked with you, that you asked him if you could talk with him of nonviolence and learn about us.

Gilberto and I, more than anything, want you both to know that we are fine, in body and spirit, and thinking of you and missing you so much. The countryside we are seeing and have seen, especially the rivers and streams, is beautiful; some day, Lord willing, I would like to travel this area with you and the kids. I have decided to do so when Matthew is twenty years old.

The trees, the mountains and the streams, the paths, and the cliffs speak of the greatness of God and his generosity toward Colombia; I cannot cease to imagine us traveling together in a country at peace. Paisa told me, among other things, that he would like for me, as governor, to come later to visit the country folk.

I love you so much and above all the moments we are separated are painful to me, along with the fact that we cannot share this landscape. But for now, it is what it is. Imagine creeks in which even with a machete you can catch the shad! Today, Saturday, we could not fish for lack of nylon. God will provide.

Only until Friday the 31st. we could hear again the messages of Marta Inés, Lina, Camila Pirri [Gilberto's son], and also your own. I believe the next will be Monday. I hope you tell us of the initiatives of the Solidarity of Friday (east, southeast, and Medellín) with the petition-signing campaign.

**Tuesday, June 4**: My love: Today I listened to your voice again, a very beautiful message in which you told me that "all my life is yours." I would like for us to be together and really share our lives.

Sunday I thought a lot about you. The Paisa early on put musical videos of Vicente Fernández and Darío Gómez and later movies, all of them very violent; I had to leave and took advantage of the time to pray and to reflect. Sunday we could bathe and swim in a very beautiful river. It seemed like we would be moved on Sunday, but in the end we did it yesterday, Monday.

The new camp Gilberto called "Villa Sadness" because it really is depressing; I'm not going to dwell on that. Love, I have thought it would be good to learn to cook better, and not only to cook but to cut up the animal.

Today I talked a long time with the Paisa, continuing your message about rural housing, integral farming, research of jungle materials, and about the road industry. And also about bartering and the market for farming.

**Wednesday, June 5**: My love: Today we changed location; it seems this will be our camp for a long time. The big surprise was that we found ourselves with eleven kidnapped military officers of the army. Some have been held for five years, others three and a half, others two and a half.

For them and for us the encounter was a reason for great joy and optimism. They have made every effort to take care of us, even down to our smallest desires or needs. We are learning about their lives, their families, and the difficulties and stories they have lived during these years.

Today you did not send me a message. I know you cannot do so every day; even so, when I miss them, Gilberto says, I transform myself and my attitude is ruined. I need you to send me news of Matthew and Daniel and to talk to me about your children and my mother and brothers.

I am aware of the complaints of my father; I understand him well and know that he was never in agreement with my jeopardizing myself this way. For the time being, it is not necessary to change him.

Love, you are my sustenance, and your voice, your messages, your activity, and efforts to find funds for nonviolence makes all the pain of being separated bearable.

Love, the Paisa told me that he talked with you and that you sent some things for us. Please, follow my instructions. I cannot be the one who ruins the philosophy that I have wanted to promote.

*Mi vida* [literally "my life" but Spanish retained because this usage is common in Spanish but less so in English], if you want to send me something, I would like to receive music and a way to listen to it; among other songs that you choose, I would like to hear songs of the struggle, and the Our Father, and the Hymn of Joy. Photos and news of you all are the possessions that I desire here. The bonus would be news about the progress of the business in Antioquia.

**Thursday, June 6:** Love, it seems that you have heard me. Today in your message you spoke to me about the four-lane highway and the tunnel. Thank you for being so beautiful. Really, I believe that God and the Virgin are with us and protecting us.

The trips full of dangers which we have been able to engage in without a scratch, and the fact that almost daily we could hear of you both, are miracles which confirm it. Love: today I learned of the selection among the AU of Andrés Uriel Gallego and Fernando Londoño as ministers.

**Friday, June 7**: Love: Today your message speaks of the advances of the nonviolence program in the Bellavista Prison and the very valuable demonstrations of solidarity by the prisoners. Also you tell about the election of the beauty queen. I'm glad that you're also spending some time with this topic; I wish you good luck with it this year. I love you.

When I experience the enormous absence that I feel for you I do not understand how these guys (the military officers) have been able to hold up for so much time without their loved ones. Each day I spend far from you is like a piece of my heart being pulled out; also I think of Matthew and Daniel, of your children, and of Mafer [daughter of Yolanda Pinto de Gaviria].

I would like to know about Aníbal, Claudia, and Emiliana [wife and daughter of Aníbal Gaviria, Guillermo's brother], I do not want to think that my situation can cause them worries; he should know that what I do will bear fruit sooner or later, and it will have been worth it if the FARC opens the opportunity to nonviolence. I have nothing but gratitude and admiration toward him.

Reading the books the military officers have has helped me pass the time; some permit a critical look at the country's history; others are motivational and entertaining, and others address culture in general. Also we have been able to exercise regularly, and since there are several of us, I think we are going to persevere six days a week; now I have a long beard, which helps ward off mosquitoes and takes care of the fungus, according to the officials and the sub-officials.

Today has been a particularly cold and gray day. The military officers continue treating us with great examples of appreciation and friendship, and we have heard a good part of their family histories. Perhaps it would be a good idea if you tried to contact their families. Later I will give you their contact information.

After reciting the evening rosary, I go to bed always thinking of you and of my three children. I love them and miss them so much. Good night, my love.

**Saturday 8, Sunday 9, and Monday, 10 of June**: These three days without hearing your voice have been very sad and gray. I hope that I can hear you tomorrow. We have learned of all the radio programs that allow sending messages to the prisoners.

**Tuesday, June 11**: Love: Today again I didn't listen to you. You have probably been very busy; you don't know how much I miss your beautiful messages and to know how you are, to sense your feelings, your strength, your love; if you could know, I'm sure you would not miss, not even one day. On *How Medellín Woke Up*, at 7:30 a.m., is the best way; there you can do so every day, except Sundays, but including holidays.

If this message gets to you, I ask you to take our voice of gratitude to María Victoria Jaramillo, to Edgar Gallego and Oswaldo González. It is good if the messages are aired after 7:30 a.m. because before that it is very hard to tune them in, other stations get in and the signal is very weak; after that time it is much better.

**Wednesday, June 12**: Love: Today we listened to your declarations about the news published in *El Colombiano*. You were very good and prudent. We are preparing a video and evidence of survival. Everything indicates that our captivity will be prolonged, and I sense that as high as I've been able to take this, the FARC is not interested in statements that I have prepared concerning nonviolence.

I cannot lose faith, I'm going to continue insisting, but with sadness I have to recognize that up to now I have found only closed ears to this alternative.

**Thursday, June 13**: Today you did not send a message, but instead I was able to listen completely to your declarations through Radio Caracol with Darío Arizmendi. You were marvelous in every sense of the word. I send you a huge kiss.

Here everyone was happy about them. Please, don't let so many days pass without hearing your voice. The environment here feels very positive about the exchange. God has brought reasons for hope to the guys, who already have had two-and-a-half, three, four, five years in captivity.

Their names are—
Lieutenant Alejandro Ledesma Ortiz, two years, six months
Lieutenant Wagner Tapias Torres, five years
Sergeant Pedro J. Guarnizo, five years
Sergeant Héctor Lucuara S., three years, ten months
Sergeant Heriberto Aranguren, ten years
Sergeant Francisco Manuel Negrete, three years, ten months
Sergeant Yercinio Navarrete, three years, ten months
Sergeant Samuel Ernesto Cote C., four years
Corporal Agenor E. Viellard, two years, six months
Corporal Mario Alberto Marín, three years, ten months
Corporal José Gregorio Peña, two years, six months

Some have never met sons or daughters born after their capture. Nevertheless, it was comforting to see their spirit, faith in God, and hopes.

Love: We are preparing to record a video to be sent to the media. They have talked to us about recording some images for the families; if it happens to reach you, please make copies for the families of the military officers.

Love: I hope that this contributes to your peace of mind and our quick liberation. God bless you, mi vida.

**Friday, June 14**: Actually, love, yesterday they filmed our video; I think it will be news next week. There we spoke of the decision of the secretariat of the FARC, that they consider us subjects of exchange. What we understand up to now is that they are thinking of freeing us as a beginning in the exchange process that will include all kidnapped prisoners.

The bad news is that our communications will have to wait, and the video for the families is on stand-by. Today we left very early in the morning; luckily it was after hearing your message, the only one in the whole week—very beautiful, and it gave me endurance for the journey. The journey was very hard, perhaps the most unpleasant of all, although not the longest, because of the swampy land we covered.

The mules became very tired so that amid a downpour Gilberto and I had to get off for them to continue. Gilberto's mule fell and trampled him; his back was really injured. We woke up in the house of some peasants; they loaned us their room and we both rested in the same little bed. It helped us recuperate.

Today we haven't even bathed. The lady of the house gave us some small sweet little bananas, *murrapos* or *chibiricos* as they are called here. Also they are called "queen's bite." Now I believe they live up to their name.

It's a beautiful evening to think of you and the kids. Here there were two kids, very kind, with whom I could talk a little; I think they were less than five years old.

**Saturday, June 15**: Love: Gilberto and I continue by dug-out canoe, the military officers walk. Our trip was very slow and full of obstacles, but it was pleasant and less difficult. We arrived at a hut that appeared it will serve as temporary lodging.

Upon our arrival, the military officers and the fighters of the FARC were there. Cockroaches are all over, but it is much more comfortable, and the two guardian angels that they gave us (Sergeant Aranguren and Corporal Peña G.) had organized and cleaned our room to make it pleasant. The mattresses have not arrived because of being overweight in the dug-out canoe. Tonight we will have to sleep on the palm hardwood on the floor.

The night with the rising full moon is very clear; I can see the Big Dipper, some planets, and some shooting stars. My head was full of thoughts and memories of you. My last thoughts of the day a long time ago are all yours and of my children, as well as Yolandita.

**Sunday, June 16**: There is hope. Yesterday the Red Cross should have entered the region. The military officers hope for packages from their families. Last night we stayed up all night. There is a program called *Wake up in America*, and one of its sections is called *The Voices of the Kidnapping*, through which messages can be sent to the captives. There are two hours for this, and only for the World Cup soccer games is the schedule changing to Saturday night.

Love, this also is a good way to receive messages from you, from the family or any person, and they can also be sent by e-mail. We hear Mass at 10:00 a.m. Gilberto received a huge gift on Father's Day: Mono, who had never spoken on the radio and who had him a bit worried, greeted him and spoke to him about hopes for work.

We all congratulated each other on Father's Day and tried not to dampen our spirits. Also there is optimism regarding the trip of the president-elect to visit the UN. My hopes are lifted by listening to your voice and knowing you all are fine. Today I could go out and fish, but what bit the best was the mosquitoes (*chitras*)!

**Monday, June 17**: My sweet love: Today I heard Daniel's message. I enjoyed hearing him but I felt an enormous sadness for his feeling so sad about this. You should try to calm him and tell him that they treat us well and there is good hope. He spoke of a couple of projects that he turned in; I would like to know about them when I return.

I hope I can get the letter to you that I have for him. I would have liked to hear from you on Father's Day. Today I'm going to work on making a fishing pole. I'm going to make it of hardwood palm or *macana,* as I call it. Love, I spent almost the whole day on it, I can hardly write, with so much wielding the machete. I'm going to try to get them to let me go fishing to try it out and to think more of you. Sweet dreams, my love.

**Tuesday, June 18**: Love: last night I was able finally to catch sea fish, flat fish, and shad, but I returned very late and everyone was asleep. Today, early in the morning, the surprise of your voice and the beautiful message filled me with joy.

It seems that the FARC does not look favorably on the first gestures of the president-elect, Álvaro Uribe. Nevertheless, I believe that it is possible they may follow them right before the meeting with Kofi Annan; one has to wait a little to see what happens.

Well, my love, tonight I'll write you a little more, I love you.

**Wednesday, June 19**: Love: today I didn't hear from you, and I couldn't go fishing either. Instead we organized a chess tournament among us, with ten participants. Navarrete took me out on the first game; in the end, he was the champion.

Tomorrow Gilberto and I will have a meeting with the commander here. I want to know when the things you sent will arrive. Love, I don't really need anything, but I am eager to see what you sent. I love you and I miss you so much.

**Thursday, June 20**: Love: today I have very bad news for you, I had a very ugly disagreement with Gilberto, and he has decided to stop talking to me. I think after living so close together in this forced captivity, we are both very sensitive and the stress has finally overtaken us. I hope we can get over it. It would be very sad if an insignificant incident ended the great love and admiration I have for him.

Today I prayed more than usual, and last night a huge downpour flooded the whole area. The little house where we are was saved, but all the fighters suffered the flooding of their camps. In an earlier note I told you I wanted to learn to cook. Well, here Heriberto Aranguren knows how to make Toliman hog, tamales that would compete with those of your mother, and bread. We'll see if it is possible for us to get the cooking utensils and if they let us do so.

Today I feel your absence even more; it seems that the only thing I'm interested in is you; nothing else motivates me. I have to expand the letter to Daniel and tell him of the chess game and tell him I listened to his message. I would like you, love, to try to talk with him.

**Friday, June 21**: My sweet love: Finally today I listened to your message, in which you speak of the solidarity of the governors and the Mass celebrated by the archbishop in the cathedral.

Let me tell you that after listening to your message, Gilberto presented me with his verbal resignation of the work as Commissioner for Peace in Antioquia. Everything indicates that his position cannot be reversed, and he was really indignant with me. I think that the one who should be indignant is me. I am aware that his attitude is not exactly a reason for tranquility for us here, because if we are at odds, the truth is that the whole environment is tense and gets heavy. It's very lamentable that this ends like that here.

**Saturday, June 22**: My love: Today in the early morning it rained, but yesterday afternoon it was sunny and very beautiful; I thought of you and when we can be together again. Your strength, which I perceive in each message, and the negotiations that you are furthering fill me with pride and motivation for me to do so here.

Gilberto has completely stopped talking to me. I'm going to try not to think so much about this, but the truth is that it is a great loss. I never imagined that it could happen, but it did—and there is no remedy.

The news of last week about the corruption of some of the police close to General (Luis Ernesto) Gilibert will give reasons for the guerrillas to justify their struggle. Early today I heard threats against the mayors of the eastern part of the country by the Front *José María Córdova*.[7] In Switzerland, the spokesmen for the FARC argued about the merits of having secured the popular elections of mayors and governors. What a contrast.

Aranguren, who today marks three years of being captured, is making a chess game from cumin tree wood. Today Montoya won the pole position and tomorrow he runs in Germany, the land of the Schumachers.

We have baptized this camp "*Villa Ladilla*" (Crab Louse Villa); we all have suffered from these almost microscopic animals. I'm going to try to fish for a while.

Today it is very cold, maybe I'd better wait until it warms up a bit; since two days ago it rained so much a lot of fish came down the river.

It went very well with me, love, with the guard who is assigned to accompany me. We got thirty sea fish and shad; each military officer had three fried fish. I'm going to make two poles of hardwood palm, one for Papo [Yolanda Pinto de Gaviria's son] and the other for Matthew. Here they also fish with reel and harpoon.

Love, in the afternoon a red and blue knapsack arrived; from a distance I think it is mine. But today they did not give us anything. During the night we awoke to listen to *The Voices of the Kidnapping*. I was awake from 1:00 a.m. to 3:00 a.m.; I would like you to listen to it some day.

Meanwhile we smell the juice of a sugar cane mill, a manual one where the military officers and the fighters grind to take out the sugar cane juice and then the molasses. I could calmly and peacefully think of you, of our last trip to San Gil, I saw you making taffy, I remembered your hands, your happiness to return to the places of your childhood and find loved ones of the past; memories of you filled my heart with joy, then the captivity did not seem more than a short physical separation which has united us more.

In the distance we heard frogs and toads, so many and rhythmic that they seemed like a great drove of monkeys; and they kept it up all night. After the flood, they have simply been agitated.

In the early evening we listened to the communication issued by the mayors of the east in which they resign their offices after a long meeting with the state government. This fact, of great political importance, should generate a strong reaction of citizen solidarity. It is the moment when the whole Antioquenian people reject these threats that attack the essence of our democracy and that is the obvious will of our people at the polls.

But more than motivation, a spontaneous will of all the people should arise. Here again, the rural people, the humble and marginalized, should express themselves to prevent the mayors from resigning their responsibilities.

**Sunday, June 23**: My love: Today I am anxious to see what you sent me. Today I woke up with coffee—for several days it has been used up. I remember that the first thing you would do when you woke up was to look for your coffee. Corporal Peña also likes the *vallenatos*[8] songs; he could listen to them all day long. Today at 9:00 p.m. there will be a program of old music on Caracol. I'm going to try to endure until then.

Love, I received what you sent me; today here it was a sensation, everyone wanted to know what I had gotten, and your selection was extraordinary; especially your radio, which you never missed listening to each morning. Thanks to that radio, I can listen to the program of *boleros* interpreted by Genaro Salinas, and what I liked the best was *A Great Love* (Un Gran Amor).

Your letters are very special and have been a marvelous help and motivation. In them I found how to clarify my anxieties and unrest and also the news about the acceptance of nonviolence. And the good relations reigning in the group calms me. I'm pleased to see that not everything I talked about just stayed in the air.

Eugenio really is doing well. I feel it in his prudent speeches, and I am aware that he is going through difficult times.

Returning to your letters, mi vida, I'm especially filled with happiness with your expressions of love and the way you have received this difficult blow that temporarily separates us. Love, I believe that as long as I receive your messages and the messages that come in these letters, I am capable of enduring any torment. Without your support and your strength, I could not resist even a minute. Remember, "you are my fortress and my refuge."

Also I loved your words for Gilberto, don't ever forget to do that, neither in writing or in radio messages. Mi vida, everything indicates that tomorrow we will change camps. This Cockroach Residence in Crab Villa will be a thing of the past. I love you. Kisses.

**Monday, June 24**: My sweet love: Today they actually moved us to a new camp, in the interior of the jungle. This does have the appearance of being more permanent.

In one sense, I'm pleased since the marches have been very traumatic; on the other hand we feel more anxious, since we could be here months or even years and the prospect of our captivity is prolonged. We are still worried about not having any word about the two mayors and Felipe Palau. We fear they might be held.

Mi vida, today will be a day of work to arrange and accommodate this place. I think about the little table so I can write you. We have to pave the way with stones and fill the ground and muddy places with sand, so that it will be the floor of our quarters.

We have to build the two beds for Gilberto and me; the fighters built a cabin for ten military officers and one of them, Hector, will sleep in a hammock. Today I worked with them bringing material from the river and I'm really tired. I think I'll wake up dead.

The little river that crosses the camp is very beautiful, and its crystalline and fresh waters give me the idea of building a "swimming pool." I believe this is an ideal place to dam it and take advantage of the space of some forty meters long by six or seven meters wide, and I think we could get to a depth of sixty to seventy centimeters. We'll see if they give me the authority for it.

The fighters have become very harsh and give us almost no tools. I hope their attitude is a passing thing and is because of the need to have the work advance to make it adequate for a camp.

I think a lot about Eugenio; the crisis of the mayors should cause him a lot of worry, and I'm sure you also are participating in these decisions. The truth is it seems to me that the new strategy of the FARC is incomprehensible and damaging. They are abandoning their own democratic positions; these actions will not help them advance; on the contrary, they will inflame more of the militarists and those who think that the conflict can have a solution by military force.

The positions concerning martial law, the proposal of the assigned minister of Justice and Government, are showing how, with these attitudes of the FARC, the answer has to be a greater radicalization and preponderance of the militarists' positions. I fear that if the FARC continues their strategy, and goes to assassinating the mayors, this will open up a wave of violence, and eventually the society could end up giving the militarists more liberty for military action, looking for quick solutions which I believe do not exist.

The FARC's relative success could prompt them to advance in a way that, without a doubt, takes them away from their true objectives and would make more difficult and distant the possibilities of dialogue, negotiations, and mediations. Good night, my love.

**Tuesday, June 25**: Today there were no messages because of the semifinal of World Cup soccer; Germany won over South Korea.

Today Gilberto and I recovered our calm, because we had been fearful about the outcome of William [Ospina, then mayor of Sonsón], Humberto [Restrepo, then mayor of El Carmen], and Felipe [Palau, then coordinator of the Peace Plan Consistent]. They returned with a message which we will probably know tomorrow.

The threats to the mayors and authorities have been extended to Santanderes (North and South), Cundinamarca, Llanos Orientales, and other states, and everything suggests they can extend even more.

A question comes to mind: What is the FARC going to do if the governors do not accept the resignation of the mayors? Are they going to proceed to execute these mayors? The mayors are very timidly criticizing the measures announced by the president.

I fear that this relative and partial success encourages the more militant sectors of the FARC and makes them believe that this is the way to advance their struggle. I'm concerned because the radicalization could be very bloody and destructive. The attitude of the president-elect has seemed to me prudent.

Love, we continue working on preparing our new dwelling; we still have not given it a name, but we have considered the name "Villa Waiting," since we think we are going to spend a long time waiting for our release, Lord willing. Good night, my love.

**Wednesday June 26**: My love: Today again we did not hear any messages; the soccer game between Brazil and Turkey dominated the radio stations.

The mayors and Felipe Palau arrived speaking on two topics: the decision of exchange and of promoting a "Law of Interchange" and the announcement of a proposition that the FARC will make to the president-elect. There is no more information about this last topic. Also, they mentioned that they had not received information about us. It seems strange that the video we filmed was not made known.

Today we also worked hard on making the "cabin" and its surroundings serviceable. One of the nice jobs is launching the antennas. The military officers throw some small stones tied with cords toward the highest branches in the jungle, and when they have those branches secure, with these cords a length of wire is strung. This wire is used as the antennas for the radios.

As you can imagine, the radios have become the most precious possession here. To hear messages from loved ones cheers us, and without them we surely would come undone. They also help to fill the enormous emptiness with news and everyone's favorite programs. At times, we spend hours trying to throw the stone several meters higher, only to discover that it is not an adequate place for one reason or another, and we must stop it until the next day.

The books that have arrived are being avidly read, especially those of Gilberto, since mine are both in English and the ones for Herbin Hoyos were sent to him. Good night, my love.

**Thursday, June 27**: Early today we didn't hear messages, none for either of us. Yesterday the deadline of the FARC to the mayors expired.

Gilberto listened to an interview of General [Rosso José] Serrano; they asked him a lot about the accusations of Pedro Juan Moreno. In the afternoon they gave the information that General Serrano had to return to the clinic in Panamá, where he is now.

Here we continue working on our cabin, with difficulties and lack of tools, because all the fighters are doing the same work: making the camp and its dwellings serviceable. I already presented our plan to the commanders to build a swimming pool, and they were in agreement. We will wait until the tools are more available.

Love, at night we listened to the speech of President Pastrana. In it he announces means to protect the mayors and compensation for whoever gives information that leads to the capture of members of the secretariat of the FARC and their block chiefs.

Love, I continue hoping for and missing your messages; now at least I have your letters and can read and re-read them when I don't get the messages.

In this camp there are not so many "*chitra*" [very small mosquito]. In exchange there are many gadflies. The repellents that you sent me are giving us excellent service. Among the medicines that are most needed are antibiotics. Other plagues are the ants (*congas*), spiders, and snakes. But as we go along and control the place, these annoyances will be disappearing.

Well, mi vida, I anxiously wait to hear your messages tomorrow and will try to listen to your messages on the Uraba radio stations tomorrow. Good night, my love.

**Friday, June 28**: My love: Today I finally heard your voice again. I'm very glad for Mafer. I know the trip is going to suit her well, but I feel sorry for you since I know you will miss her a lot. I promise you that at the first opportunity we will visit her and Daniel. Also, I'm glad that Papo is with you.

I hope you take care of your throat. Since they have retained me and I listen to your messages I am concerned. You had a cold and I have felt you are very hoarse in almost all your messages. Please, take good care of yourself, mi vida, we need you a lot.

Also, we heard Martha Inés and Lina, and felt they were very encouraged and strong. Last night we had a meeting among ourselves to organize ourselves a little and try to establish some minimal agreement regarding living together and procedures to allow our situation to be less unpleasant and to maintain harmonious relations with our captors.

A new day has begun and the military officers are each doing their own thing; some getting gravel, others reading, others cleaning the weeds, others chopping down, and the rest washing.

I'm going to re-read your letters, mi vida. They are the most precious treasure, along with your radio and these notes for you.

My love, I want us to take up again with conviction the topic of children's camps for nonviolence, and for us to do it every two or three months, and look for a way to guarantee their continuity in the future. I would like to find a way to assure that it is incorporated in all the public schools and high schools. I was very enthusiastic about your announcement regarding the success of the camp; it would be good to follow these young people and continue their nonviolent formation.

Love, I interrupted here to go fishing. They gave me permission this afternoon and I was lucky, I caught twenty or thirty little shad, sea fish, and catfish; I arrived late and soaked. We could only clean the fish and salt them, and tomorrow we will fry them for breakfast.

Today they gave us cornbread for supper, a great delight; it's the first we have tasted. While I was fishing I was thinking a lot about you, I think you would really like this type of fish and also the kids would like them. I heard on the news that Mono Jojoy had given the orders to execute the mayors who do not resign. The information showed that army intelligence intercepted the communications.

I have begun to read one of the books about Napoleón they sent Gilberto. Well, my love, I send you a thousand kisses, good night.

**Saturday, June 29**: My love: I'm writing by the light of a kerosene lamp that they put in the dwelling to keep guard during the night. The insects fly around it attracted by its light, and there they die or get their wings burnt.

I think of you. Tomorrow will be the program of *boleros;* I hope to hear new ones so I can dedicate them to you later. I'm looking for a very special one that we can always share. I love you and above all else, I hate being separated from you.

Today I didn't do anything except read; I didn't even bathe. All day I sat reading the history of Napoleón. In the morning they brought us the fish I caught yesterday, but they were very salty and not fried enough. Also, today they gave us corn, not in a cake but in rolls. I kept a little for lunch and a few pieces that the military officers gave me from their rations for supper.

Today it was cold and now it is raining. I didn't even listen to the news. The military officers are preparing to get up and listen to *The Voices of the Kidnapping* in the early morning, since they receive their weekly messages there.

I know there were statements by Álvaro Uribe about the members of private security companies and their plans to unite with the public force around the event that is celebrated in Cartagena.

I think of your kisses, your smile, and your happiness which filled my thoughts: Today they are a memory that feeds my spirit. Without the certainty of your love, I would not have the strength to put up with this absence of everything. I also think of Matthew and Daniel; it causes me immense pain to know that they are sad because of me.

I hope these letters reach them soon and calm them. Mi vida, I'm going to bed and pray. Receive my kisses and my love, my sweet princess.

**Sunday, June 30**: This morning at 3:30 a.m. I again heard your message from Friday, also that of Ángela de Pérez [wife of Luis Eladio Pérez]. I loved hearing you again and to know that you are aware of *The Voices of the Kidnapping*. I hope that someday you will try to listen to the whole program. I think it reveals many things to anyone who listens to it.

Today I continued reading about Napoleón. I only stopped for a meeting Gilberto and I had with the commanders about the standards of conduct here and the possibility of beginning some activities, like for example building the swimming pool. Everything seems to indicate that soon we can begin it, together with the construction of a small oven, the gymnasium, and a little field for mini-soccer.

Last night it was really cold. The cover I had was not enough but your voice compensated. Your words have made me feel the strength of your love. This beautiful feeling fills me with joy, even amid uncertainty and anxiety. I was imagining you being with Papo, in our room; I hope that the passing of time does not diminish your feelings and each day illuminates my negligent hope in this jungle, exposed to the will of other people who seem to not share nor want to understand the message of nonviolence.

Love, I have put on the long-sleeved yellow T-shirt. You know what it means to me, and so I feel more melancholy in your absence, but for some strange reason I also believe that way I have you closer.

Today we talked with some of the military officers about typical meals. There's one, love, from San Pelayo: Negrete. Remember that we were going to the fiestas of the *porro* dance? I promised him that you and I would go with him the next time, but with reveille and all.

The kerosene lamp trembles and crackles when the mosquitoes, gadflies, gnats, and even fireflies pass through its flame, attracted by its light and heat. I have asked for permission to fish early tomorrow morning since yesterday it rained so hard and I believe the shad will be biting; I don't know if I can go, but it is the only entertainment I have here.

The rest of the time, my head is spinning a thousand revolutions. Only memories of you and your letters and messages bring me peace. If I had a mask with a snorkel, I could dive and fish with a harpoon; I'm making one of hard palm, to see if later I get a chance.

Today the soccer World Cup ends and I'm surprised how little it interests me. Only your image continues unharmed and stands straighter above all I value and want; only your promise to wait for me encourages me to not lose hope or despair.

Well, mi vida, I'm going to try to listen to the programs of *boleros*. A thousand kisses, love: good night, greetings to Papo.

**Monday, July 1**: Love: Today being a holiday, we have not listened to your messages; so energy to pass the day has been low. I have been reading all day. Last night I could not listen to the *boleros* program, since a transmission of the National Reign of Bambuco[9] competition was put on by the radio station which constantly competed with *The Voice of Antioquia*.

We have progressed a lot in cleaning around the dwellings and that helps lessen disease. Nevertheless, since we have a nest of *congas* ants a meter from the dwelling, we are waiting to see what solution they have. The ants are really savage. The military officers compare them to the bite of a scorpion.

Love, I hope to be able to make sure these notes get to you very soon. I'm anxious that because of the circumstances the country is going through, our captivity could be greatly prolonged. You and Martha Inés should prepare yourselves for this possibility.

We are trying to generate activities to fill up our many hours of idleness but are hampered by the limited materials, books, and writing supplies in our efforts to at least make our time here a little productive. I believe we are going to try to turn over our minds to write.

Today we listened to news about the beginning of a new Episcopal conference and the announcements about the candidates who will follow Archbishop Alberto Giraldo. I believe that now he can have greater liberty to act on our matter; we have talked here and think that he should continue.

I have also thought of our daughter (Yolandita) and I rebuke myself because of the indecisiveness that hindered us from doing things earlier; each day that passes goes against us. Today I'm too melancholy; I don't want to overwhelm you with such bitter sentiments. I will continue tomorrow.

My love, sweet dreams, I send you kisses.

**Tuesday, July 2**: Love: Today we listened to messages for Gilberto from Vivian [Gilberto's daughter-in-law], Martha Inés, and Lina. I still haven't heard your message of today, but Friday they put it on Caracol National. There's very good news: the declarations of the archbishop in the headquarters of the Episcopal Conference are optimistic; they convene the solidarity with the mayors and call for dialogue.

Also, the Communist Part, through Jaime Caicedo, its president, raised the need for dialogue over facing each other militarily. The mayors of the east have proposed, with courage and great integrity, my condition as bearer of alternative pacifist proposals as the axis of their humanitarian actions. In short, there is a milieu that I perceive as full of convictions for the need to help negotiations.

Today we began the day with corn bread, which made everyone happy, especially me. My love, today has been a calm day, I have dedicated it to thinking of nonviolence, to reading the novel on Napoleón, and to chess; in this I have improved a little but I still play very slowly; I hope to be a good challenge for Daniel when we can play together again. With Aranguren I am making a chess set of wood for him so you and I can take it to him.

The night brings the most peaceful memories of our life. Here I remember so many days we shared together. Reading Napoleón in his wars with Russia have brought to mind the days in Moscow and St. Petersburg, our visit to the Hermitage, and the cold that we put up with, my love. Also the trip by train and Red Square at four in the morning.

It is raining and some glowworms have taken refuge under our roof; they are really special and they produce in me a very beautiful romantic sensation; I would love to share with you the fireflies, just not this captivity.

Sometimes, thinking of you, I have come to believe that you are capable of appearing here; I hope that very soon we can be together, to allow me to hug you, to kiss you, to look at you. To make ourselves happy.

I insist that you go ahead with the necessary actions so that we can ask for Yolandita. I don't know when we can send these notes; it seems it may be possible to do so when the Red Cross comes into the region, together with the correspondence of the military officers. I hope God permits that soon.

I just heard that Monsignor Rubiano was chosen as president of the Episcopal Conference.

**Wednesday, July 3**: My sweet love: This morning I listened to your sweet words and it seemed to me that you were sadder than at other times. I well know that some days the pain of being separated is harder than others. I also know that for you and those who are there it is much harder than for us, due to the uncertainty and the lack of news of us.

In one of your interviews you said that you "never doubted that they were treating us well." You are right, and that is what you should think when doubts attack you. I would like to calm you in my arms so that you continue displaying your marvelous strength and your faith.

I'm glad that the children are here in Colombia. It's really good for Matthew to see his brother, and it's possible that together they will decide to send a message by radio. I understand from your letters that they have told Matthew that I am traveling. If it is necessary I think the truth could be explained to him. It is very harsh news but most likely his little friends already know.

Daniel should be strong and calmly explain that kidnapping is a job risk for any government worker committed to nonviolence. This effort is worth it if we succeed with him to offer the children and young people of Antioquia a peaceful future and an autonomous and more just state.

I heard on the news of the creation of the foundation of [Enrique] Peñalosa. I'm glad that it has been decided to work for the future of the country and to explore its points of view. Also, we listened to the offer of Monsignor [Luis Augusto] Castro to work for the liberation of the official and sub-official prisoners. This pleases us and it creates great enthusiasm among them, our companions.

I have various questions; every day I think intensely about where these threats of the FARC might lead. Where will this process end? What will their attitude toward me be? What do I feel, what is my view in light of these circumstances? Why do I feel like there has not been enough action by the people to support their threatened leaders? What can we hope for from the threatened mayors? If this "new weapon" is not challenged, who will be threatened next? What are the feelings of the people in the threatened municipalities?

Sweet princess, I adore you. Receive my kisses and good night.

**Thursday, July 4**: My love: Today we listened to your marvelous message. It is really a luxury to hear you every morning. The news about the prisoners of Bellavista (who declared themselves a nonviolent jail) generated great joy. Every day I am more convinced of the possibilities of nonviolence. I know that it will be opening the way while there are leaders who take on the firm commitment of advocating it based on convictions like ours.

Love, today they gave me permission to fish, and it went very well: I caught twenty-three fish. They were biting well since in early morning it rained and the river rose and this agitated them. Returning early, we were able to prepare them, and before supper they brought them fried. This is a simple morsel, but here it is a special dish.

In the afternoon we played chess, and I admit that last night I did not write you since we were absorbed in a checkmate play over which we had a big discussion; in reality we went to bed without resolving it and Friday morning we will finish it. It was over the checkmate between the king and castle vs. the king and bishop. Today, Thursday, I *am* writing you.

Well, mi vida, I have thought a lot about you; I send thousands of kisses. Receive all my love.

**Friday, July 5**: My sweet love: Today was a marvelous day. On the one hand, we listened to your beautiful and comforting message and that of MI and Lina; on the other hand, we could see the video of the march with the fighters and the commander who guard us.

Let me tell you it was marvelous because besides seeing you again and listening to you speak and see you at my side, the recounting that they sent, my love, is very complete and in a very congruent way unites the statements that we have been doing. To be able to see again the faces of the marchers and some members of the government team and the evidence of the success of the Conference of Nonviolence has really been unifying. I feel that all has not been in vain, that the seed has been planted.

Also, we have had the opportunity to see a couple of movies. You are not going to believe me, but now I don't have any desire to see television, and much less pictures where violence stands out, which are in the majority here.

Today it rained all day; we woke up with it raining, it stopped a little, then rained all afternoon. My love, it is 7 p.m. We just finished listening on Caracol the news about the video in which we tell of the decision of the FARC to consider us subjects of exchange. We heard the statements of Guillermo Gaviria Echeverri and of Martha Inés.

Tonight we are going to stay up trying to wait for your statements and the different reactions. Above all, it seems important to know what president-elect's attitude will be. I believe this juncture can serve to resolve two problems: that of the threats to the mayors, which you know worries me a great deal, and that of our liberation.

There is great hope and we will be very attentive. There is a positive air among us; I think that at least it has served so they see us and that they know that Gilberto and I are together, and also it serves the families of the military officers. It is probable that this will motivate the relatives to make contact with you my love.

More good news this very dense day: tomorrow night, that is early Sunday morning, the program *Wake up in America,* which has the section *The Voices of the Kidnapping,* will originate from Medellín. Since they have published it, I imagine that you, and hopefully all the Antioquenian people, can participate with enthusiasm; a good sign would be a great referendum of support and solidarity.

More good news has to do with the well-timed challenge questioning the appointment of Fernando Londoño as minister. We hope that these criticisms, made with high quality and supported with serious information, will prevent someone who does not have the proper requirements from holding such an important office.

My sweet love, today I see you so marvelous and beautiful. You made me feel full of pride and here they praise you so much. I'm going to sleep with my spirit exalted and with more optimism and tranquility. Receive thousands of kisses and all my love.

Good night, princess. Love, it's 9:15 p.m., I just finished listening to your declarations on RCN [National Radio Network]. I hope that soon we can give each other the hug and kiss that you spoke of.

**Saturday, July 6**: My sweet love: Today we dedicated ourselves to listen to the different reactions to the video. At night we went to bed early so we could get up at 12:30 a. m. to hear the program of Herbin Hoyos.

There was a double hope: on the one hand, the appearance of the video and the hot topic of prisoner exchange, and the other, what was happening from Medellín. I loved hearing you both times, and I was very pleased that you stayed for the messages of the families of the others kidnapped. I'm sure you could hear the messages they sent to the military officers and those of Gilberto.

It is a delicate moment and there must be much prudence to not send a mistaken message. I feel the balance is positive. You, Martha Inés, and the families have received our messages, and the FARC has notified the country of their intentions; now the only thing remaining is to commit us to the Lord and the Virgin and wait for the decisions of the next government, whose prudence gives us the idea that there are possibilities.

Also, we spent a bit of time with chess. I ask myself how Daniel and Matthew are. And how is Papo's stay in Medellín? I would like to know about them and also if you have received news from Mafer, how he got installed and the details.

There are moments in the day and night when I would like to draw or photograph. I think we could take some works of art, since there are images that I would like to remember all my life. Early in the evening, by the light of the kerosene lamp, some evenings and some daybreaks, the chess game, the aspects of our dwelling, the mixture of jungle and camp, our reactions in some special moments and the river, fishing, etc.

Many moments nourish the spirit, and I would like to share them with you later. I suspended my life a moment to think of you, of your love, of Yolandita, and to pray; now it's 8 p.m. and already dark.

We are using the kerosene lamp, we listen to soft music, because some are already sleeping, and Marín, Negrete, and I are writing to our loved ones. In the early morning you were marvelous; I love you, mi vida. We heard the papal *nuncio*, Beniamino Stella, motivate the entering government to look for a solution to our captivity and sternly criticize Gilberto's and my captivity.

The predominant note in the statements of the families has been the criticism of President Pastrana and the recrimination of his lack of interest. Good night, love.

**Sunday, July 7**: Love: Today the sun reappeared after rainy and cold days. The news of an exchange continues to fill the airwaves. Here the day was very slow; we tried to distract ourselves by reading Napoleón, playing chess, and talking about nonviolence.

Fortunately you sent me Micofix. With it I've been able to control the fungus that was beginning in my feet because of the humidity; that is a vital drug here.

Today I listened to Mayor Luis Pérez outline and explain his views about the power vacuum generated by the threats to the mayors. He was very strong toward President Pastrana. Love, tonight at 9 p.m. I'm going to try to listen to the program *La Hora del Amor* (The Hour of Love) on Caracol. They broadcast the *boleros* of Chucho Avellanet. I hope to hear some for us two.

Receive my love and kisses. Good night, mi vida.

**Monday, July 8**: My sweet love, I love you immensely and I miss you. Today there was no message from you, but in exchange, at this hour you made excellent statements to Caracol. You are developing the themes in the right direction, finding creative alternatives rather than closing your mind.

*El Tiempo* wrote an editorial about Fernando Londoño. There are announcements about other assignments of the government of

Álvaro Uribe. Last night, my love, I heard two marvelous *boleros: Cuatro Vodas* (Four Lives) and *Mil Violines* (A Thousand Violins) sung by Chucho Avellanet; I hope you listen to the program.

We are moving forward in the building of the gymnasium. I think that tomorrow I will begin daily exercises again.

Here Lieutenant Alejandro Ledesma seems to have hepatitis; we are concerned that it doesn't spread and that he will be healed soon.

I'm getting better at chess. I've insisted on practicing. Last night the sky was beautiful, starry and clear; they are fleeting joys, since among the trees of the jungle there is little to enjoy and the plague advances rapidly.

**Tuesday, July 9**: My sweet love: Today we listened to the news about the attacks against the mayor of Santa Bárbara. Although the reporters speak of the FARC and they put them in the package of threats, it does not seem clear to me that they follow the process of threats delivered by the FARC.

On the one hand, the FARC gave time until tomorrow, the tenth; on the other hand, if there had been twenty well-armed men of the FARC, the results would have been different. Also in that region the ELN and common criminals are active, which makes it seem likely that the activity came from these last two groups.

Today, my love, we begin doing exercises; in the gymnasium we have parallel bars, and we're going to build a bench to do abdominals. The exercise helps to use the time, and it clears us of the stress that we are accumulating because of the inactivity and, in my case, of knowing that I am separated from the charge that the people of Antioquia entrusted to me.

Today I also began to give the military officers English classes. There is a lot of enthusiasm. If they continue like this they are going to learn a good vocabulary and probably can even practice reading Gandhi and King.

I'm trying to form a routine; after getting up about 6 a.m. and listening to *How Medellín Woke Up* looking for your messages, which have been scarce this morning, I eat breakfast and then exercise until about 10:30. Then we bathe and prepare for lunch.

We listen to news through the day. After lunch, I spend three or four hours reading and before it gets dark, English classes. About

6:30 p m. after praying, I dedicate myself to writing you and thinking about you and our children and our future.

I think of dedicating the afternoons to nonviolence and the government of Antioquia while I finish the readings I began about Napoleón, Bolívar, and the Colombian military history. Well, mi vida, I'll say goodbye with thousands of kisses.

**Wednesday, July 10**: Love of my life: Today again you did not send messages. I miss them so very much. Also I don't understand why the family doesn't send me messages. Today on Caracol they talked about the polls on the topic of the day. They asked about the need for a legislation of war. Also the controversy of Fernando Londoño continues with the Supreme Court. Personally, I think that he is preparing a justification to leave for a cause different from the scandal of Invercolsa.

Love, it is nighttime, it's 7 p.m. We are writing by the light of the kerosene lamp and at the same time listening to some news and one or two songs. I was happy to hear the plan the government is putting into practice in relation to the threatened mayors. I'm moved to know that more than eighty mayors and more than fifty council presidents met with the governor to look for a better way to proceed in the face of the threats.

This way of proceeding also permits offering the citizen a more united front and motivating their solidarity, which is valuable for subverting the results of the fighters' ways of proceeding.

Love, I think of you all the time; this separation is so sad. I can't help but think that these circumstances will get complicated and we will suffer this unjust and cruel captivity for a lot longer. The decision of the FARC is made; our plans of nonviolence do not interest them. They brought up your mention of my intervention in the video that you all saw last week. We're going to bed with the hope that the program will be broadcast tomorrow on different stations between 8-9 a.m. I would love to give Daniel and Matthew a hug; I would love to send a kiss to each one.

My princess, I love you and I miss you with my whole being. Receive my kisses and good night, sweet dreams.

**Thursday, July 11**: Love: Today you opened the program of solidarity on the radio network with those kidnapped and their families on *The Voice of Antioquia*. I hear you very well, my love. Your reflection about the effect of the kidnapping on the family, in our case, in Antioquia makes me think that the kidnapping is like a type of death from which it is possible to return.

This is the only difference: it gives us a second chance. What is constant is the faith of these persons. What could we do without them? At this moment, you are giving a just answer to critics like those of Gardeazábal.

Very good, mi vida; If I had not known you and loved you, today I would be loving your valor and integrity. I hope that you apply your intelligence and strength to multiply the solidarity of the Antioquenian people toward all kidnapped and disappeared persons.

Nonviolence is to denounce, without fear, injustices and crimes—and nothing is better than that the families themselves expose the real situation of the country in this field. At the end of the program you closed marvelously. It is necessary that first Antioquia, then Colombia, and finally the whole world unite against kidnappings and forced disappearances.

Mi vida, this hour has been crucial; if it is possible to multiply this effort, very quickly the national conscience will be touched and the Colombian people moved to gather around concrete nonviolent proposals for solutions. I congratulate you; I feel so proud of you, my love.

My love, it is mid-day, the signal is very weak. I heard your conversation with Yolanda Pulecio. It pleases me that you continue agitating on the topic. Today they have given the kidnapping the treatment it deserves and you have nobly led the process.

I just read parts of the will of Napoleón. My attention is drawn to what he says to his son of whom he has not received any news for several years: "That my son read and meditate regularly on history, the only and authentic philosophy.... But all that he learns will serve him little if in the depth of his heart he does not cherish the sacred fire and the love of the good that makes great things possible."

Love, the day has finished and it is cold, a heavy rainstorm with lightning just finished. Today I finished the book about Napoleón, and I have begun one about Bolívar which promises to be very interesting and instructive like that of the Corsican emperor.

We hope that in any moment the delegate from the Red Cross will arrive, and I think we can send all the correspondence that we have prepared and these current notes. For the time being, you were marvelous.

The day was very valuable for the cause of solidarity with the families and the kidnapped ones.

I love you, receive my kisses and rest. I hope to see you soon. Love, you haven't told me how it went for you in the session of solidarity. I hope that tomorrow you send the message of the week and that you don't forget me on the weekend.

**Friday, July 12**: My love: Today you did not send me a message either. But it comforts me that I heard you so well yesterday. Last night I dreamt that we were freed. Can you imagine the happiness and later the sensation of frustration upon awakening? Nevertheless, I know that when the dream is a reality, the joy of being able to hold you will be unsurpassed.

Love, now I'm conforming to a good routine; one believes that one has all the time in the world and it will be more than enough time and will be most profitable. But more important than that is reading. I'm going to ask you to send me books. In the next few days I'll make you a good list.

Early in the morning, a deer appeared in the river. The fighters saw it and they shot it three times. Tonight we dined with venison, very delicious, and a couple hours after it had been killed another one almost got into the quarters.

Love, I have decided that we go to Cuba for the Festival of the Bolero when we can be together. Remember that place in Bogota where we would go to listen to *boleros*?

Today was the news of the honoring of President Álvaro Uribe at the University of Antioquia. The news about the subway annoyed me very much; one has to ask Eugenio [Prieto Soto] what happened. They should find out the truth, the charge, the votes, everything, and possible meddling of the federal government in local affairs. I hope we can have everything clear for when I return, but if they have the battle before, it has to be done.

They do not send me news about housing, reforestation, and child nutrition. I don't understand the reason for so much silence with respect to the standard programs. Well, my love, I'm going to sleep. Receive my kisses and my heart; I love you, good night.

**Saturday, July 13**: My sweet love: It is 3:00 p.m. and I write you excited and happy. You just intervened in the institutional program. You spoke extendedly, clear and very certain in putting emphasis on the error created in having us denied liberty. Without a doubt it is the best message of those sent to the radio; it only compares to your beautiful letters.

I would also like to hear about housing and the other topics related to the *bandera* program. Love, this compensates and exceeds everything of the week. I love you and miss you with my whole heart.

**Sunday, July 14**: My love, good morning. In the early morning we were listening to the messages to those kidnapped; I did not hear you, but there were messages for all the rest. You had sent a very beautiful one yesterday afternoon. From your message we learned of the support of the Network of Solidarity and Permanent Help to the families affected by the flooding of Murrí, and the humanitarian relief efforts in the Atrato Medio.

The mention of my mother's sadness left me very upset. I hope you can quickly get these notes to calm her, since the conditions of our captivity are very different from what she suffered. Additionally, there are two sub-officials, Peña and Aranguren, who, since Gilberto and I arrived, have offered themselves to serve as our helpers, and they have been doing so with much love and generosity.

I'm so pleased to hear new and good news about Matthew, Daniel, and Papo. I'm glad that you are surrounded by these loved ones. From the program last night, I have a suggestion and petition for you: José Pablo Uricoechea also is kidnapped. Last night his wife sent him a beautiful greeting. I'd be so pleased if you would call her and find mutual support. It is also something that you can do, and you have been doing in your messages; generalize and try to identify with the families of the kidnapped Antioquenians.

Yesterday Gilberto told us of an experience with his father before his father died. His father left as a lesson: ten suggestions for life which have been enthusiastically received by all of us, which are:

- Love your mother
- Love your country

- Be considerate of your spouse
- Live honestly
- Do not harm a friend
- Do not make decisions in moments of anger
- Think negatively and it will surely happen that way
- Practice loyalty
- Study and cultivate knowledge
- (missing in the original)

I have thought a lot on the topic of the depression in the rural economy. I would like you to insist to Sergio [Trujillo, secretary of Agriculture in Antioquia] the model of Colanta[10] and the Promoter of Social Commerce. The investigations of the University of Antioquia on the topics of technical development in agriculture also have to be watched (LOOK! Applicable for the rural person).

I heard that the program *The Voices of the Kidnapping* next week will broadcast from Bucaramanga. Love, during the noon meal we listened to comments about the article by López [Michelsen]. Everything seems to indicate that it is possible, and López considers it desirable and he proposes it, that will accomplish a special agreement with those kidnapped and guerrilla prisoners who are not guilty of crimes against humanity.

Without a doubt, the statements of the ex-president are going to contribute to the atmosphere, indeed very excited and favorable, of looking for solutions for our captivity. Additionally, I believe that if Lopez has come out to arbitrate, it's because he sees the field as very fertile. With Gilberto, we believe that ,from the point of view of possible liberation, it is perhaps the most positive news.

**Monday, July 15**: My sweet love: I have reflected about the FARC. Without a doubt, if the society, and especially its leaders, could carry out an objective self-analysis they would see that the fighters are offspring of their violent activity, the product of their surroundings, which is the constant reality in our fragile and hypocrite democracy. Rather than insisting that everywhere these persons be called fighters, we should look for another way to transform this costly and destructive attitude, which, in the end, is a product of a society and that looks similar to the proposed violent solution.

Love, our topic has reached unsuspecting levels of national attention. Everything indicates that you pointed in the right direction with your suggestions that, with creativity and imagination, we look for alternatives. Among the military officers there is a lot of optimism. Ex-presidents like Turbay and Samper, judges like Jaime Bernal Cuéllar and Eduardo Cifuentes, and almost the majority of those surveyed have supported the idea of López.

Today also there is good news in sports and medicine, led by Antioquia: Botero won the stage in the Tour of France, and the San Vicente de Paúl Hospital successfully did a transplant of trachea, pharynx, and larynx. Imagine what possibilities there could be . . . as Father Yépez says, the ways of the Lord are mysterious; maybe our kidnapping was necessary so the country will give the attention that these families and the problem deserve.

The country should try to face them and find solutions that can end the cancer of kidnapping. Oh that so many minds dedicated to giving the same repeated opinions might dedicate themselves instead to changing the structures of society and bringing about solutions. Two countries face each other: The one attached to the status quo, and the other the one struggling with the essence of the problems and cries for solutions.

**Tuesday, July 16 (Virgin of Carmen Day)**: My love, this morning I listened to your message; it was very beautiful. Also, we listened to Martha Inés, Lina, and Camila; and the rural folk of the area sent a beautiful message to Gilberto.

It looks like tomorrow the messages of the families of the military officers and news for them will arrive; probably at that time we can send our letters. We hope that God permits that we are able to get our news to them. I want you to know (together with Martha Inés) that we are listening and how much they feed our optimism.

I include you in this type of diary and also want to update the list of claims. They have informed us that the second package is on the way but they have said that it will be delayed.

The military officers fell in love with the white shirts of nonviolence in the march. If you can, I ask you to send one for each one of them. Everyone is filled with hope for a solution soon. Nevertheless I ask you to send me five or six books on nonviolence. I consider that the most important thing is, via e-mail, to ask Mario López Martínez, at the University of Granada, to recommend them and then for Sofía to buy and send them to Colombia. Hopefully in Spanish, if not in English.

Among the medicines, the most important are the antibiotics, in pill form and the Micofix for the fungus, together with Cuadriderm and Canesten. Also it would be good to have the "vaccination" against colds (pills). In the list I update it for you.

For the messages it will be very good if you (and Martha Inés also) continue them with *How Medellín Woke Up*, hopefully after 7 a.m., since before that the signal is very weak. Also, we enjoy listening in the early morning on Sunday. There you can record them before hand so that you will not have to stay up late at night; also the cabinet and some of the members of the family can do so and comment to me how the *banderas* program are going.

**Wednesday, July 17**: My sweet love: Today was a very happy day here, despite not hearing your message. For the military officers the packages for each one arrived; one from the FARC with clothes and the other from each of their families with personal cleanliness items, medicines which they have not given them yet, and letters and photos of their loved ones.

Today they gave Gilberto and me the grey knapsack you sent us with books, letters, caps, and ponchos. Each one had a fiesta with their things. They got a lot of candy and gave some to Gilberto and me. In this way the strict diet I made for myself to not eat or drink sweet things was broken. Chocolates, candy, cookies have come to complement the happiness of receiving letters from you. The letters from Anibal and my mother were very timely and yours very precious.

We are thrilled with the books. For me, those of nonviolence and for Gilberto the novels are going to greatly entertain us. Also, we celebrate the notebook that they published with nonviolence topics and the fifth conference, very well done and explicit.

My love, the thick poncho of Idea[11] I have on right now and with it I think I have conquered the cold I got on the rainy days, which are not a few here. The caps I have distributed among the military officers, and I gave Gilberto one to replace the straw hat that, like my cap, suffered an acute attack of "dirt illness." Despite this fact, we had decided to keep them until we are released.

The English classes I'm giving them have them very busy; almost the whole day, and I mix nonviolence in them. The message got through to them, thanks in part to the video you sent, in which an excellent summary of the march and our efforts of nonviolence were made. In fact, they had time left over and didn't know what to do with it; now there isn't enough, and also we have been doing an hour of exercises each day.

Love, I tell you that I have lost a little weight and my health is very good. Returning to the topic of the packages, we are very concerned that at the moment they have not allowed us to send our letters. Gilberto and I want nothing but to let them know that we listen to you both and how much we miss you.

Love, at this moment it's 8 p.m. and I listened to *Melodías* (7:30 a.m.) a program of *boleros*. Javier Solís sings *Este Bolero Es Mío* (This *bolero* Is Mine). I would like to dance this with you and many more. In your letter you tell me about the landscapes, so, among the requests is for a camera and film.

If the gentlemen of the FARC authorize it, Gilberto and I can dedicate ourselves to taking some really artistic photos and thus manage to share with you those moments we can call beautiful amid our captivity. Aníbal should give advice about the ASA of the pictures so as to take photos with little light, with much light, and at night with the light of the kerosene lamp.

The crazy idea that we have is to try to take Ansel Adams-style photos. Well, my love, thanks for this day. I love you and miss you so much. Receive my kisses and my love.

**Thursday, July 18**: My sweet princess: Today also we listened to your message. You talked about the things happening at the University of Antioquia. The president was in Medellín, Bucaramanga, and Barranquilla; in each city he gave information about the increase in force, a discourse that did not inspire in me any confidence at all.

Today the other knapsack of the second shipment arrived, the mosquito nets and some other books. The report and the texts on nonviolence are very interesting, and the report they prepared about the march was excellent.

These days we have been eating a lot of candy, since all the military officers received packages from their homes and each has taken a little of theirs to share with us. Gilberto insists that I am an incorrigible glutton. Despite this, I am very well behaved controlling calories in the daily meals.

We have not progressed in the plans for the swimming pool or the playing field since the attitude of our captors has turned very hostile. The English classes continue motivating the military officers, and Gilberto and I have been impressed by the zeal and the progress.

We have been learning to live with excitement and valor in these conditions and this jungle, and thanks to the daily exercises and reading we have been very occupied in body and spirit. I love you, mi vida, receive my kisses.

**Friday, July 19**: My love: Today we also listened to your message and obviously knowing that you were going to be in Frontino, we tuned in to the municipal radio station. There were some bits of news but really we could not hear anything concrete, nor your statements.

We know that tomorrow will be the morning rosary from the Cathedral in the Bolívar Plaza and will be repeated in all parishes. We hope that the stations cover it so we can know how it develops.

I can't imagine how your trip will be tomorrow to Santafé de Antioquia and the day after through Guarne. I hope it goes well with you and that the events are productive. This weekend I'm going to study the management report. Gilberto heard that there will be solidarity events in Mutatá, Sonsón, and Girardota. Also, we understand that they will give expressions of solidarity.

Yesterday and today the news of the attacks with pipe bombs, which fortunately were frustrated, concerned us. Yesterday the FARC, by means of Mono Jojoy, widened their threats to all government workers of a dozen states. One can see an attitude of triumphalism fed by the political energies generated by the first threats, and now the solidarity and civil valor that are vital to putting a brake on this attitude that I consider erroneous. Samper, firmly expressing himself in favor of a contract of amnesty, presented the example of Clinton, and left clear that the question is wanting to.

Your few words about the visit of the president confirm my suspicions that more than solidifying it, he went to take advantage of this space. My readings on Bolívar have been revealing. It seems to me to be very useful that you and also the cabinet be concerned to study in depth the true father of our country. It is difficult since the official history seems very complicated.

Well, mi vida, I just have to say that the days are different and happy when I listen to you, and they are long and gray when I do not receive your love in your messages. Receive my kisses and my love. Good night. Now I have the yellow T-shirt on that you know that is my favorite. I don't take it off, not even to sleep.

I have been thinking about the prisoner exchange; tomorrow I'll tell you about it.

**Saturday, July 20**: Love: Today you are in Santafé de Antioquia. We could not hear the news of trips to Frontino, Santafé, and Guarne on the radio but I'm hoping that Monday you'll tell us how it went. I know it went well. Today Luis Alberto Ramos and William Vélez were elected presidents of the Senate and the House. Antioquia consolidates a lot of power with 31 congressmen (14 senators and 17 representatives) with the national president and the leaders of both chambers.

Oh that this political capital would jointly apply a solution to the problems of the state and not satisfy personal interests. The regional autonomy, the subway, and nonviolence seem to me to be the three most important topics.

All afternoon I have been thinking of you. The book of poems that my mother sent, with some of Neruda, moved me to Black Island. The poncho that you sent me warms me and the company of the rosary of rose petals almost makes me happy.

Your absence, however, is so great that it crushes any other sentiment. At times I think that the "happiness" of our life here and the small pleasures, like going to fish, which for weeks they have not authorized, to do exercises, to read, can confuse the perception of abandonment, solitude, injustice, and almost permanent anxiety of finding ourselves at the border of an imminent tragedy.

There's a notable contrast between the availability of time and the latent danger that surrounds us. Love, I confess that I have smoked a few cigarettes; at night at times they help me drown the sadness of being without you. Good night, mi vida.

**Sunday, July 21**: We heard messages from Martha Inés and Pirri, also Blanca, Lilia, and Margarita Tabares sent messages via the Internet. We know that in the edition of *El Espectador* there is the great priority for our liberation. Also Bishop Castro and Marlene Orjuela have been interviewed. We have heard [from Castro] that López returned to write on the topic.

There is news about the kidnapping of a three-year-old girl by the Southern Block, who will be released when the threats of the FARC that demand the resignation of the elected officials are realized. Love, one of the sub-officials was working with the fighters and brought very encouraging news; it seems that the attitude of the FARC is very positive toward a humanitarian interchange and that they are prepared to do so before Pastrana leaves office.

The reason why they have not authorized the release of these letters is, apparently, that our release is near. Undoubtedly your actions and the enormous pressure of public opinion and the perseverance of the families have created the favorable milieu in the government to crystallize an accord, and it seems that luck has again smiled on Pastrana. Today there were events of civil resistance in four cities. Luis Pérez seems to have left the country.

I continue being convinced of the importance of nonviolence, a little frustrated for the lack of an answer from the FARC, but I'm sure that it has to be worked on at other fronts that society offers: poverty, exclusion, interfamily violence, unjust exploitation, unemployment, and so many faults that injure our people.

With this good news I'm going to listen to the *boleros* program. Kisses, my love.

**Monday, July 22**: My sweet love: Your message was marvelous, I'm happy to hear that your weekend visits went well and to perceive that solidarity continues in Antioquia's towns. I swear that Gilberto as well as I and the military officers heard in your words a special hope. It seemed that you knew something and we have the impression that it could be something that the president told you.

Love, today the news centers around the visit of Uribe to Venezuela and the reception that Chávez gave him. Also, I heard on

*La Luciérnaga* (The Firefly) that Édgar Artunduaga has retired from congress to "not listen to the lies" in the president's speech.

Love, I am listening to *Radio Melodía*. The moon is astonishing, it lightens the branches of the trees of the jungle, and the light is such that we even perceive the colors that surround us.

The idea has overtaken us of an imminent return. We all begin to think seriously about that moment and how that reunion with loved ones will be. I think of you and Daniel and Matthew. I hope I can return before Daniel travels.

By the way, what do you know about Mafer? I expect you would be able to bring up the subject of Yolandita. Well, if God wills, we will see each other very soon. Until then, take care of yourself, please, mi vida.

Kisses and good night; I hope to hear your voice in the morning.

**Tuesday, July 23**: Love, it is 2:00 p.m. After lunch we listened to the news about the crime in the Tertulia and the sad death of Hildebrando [Giraldo Parra]. My heart feels like it lost a political friend, and my head alerts me to the consequences that can give way because of these actions.

It is now when my captivity concerns me most; when I feel its chains the most. Now is when nonviolence is most needed. The answer that society gives, and in general the political leadership, will depend on whether the intensity of the conflict is reduced or retaliations and atrocious crimes increase.

I hope that Eugenio does not lose the line of conduct that he has maintained until now. Today, with much pain, I will dedicate myself to pray for the soul of Hildebrando.

About the proposal of peace bonds, I feel that really the country should make the sacrifice to collect two billion, and they can be businessmen and groups and families of means who should give their support; however, I believe that the beneficiaries of this initiative should be the most needy sectors—rural farms, low income housing, and generation of employment.

I do not share the idea that an effort of this nature should disappear in arms and military tools, which then would be repeating history. We have to wait for the results of the investigation and inquiries about the crime. I'm really afraid that it is related to the actions of the communities. I believe that what is required is a change of attitude of the whole Antioquenian society about the causes of our difficulties; more solidarity from the well-off sectors of society, towns that refuse to use violence but still demand a solution to the wretched wounds of marginalization and the lack of equity.

**Wednesday, July 24**: Love: The day began sadly because of what happened yesterday and more so because there was no message from you. Because of the hopes of leaving that have germinated among us, I was overtaken with a great anxiety. I spent the day and part of the night thinking of you, of how marvelous and sweet will be our reunion.

I think that one of the best things about this kidnapping is to have discovered the immensity of love that I feel for you and the marvelous examples that almost daily I receive of your love. Perhaps this painful separation is responsible for my discovering how stupid and irresponsible I have been when I don't understand the greatness of your love.

I anxiously await the moment when I can embrace you again and sleep in your arms. Mi vida, I love you and I send you thousands of kisses.

**Thursday, July 25**: My sweet love: The sweetness of your voice this morning contributed to calming my soul, but I am sad over the death of Hildebrando. I think of Dr. [José] Prieto and I imagine his pain; for him it would be like having lost his son. I think I have pending a conversation with him. I hope my attitude and having left Eugenio in charge has been able to take a comforting role.

My love, until now, I've been able to battle sadness, but I begin to feel myself flooded with a sensation of sadness that I cannot contain. The country is ready to go to war. I do not believe that is the solution, but I cannot see how nonviolence will gain strength when in the words of all who make declarations there is the conviction that subversion is finished only with arms.

My brief but illustrative contact with the FARC makes me feel that they too desire a test of their strength and military strategy. Their capacity to do damage by mean of attacks is great and truly surpasses the ability of the establishment and society to be alert and prevent them.

Nonviolence will have to do with a genuine change in the attitude of the people before the conflict, before the injustices and the solutions that we in the government offer. Strong centralized government should be changed, but everything indicates that the opposite is happening. Against the threats of the FARC the military option is strengthened, and this will demand greater freedom of power for the president and as a consequence there'll be a centralizing of power.

Nevertheless I heard the very satisfactory statements of Minister F. Londoño in relation to the States. Love I'm going to continue my readings of Bolívar.

Love, in the news today, that of Santiago Botero stood out, since now he occupies the fourth place overall in the *Tour de France*, and the march of the women for peace; I suppose that this would have more coverage on TV than radio. At this moment, President Pastrana speaks (explanation: about a country supposedly well governed).

Love, I confess to you that I'm going to smoke a cigarette. Love, we just had a scare with a snake; the guard who watches us at night saw it. He said that it was a Mapaná X [a poisonous snake]; in the end we looked for it with torches and flashlights but could find nothing. We went to sleep very psyched out.

**Friday, July 26**: Love: Thank you for your message. By the way, very good initiative that the secretaries gave a brief report, but I would like it better if they were more precise and deeper.

Today I finished the book on Bolívar. I confess that it cemented in me the view I had of him as a great man and at the same time it raised some doubts and big questions about a lot of the things people consider a part of his heroic liberating deeds. Now that you are going to be in Bogotá, I'm sure you can consult authorized opinions about the progress of the conversations between the government and the FARC.

We heard a declaration of the Federation of Governors in which they point out that they will not accept resignations caused by FARC threats against the mayors. Yesterday Anne Patterson[12] seconded a request that Luis Pérez is making to call into service the military reserves. In another time, that would have been considered an unpardonable intrusion in Colombian affairs.

Colanta lowered the price of milk, good for that. I ask myself about the children's nutritional program. Love, I have not told you that the ants [large, edible ants of that region] have fascinated me. I have been saving them carefully; the first day I gave a taste of them to everyone, and later with much discretion. With each one I remember how you love them. Also, the beautiful rosary goes with me and comforts my times of prayer. It brings your precious image to me.

**Saturday, July 27**: Love: Despite not hearing you this morning, today has been a happy day for three reasons. First is the program of the personality of the week, in which they interviewed Eugenio. It was very good, since at the beginning he spoke with much control and conviction about nonviolence and he interpreted very well the reasons that pushed me to embrace it; I really liked his loyalty.

He also did very well in resolving the doubts that, I suppose, have been the hobby of the Antioquenian political class, which have speculated about the provisional character of his conduct and about the possible grafting of your or my family. Finally, I liked to hear him defend the actions of the administration.

The second reason is that I could hear the program of the state government, and I heard them speak of reforestation, the business of the Management of African Colombian affairs. Also I listened to your voice in declarations very similar to one of the last messages.

The third reason is less "noble" and is limited to the fact that in the meals they gave us cornbread, and some military officers gave me extra. So the meal was ten cornbreads and you know, love, how much I love it.

At the end of the afternoon, Gilberto gave all of us a very good talk on ethics, morale, and emphasized the concepts of ethics, morale, legality, and justice. Very good, and you know the grace and enthusiasm that he knows how to use.

We are going to go to bed with the assignment of getting up at 1 a.m. to listen to *The Voices of the Kidnapping*. I believe that you are not accustomed to sending messages, but I enjoy hearing the relatives of all who find themselves in these painful circumstances.

I send you a thousand kisses and my love. I love you.

**Sunday, July 28**: My love: Good morning. We are listening to the program on Caracol with the new committees of Congress speaking about the reforms and the possible repealing of the present Congress. I think, and I want you to remind me to not forget, that I should speak with the three women who registered me, to review their situation.

Today we listened to the statements of the next minister of defense in relation to the call for the reserves. It pains me everything is headed toward war, and besides, "recommendations" of the [U.S.] ambassador are heard rather than the petitions of our people.

There was an attack in Cali; fortunately no lives were lost. My head boils with ideas of nonviolence and my personal perception of the need to procure more radical changes in Antioquia and also in my own life, our life.

The gospel for today was the parable of the kingdom of God that is like a treasure, or a very special pearl which justifies giving everything for it. Today I hope *The Hour of Love* gives us some beautiful song for both of us. Love, I'm going to pray; a kiss, I love you.

**Monday, July 29**: My sweet love: Today I did not write you, those notes I'm doing tomorrow, the 30th. In the morning we heard your beautiful message. In it we read more than your optimism, the message that you had conversations that permitted you to know how the process of liberation is going. Your hopes and ours are very similar and the level of hopes here is very high, both among us and among the fighters.

Today for the first time we did not receive breakfast, but I don't complain. We did exercises like any other day, and I greatly enjoyed lunch. It was a healthy forced fast. I want to study the topic of fasts. In reality, in all areas of nutrition, I want to do experiments.

Can you imagine that here we eat rice, lentils, beans, green peas, and small green plantains; this they accompany with brown sugar water and sometimes with oatmeal drink. Usually the rice is combined with some grains; rarely do they give us corn, it depends on if there is a field nearby and if it is producing. I have learned to "not need" meat and I confess that I aim to notably decrease my need. I eat very little fish since for quite a time now they have not let me go fishing, but that is something I'd like to increase.

Also, I tell you my love, I have practically eliminated sweets. Once in a while I'll eat a candy, and that's when things from home arrived. Actually, I don't miss it.

**Tuesday, July 30**: My love: I heard your beautiful message in which, besides your well-oriented optimism, you speak of Daniel and Matthew; I'm so pleased that they are well. I confess that here it really hurts me to be far from them and to cause them this pain. I would really like if you would talk with them more and, if possible, shared more time with them.

I know that it doesn't depend on you, but here it happens that after wanting something and asking for the Lord's help, those desires are fulfilled. Also, we heard Josue's report, very well structured and very positive regarding the VIVA[13] business, although I'm sure due to limited time it was also a little limited in information and data on the progress of the program, which interests me more.

Listening to the program I have an idea of a program that I call Report for the People of Antioquia that daily explains in the regions the advances and programs of the state government and offers participation to the local actors. Its frequency: daily; its duration: an hour. I also have thought that the need to gather and process, confidentially, information on our social problems is critical, to insist on my continual harping on pertinent and sufficient indicators. This is the task of planning and is the condition *sine qua non* for trying any nonviolent action.

In this area of nonviolence, I want to study more deeply the experience and advances of the Shalom Group of Holland, also that of Kenneth Kaunda in Zambia, since he also, as president, applied governmental nonviolence.

For several days the pope is in America. Today he was received in Guatemala, and there they will canonize one of the two saints the church recognizes. What draws my attention is that of Diego, the country boy who saw the Virgin of Guadalupe. Curiously, the image that Taia (Margarita María Maya White) loaned me, to accompany me on the march, is the Virgin of Guadalupe.

It is also the image that helped in the revolutionary battles in Mexico, while in other parts of Latin America the church persecuted Bolívar. Coincidence? Signs?

Today the military officers went to help load the provisions. Considering "our age" they excluded Gilberto and me. I tell you that the English course is going very well. I'm really surprised at the desire and the ability of the military officers. They learn quickly. Today silence reigns and the environment permits me, ever more, to read and think of you and of Antioquia. Kisses, my love.

About nonviolence, I believe the moment has arrived to strengthen and establish real connections with the nonviolent community of the world. I plan to do that immediately after I return. A little period of study and preparation and then an intense trip to know them personally and speak about their experiences and plans and about our actual situation.

I have thought about the ridiculous "international help." I believe we lack more dignity at the hour of accepting it and appraising it. With that I do not say it's not necessary. It's more that true help is needed. Today what the "Third World" receives from the rich countries are crumbs, which is a cheap way of maintaining us in their clutches.

Love, you have to remind me to get the documents of Vatican II Council on Peace, the documents of the last popes and the World Council of Churches, especially the pastorals of the United States and Germany. Good night, mi vida.

**Wednesday, July 31**: Love, we listened to your beautiful message, also multiple messages for Gilberto for his birthday. We and the military officers got up very quietly at 4:45 a.m. and sang *Las Mañanitas*. We woke up and we gave him very humble gifts and cards prepared by some with artistic talents. The gifts were from *arepas* (griddle cakes) to undershorts (second hand), a much desired item here.

Until 8 p.m. we listened to many messages and optimistic news and of great solidarity. Eugenio's message at mid-day was excellent; until now I feel that I have been right in his election. I hope that the experience serves him for the future; he has demonstrated valuable virtues.

At this moment we are listening to an historic dissertation by Gilberto about the chronology of violence in Antioquia. Very interesting. Yesterday the fighters returned at 4 p.m. We had a calm day, and when they arrived they were tired, and they brought good news. The enthusiasm and friendliness of the fighters, as well as their conversations, indicate in an unmistakable way that our release "is done."

I feel that you all have been suffering unbearable levels of anxiety. With God's help and that of the Virgin, soon we'll be together, mi vida. The statements of Dr. Camilo Gómez are very unfortunate in that it seems he is more interested in seeing the failure of what President Pastrana claims to be his biggest hope.

**Thursday, August 1**: My love: Today you did not send a message and the attitude of the FARC has changed. It seems that they do not want to move forward with Pastrana. The blow to our state of mind has been great, even though Gilberto and I were prepared to concede that solutions are not so rapid and we do not believe in the willingness shown by the president and his commission. In any case, we should continue with enthusiasm and optimism.

Love, the figures of DANE[14] are a real cause for concern, also because I believe they hide the truth. Unemployment and underemployment have climbed, and even the Ministry of Public Funds has been frustrated. They won't delay in justifying themselves and painting their picture. I hope that the solution has a different focus.

We cannot accept that the same remedy of "blood and tears" be continued, applying the same that all the ministers of public funds use. It seems it has become known that the proposal by Pastrana to the FARC was forty fighters for seventy-five kidnapped persons. It is possible that this could cause the FARC to react by not continuing to advance with Pastrana.

The good news is that we perceive in the FARC, at least among those here, a good reaction to the efforts of Álvaro Uribe and the mediation of the UN. The realistic time frame, my love, is of several months.

I continue thinking, each day with more conviction, about the alternative of nonviolence. The most practical application would be a "nonviolent social defense." The transformation is urgently required; it is imperative that the government of Uribe takes on the role of nonviolence education. I have arrived at the conclusion that without nonviolence no democracy can exist.

**Friday, August 2**: Love: Today I really missed your message. In reality, my spirit is very low. I have to get out of this hard cycle.

I listened to the criticism that the president is making of the Assembly, Rodrigo Meza, and the situation of the state. He showed that there was a surplus of 57 billion, and yet there are hospitals in bankruptcy.

I think this time should cause me to think more deeply about the changes that we would be required to make to give a real boost to nonviolence. I would be thinking of a series of campaigns and shaping the structures and curriculum so that the people of Antioquia really learn and we can begin changing attitudes concerning violence.

Today I have no doubt that Antioquia, if it accepts this philosophy, would be called to play a role of transcendence in the context of the world. I hope Luis Javier Botero (consultant on nonviolence in the state of Antioquia) is advancing and that these sacrifices are not in vain. I know how hard the process will be. I myself realize how much I miss it, despite the fact that I am convinced that it is the better way.

**Saturday, August 3**: My love: Good morning. I hope that you are resisting this prolonged separation better than I am. I continue in low spirits. Neither the exercises, nor reading, nor prayer, nor the classes help to get rid of the sadness of my heart. I hope to leave this condition soon.

I listen to the problems in Meta, in Puerto Alvira. Also in Facatativá there was the explosion of a pipe bomb.

I love you and need you. I would like to know how Papo and Mafer are. For next week, Mockus proposes an excellent campaign: "The week of self regulation and living together." This suggests to me a week or a month of nonviolence, after an adequate period of formation or training with some ingenious campaigns. Receive my love.

**Sunday, August 4**: Love: Today in the early morning, like each Sunday, we listened to the program *The Voices of the Kidnapping*. I know that you do not send messages by this means; nevertheless I listen to it with the hopes of hearing you and of knowing the feelings of the relatives.

In the middle of the night they gave the news and the communication of the FARC, in which they pointed out that they had received no proposal from the government of Pastrana. If you review these lines, you will see that this news confirms the doubts that I have always expressed concerning the sincerity and will of the president.

Today breakfast was very deficient, and it doesn't appear that they will be giving us lunch. Something is happening with the provisions. I heard that the ANIF,[15] alarmed by the numbers and the behavior of the dollar, are asking that an economic emergency be declared. It seems like they are repeating the errors of the beginning of Pastrana's government, which caused panic that later affected the national economy in an irreversible way.

Gilberto shared with me one of his very precious gifts, a can of flan custard from arequipe; it was a good substitute for lunch. Yesterday we missed the radio program of news of the state; today they are going to begin it, so I'm going to listen to it.

A kiss. Various news: The best one was to hear your voice repeating the message that you sent us on Gilberto's birthday. Your voice made my soul rejoice. Finally, lunch arrived; the delay was due to a defect in the oven.

Already we have heard some news in which the government pretends to show its will, but the truth is it does not achieve it. Last night the father of Malimud (kidnapped by the ELN) said in his message that he had "spoke in plain language" to Doctor Camilio Gómez in a meeting in the Moroccan Embassy. I think that the liberation will be given, only that in the beginning of the government of Álvaro Uribe it can easily be swamped, but the fundamental elements are given: The FARC wants to get out some of their men and public opinion desires our way out.

I have already said and written it, but it fills me with deep sadness and loathing that the president plays with the sentiments of the families and the hopes of public opinion. Well, my sweet love, I hope to hear you early tomorrow. Kisses, and receive my love.

**Monday, August 5**: My sweet love: You did not send a message. We only listened to Martha Inés and Lina, but very poorly since the signal was very bad.

Today President Pastrana and his ministers, Garzón at the head, gave statements saying that they will wait until the last minute for the FARC to send a fax or some sign of interest in the humanitarian exchange. Horacio Serpa wrote a very critical article against the government of President Pastrana. Minister Rómulo García has tried to answer him and refute it but was limited to morally disqualifying it for having participated in the government of Samper.

Yesterday I heard that they are going to summon the Minister of Transportation to speak about the enormous costs that, according to the parliamentarian Álvaro Araújo from the state of Cesar, has come having to elevate the nation through a bad contract of concessions.

I would like to know if a debate will be given tomorrow and what numbers are real: At first sight I think that he is not taking into account the actual value of the infrastructure, and undoubtedly neither does he take into consideration the savings this can offer the country.

My spirit is better today, I miss you immensely. Today I gave a written exam to the military officers on English—they are improving notably. Well, my love, I adore you; receive thousands of kisses and all my love. Good night. I hope that tomorrow I can enjoy your voice.

**Tuesday, August 6**: My love: I'm happy. I just finished communicating your message, now we're going to listen to it; those of Martha Inés and Lina have been heard. Yesterday they were at Mass in Isagén, today they will be accompanying Álvaro Uribe in a Mass; it's not clear whether in Bogotá or in Medellín. Uribe received the prescribed military decorations.

Your voice was very broken, I'm sorry you are suffering so much. I hope that you can speak with Uribe and he will help you know what to think and what possibilities he sees for a humanitarian exchange shortly. In these last days you have been very absent, I don't know what the reason is. Listening to you, I believe you have been a little sad. The cruel way hopes were generated about our release would have really hurt the families. We here also feel the hard blow.

Love, things here go on without major changes. I put forth the effort to keep occupied in productive things. Right now I'm preparing a speech about nonviolence. I'm also reading a book that arrived for us in the second parcel, about (Rafael) Nuñez. Really surprising is the vision of those years that had so much influence on the nation, and I see how much influence they have in the present time.

I have not heard again the messages of the cabinet. I hope they can continue. They are very beneficial to me, and I believe that it would be good to make them available so the Antioquenian people can hear them.

I miss you so much, I miss the boys; I don't know how the military officers can resist being absent from their families for so much time. Some of them don't even know their own daughters. Well, love, receive my kisses and my love.

**Wednesday, August 7**: Love: Today we do not expect messages from you all since it is a holiday. On Radio Caracol, López, who was in Medellín spoke. I wonder if you were able to speak with him, since I know how much you admire and appreciate him. I wonder what you are doing now, but I hope you are more serene.

I would like to know how the initiative of the floral banner of Liberty is going, how the Floral Fair is doing, and how you have participated. Love, don't think that I have forgotten our anniversary which will be this Sunday. We are expecting with the swearing in of Álvaro Uribe, the FARC will decrease the escalation it usually carries out during the change of government, and this can open the way for mediation by the United Nations and through them a process of peace can be cemented. López also expressed that today.

To the question of what was most important for the government of Uribe to begin doing, he said, "To provide steps toward peace and these steps are negotiation, since the peace of arms is not lasting." We are prepared to listen to the program at 9 a.m. (Caracol) about Uribe and in the afternoon the inaugural speeches. Love, remember that I was never good at listening to the radio? Well, now I have improved greatly.

Another thing that did not make me enthusiastic was the rice, but now I think it can compete with you. I love and miss you so much.

Love, we listened to the conversation of captivity. I find it very positive for the country; however I do not see a way out of our situation. I believe that again it is in your hands and the success that you can have by keeping the public motivated, something that will be more difficult each time topics like the proposed reforms are discussed.

The attitude of the FARC reveals even greater difficulties in this respect. It insinuates that the space for nonviolence is reduced. I confess that in the conversation I did not hear mention of regional autonomy, but it is also probable that they think that with the threats to the stability they seek to make it necessary to maintain the power concentrated at the central level.

You know that I consider centralism as the worst defect of our system and the source of vices and the cause of the mediocrity of our state. This I say based on my experience on the central level, more than as a provincial authority.

The hour to say good-bye has come. The night is very dark and your absence makes it solitary and sad. I hope that even my kisses and my love arrive. Good night, mi vida.

**Thursday, August 8**: My sweet love: Today I heard your marvelous message, in which you tell me all the activities programmed for this month. I really like your allusion to the "chair of liberty."

Just yesterday I was thinking of Aníbal, Emiliana, and Claudia. I hope they can enjoy some of the events at the fair. What drew my attention the most was the orchids, birds, and flowers of the botanical garden.

Mi vida, I am very pleased to feel more encouraged than yesterday, I know how difficult it is. I have to force myself so as not to let myself be overtaken by sadness. I am doing exercises daily. When I get out, I'm going to have to be very strict concerning food and time to do exercises every day. I would like you to accompany me in the exercises.

I want to do so many things with you, beginning with our daughter. If time permits us, if I do not stay here much more, and we can proceed without much risk, I would like this to be the first. I want to go deeper in the life and thoughts of Bolívar, visit places that were important, review his writings, etc.

Another thing I want is to strengthen the bonds with nonviolent entities in other parts of the world and to explore the study of this literature, which is more abundant and serious than I first thought. I have been trying to make a decision about our moving to "another place," like we have discussed, and I confess that I have not yet decided.

I believe it is necessary to know your opinion, to know your desires and your point of view in this respect. Love, the news about the acceptance of mediation on the part of the UN and the hard position on Chirac before the terrorism of the FARC are crucial. We hope that they lead the country toward opening spaces for really productive dialogue. With Hernán Peláez again in *La Luciérnaga*, I have thought that you will be enjoying it much more.

Today, more than usual I've been thinking of my parents and brothers and sisters. What are they feeling and how are their lives going? I have also asked myself how Mafer is doing in her English.

Well, it is late and it doesn't stop raining. I'm going to bed to think a little more about you. I send you kisses and all my love. God bless you.

**Friday, August 9**: Today you were not on the air. We listened to Martha Inés, Lina, and Vivian. The news has to do with the declarations of the new Commissioner of Peace, Luis Carlos Restrepo. Very serious, organized, and very exaggerated; he clarified some aspects of the president's speech. The most important has to do with the mediation of the UN, about which he clearly expressed that they have taken the first step, but it would be better if the FARC would speak up.

They didn't wait. Before midday they said that a real change in the Colombian state was necessary and as long as that wasn't done, all mediation was discarded by them. We should wait to see the reaction to have a more clear idea. In the meantime, today we are sending a letter to see if the secretariat will listen to us, to present the proposal of the Laboratory of Nonviolence. We have it, but the circumstances have not permitted it.

Well, my love, it's close to dinner. I love you, kisses. In the afternoon Gilberto listened to a news report that the state of Santander (I suppose the capital Bucaramanga) had made an homage in our honor in which Santanderan gratitude was expressed and especially making reference to the road of Guane. I suppose that Genaro Peñalosa [then mayor of Barichara] in many ways would be responsible. Like Santander, there should be many more grateful regions.

**Saturday, August 10**: Today there was good sun. I took advantage of it and warmed my feet. Sunning myself, I thought if I had some water colors and a sheet of paper for this picture, I could practice recovering my abilities as a little painter. I would like to record this landscape, like you mention in your letters. I enjoy the nature and try to have the landscape nurture my soul to make this separation less hard.

Yesterday I was rereading all the letters you have sent. They fill me with energy and joy. They are my inexhaustible strength for this hard blow. I still have some of your edible ants; I'm going to eat one little portion. I tell you that it has been difficult to contain myself to not finish them off on the first sitting, but as you can see, there still are a few.

Yesterday we sent two letters: one for those responsible here and the other containing our proposal to make a laboratory to apply nonviolence in Antioquia, directed to the commander of Front 34, asking for a meeting with Marulanda and the secretariat and the Bolívarian Movement for a New Colombia. This, which we have had prepared for quite some time, has coincided with the declarations of the FARC in which they demand a willingness to change on the part of the government of the state.

More will for change which is stated in our proposal and the coherence of our attitudes is very difficult to find. We hope that they receive it and see its transforming potential. I hear on Radio Super some declarations about the horse ride. It seems that it is all a success.

I think of you and our anniversary tomorrow. I miss your messages on the early morning program, *The Voices of the Kidnapping*.

**Sunday, August 11**: Happy anniversary, mi vida. Today we prepare ourselves to listen to a program, in Radio Super which gives homage to Gilberto and me, which begins at 8 a.m.

We hear that an Antioquenian was elected Miss World; I ask myself if it is also the responsibility of the Corporation of Beauty of Antioquia, and I send you my congratulations.

There are a lot of rumors to explain the inside reshuffling and commotion here. I have been exercising with such earnestness that Gilberto tells me to lower the rhythm. He doesn't think I can do so with so much regularity outside. I have probably lost five or ten kilograms. I'm going to increase my intake by eating dessert since it's high in calories, and also rest on Saturday and Sunday.

Love, I have been very diligent in preparing the talk about nonviolence, and now I have it more or less structured. I believe I will have it tomorrow, Monday. Really, this is my first theoretical evaluation of the topic of nonviolence. Let's see what the reaction of the military officers and of Gilberto is. The more I study, the more I am pleased with and committed to this philosophy of life and methodology of social transformation.

Last night they gave us a lot of rice for supper, which is only rice. You would laugh if you saw me enjoying to the utmost a meal which is only rice. Now I'm beginning to see why you and my dad like it so much; it's something just like corn (in the form of cornbread). It has simplicity but at the same time, its own character of flavor, and draws my attention. Now they are my preferred snack.

Well, mi vida, I hope to hear you tomorrow. Receive my kisses and all my love. Happy anniversary.

**Monday, August 12**: Love, good morning. I'm so happy, because I listened to you. You spoke of your love and of how much we miss each other and of our project of life. Also, the little chair of liberty and of the concert of Juanes and the emotion you felt when he asked for our liberation and that of all those kidnapped.

Additionally today, they authorized us to build a little field for micro-soccer, a product of our solitude (one of the letters that we sent this week). All morning long we were dedicated to this task. In the afternoon I have scheduled the talk, then I'll tell you about my life. Actually early this morning there was an internal commotion.

Heriberto continues laboriously working on the chess pieces. He promised me one which I hope to take to Daniel, together with other little gifts of hard palm.

Hello, my sweet princess. I am awake and I got up to write you some things that are rolling around in my head. In the first place, the talk on nonviolence was a complete success, but I had to divide it into two; the second half I will finish tomorrow.

Today it was an hour and a half and we had almost two hours of discussion about the topic; later, with questions and reflections of the military officers. I believe that in this the Virgin, who I have been asking for light and help, heard me; I should say, also heard me.

Before going to sleep I heard the last romantic songs of the program on Caracol, *La Hora/Boche del Romance* (The Hour/Night of Romance) from 9 to 9:30 p.m.

We had an unfavorable reaction from those of the FARC, since the military officers wanted to dedicate only the morning hours to physical work (in the building of the playing field) and wanted us to work more intensely. I hope that the nonviolence helps us to convert this into an opportunity to draw nearer and not to the opposite.

In my being awake, I heard news about Gilibert (police), Juanes, Chávez and the milk, the naming of decentralized officials, and the income tax for the war.

Next, some impressions. The news of Gilibert and his resignation which happened after hearing this morning declarations of the minister in which she intermixed doubts, and that the government of Uribe has listened to the persistent rumors of corruption in the police, I had to remember an episode that caused me great concern and which I attended in the velodrome put together by the police of Antioquia. This annoyed me, because it was converted into a real act of worship and praise for the general.

They distributed T-shirts and caps with the image of the general and the Heart of Jesus. It goes without saying that in the stands there were huge flags with his image and banners with his picture on them, and images of them were projected. We ask ourselves here, with what money was this lip service made possible? Would it be dollars?

You mention, love, about the concert of Juanes Saturday and an interview that they just put on Caracol. It makes me feel great pride; you know how much I admire the work of Shakira and Carlos Vives in favor of the culture and the international image of Colombia. They, and now Juanes also, have achieved more than many in the government.

I hope to have the opportunity to acknowledge him with the Shield of Antioquia. I heard that criticism has begun about Luis Alfredo Ramos on an interview that he had with Chávez, which Genaro Pérez attended. The coast people pretend that there Colata is favored, and they are demanding explanations. I have thought of the inabilities that stop the congresspersons from participating in these topics in which they have some interest, that generally are those in which they stand out or for which they were elected, since that is where they have their electors—habits of the hypocrisy that reigns in our codes.

By naming regional officials through competitions of merit, Álvaro Uribe has taken a great step against politicking. As I understand it, by law, these officials of the poorly named decentralization institutions are chosen by the governors from a list of three candidates presented by the institution; they are, thus, regional "quotas."

I'm surprised that the president, having the opportunity with his novel proposal in the naming of hundreds of first, second, and third level in the central government, has proceeded there to choose them with his finger (politically) and here, we who in the statutes were his governors, he offers to generously choose them "by merit."

Finally, I wanted to share with you that, based on the Political Letter, I am thinking of publicly rejecting, for reasons of conscience, the paying of a war tax. It is something that I should talk with you about in more detail.

**Continuation, Monday, August 12**: Love, last night I ran out of paper and I tried to sleep and I didn't even say goodbye; a kiss and good night.

**Tuesday, August 13**: My love: Good morning. I listened to your beautiful message. I felt you were sad, and I grieve greatly to hear you like that. I imagine the things that are passing through your mind and with the course of happenings in the national government. As you say insistently, we have to trust in the Lord and the Virgin and hope that in their designs maintaining us with health and life permitting liberation quickly.

I hope to leave with enough time to round up the fundamental topics of the government and especially in regard to the impulse of nonviolence. We heard of the kidnapping of the ex-governor of the state of Arauca, Héctor F. Gallardo. Also, the statement by Castaño that he is ready to initiate a process of peace with the government at any moment. Yesterday I said to Gilberto that it would be very interesting if the government of Uribe could sign an agreement of peace with the paramilitaries.

Today they did not allow work on the playing field. This attitude makes us think that it is in retaliation for not having worked yesterday afternoon.

My love, I tell you that today I ate the last of the ants that remained. At this moment we are in the writing class, with the help of a dictionary we are reviewing the rules of Spanish.

Love, if in some moment you have the opportunity to again send us things, I ask you to send a constitution, hopefully extensively commented and complemented, especially on topics of participation. Well, love, I say goodbye for today; receive my kisses and love.

**Wednesday, August 14**: Love, today you did not give a message and I missed it so much. If this happens to me for one day that I don't hear you, I imagine how you are suffering, despite the fact that you can have the support of other persons. Last night, a little sad, I went to bed a lot earlier.

Today I'm going to try to avoid this melancholy, which at times dominates me. The day is beginning beautiful, despite having rained all night. The sun has been coming out cloudlessly since very early, and while the drops of water caught in the vegetation and the foliage are forming small sparkles, and the vapor gently lifts at times like the smoke of a cigarette in the twilight when it is illuminated by a beam of light, its soft rays are filtered and solemn among the trees, producing marvelous contrasts with multiple greens and browns.

These images are not permanent; they constantly change because of the little clouds that interpose and thus at times are sad, at times happy and warm. When they succeed in passing the surface of water, they dissolve, an effect of vibration on the leaves that remember the games of light.

Today I should finish the talk on nonviolence. Yesterday we began a course in writing (Alejandro Ledesma). Love, the conference became very long, so I am going to need a last session tomorrow, Thursday. I think of you a lot and I miss you immensely.

Today they announced the appointment of Campo as general director of the police. I hope he permits our proposal of nonviolence to be presented and that it penetrates into the interior of the institution. Up to now, the reactions to the talk on the part of the military officers, as well as the picture that you sent, have been very positive. This has more merit if we take into account that in them there is a profound questioning on the use of arms. Well, mi vida, receive all my love.

**Thursday, August 15**: My love: Today I heard your beautiful message, your announcements on progress in the manual for older adults, and the crucial putting into action of the school of the government and the forum about regional autonomy. Love; nevertheless it causes me deep grief to hear, in your voice, the sadness that covers you. It hurts me greatly to be the cause of your anxiety.

There is something that you don't say. As if you knew the difficulties that are coming for us and you do not want us to see them. I wish I could get through to you the news and that you would know that we are fine and they treat us very well, despite our own difficulties and the limitations of our circumstances.

Also, I want you to feel the strength that faith gives me and the conviction of nonviolence and the message that we are giving to the FARC and to our people. I love you, mi vida.

Heriberto continues working on the chess pieces; the two that are going to be a gift to the commanders here are almost ready. We have already begun what he is going to give me, which is a gift for Daniel; I'm thinking that the black pieces will be of *macana* palm, even though it is very hard; I think it will be a novelty, pretty and very special.

Well, love, today I did not finish the talk, I'll do so tomorrow.

**Friday, August 16**: Love, today, like you said, I did not hear your message since you were in Bogotá, but instead I had the opportunity to listen to you on Caracol. I heard you much better.

And you were very clear. The conversation was very placid; I liked the frank and dignified way you reproached Gardeazábal publicly on his absurd and insulting position. I hope the occasion lets you enjoy yourself a little and be happy and that you have much success. Also, I liked your decided attitude to make what is necessary.

Today, after a long silence, finally they invited us again to watch television. We saw the news on Channel One. The greatly changed format of the news impressed me, very modernized. Also the piece where they seek to generate great repudiation in the population against the fighters really impacted me negatively.

After the news a program of *Popstars* began. Gilberto and I went to bed before 8:30. The military officers stayed until late. Last night I thought a lot about you, my love, of the possibilities of having our daughter and what it would be like to be together again; I thought again of the "crystalline" and in thinking in thick lines of a true "life plan."

Negrete made you a gift: a bracelet with your name. He also made one for Daniel and Matthew. I'm using yours, and I feel very sweet sensations having you so near. I love you, mi vida. Good night.

**Saturday, August 17**: My love: Today I dedicated myself to the chess set for Daniel. Finally, my proposal to make the black ones with *macana* palm was seen that, indeed, it could be done. The pope is in Poland and has made a call to put an end to the use of war.

Here finally President Uribe spoke of creating regions. I don't know if he spoke of ending the states. I'm sure that is where it will get to since his advisor is Castro. I hope that Antioquia is sufficiently prepared to accompany him and participate in the struggle, which will be dangerous. Although the country has seen his effort of proposing the national administration to the states, with pleasure and as a example of decentralization; I think that, as such, it finally shows the goodwill of the ruler. But it doesn't advance, since it continues being the central level that decides.

The topic is delicate but it is important who (I wish I could) takes part in the debate so that the good will of the president cannot stay there and we are successful in opening the way to true regional autonomy. The initiative to end comptrollerships I really like. However, I do not see the fulfilling of promises to end the national institutes called "decentralized."Rather, they are taking away from the governors the power to elect the regional directors from triads.

Nevertheless, I am confident that, confronted with solid arguments, the president will know how to make a satisfactory decision.

Tonight we watched television. I was going to go to bed early to pray and write you, but they came for me and told me that if I did not go with them none of the officials or sub-officials could watch it, so I went with them. I tell you, television doesn't attract me. I believe that never again will it produce the effect it once did.

We saw the news, which each day has more "show" and gossip; then we finished with a movie, and Gilberto and I left. In the morning we listened to the program, *The Voices of the Kidnapping.* The good news: the liberation of Santiago Taborda and José Vásquez.

Thinking of you and the children, I slept peacefully.

**Sunday, August 18**: Good morning, mi vida. Today I'm imagining you in your house with your kids, and I hope you are enjoying them. I heard Mass today and then the interview with General [Teodoro] Campo.

Last night my reflections took me to see the kidnapping really as torture to society. With some anger, I see the pretensions of the United States so that Colombia will bow down on the position of the USA before the court in Rome; it has a real odor of blackmail. Fortunately already, the voices of public opinion begin to show themselves against it.

There are also critics of the referendum, for the lack of execution that permits strengthening political parties and little explanation about the new economic model. I'm concerned about not hearing anything about regional autonomy; I believe it is the most appropriate opportunity.

Now they permit Gilberto and me to stay here, while the military officers go watch television. They can spend six or eight hours watching it; I'm only interested in the news. I prefer to read, think, write, or listen to music. Today we killed a snake here in the bed of one of the officials. It happened to be harmless.

**Monday, August 19**: Today, love, we celebrate the Assumption of the Virgin Mary to heaven. Today has been a calm day. The military officers left after lunch to watch television. The news had to do with the displacements in San Francisco, Yondó.

I have decided to read about the history of Nuñez and the Regeneration, to think of my loved ones, you at the top, and to talk with Gilberto. At night there was a meeting of our captors that was very long and I did not wait for supper. I went to bed without eating. Kisses, mi vida.

**Tuesday, August 20**: Hello, mi vida. I just finished hearing your message, also those of Martha Inés and Lina. You are returning from Bogotá, but you haven't told me how it went for you, either in the session of solidarity nor with your children. I noted you were stronger; I suppose the trip has served for you to regain your spirit.

Today we heard of the kidnapping of eighteen persons in Chigorodó [state of Chocó]; we'll have to wait for more information.

General Campo spoke about the 193 municipalities without any police presence; they asked him about rumors of corruption.

**Wednesday, August 21**: Hello, mi vida. Today also I heard your beautiful message. We are completing four months here. Today I spent almost the whole day in making the chess set for Daniel and playing with Yim. I am really getting better.

With stones, we are building a little dam to block the river; now we have a well of fifty inches in the lower part. Today, at night the ELN kidnapped twenty-four persons in the cove of Utría [south of Solano Bay, Chocó]; these, as well as those kidnapped are humble persons; poor, municipal retirees of Cali, and those of Urabá are small businessmen.

We have been hearing the promotion of the construction of the word *liberty*. We like the idea a lot, also the footstool like this. Today the day went by quickly because of the chess. Working on the swimming pool, I suffered a little accident and cut two toes a little, nothing serious, but it won't let me exercise tomorrow. I tell you, not to worry you but that you know that even the most insignificant happenings here are set apart.

Good night, mi vida; I love you.

**Thursday, August 22**: My love: Today we did not hear your message. Yes, we did hear Martha Inés and Lina but there was so much interference that we couldn't understand anything from them. More than a month ago we asked the commander here to tell them to send messages after 7 a.m., but I don't think he has done us the favor of getting in contact.

Today we heard a sad piece of news: The FARC does not want to accept the mediation of the UN and insists on the clearing out of two states as a requirement to negotiate with the present government. Everything seems to indicate that it's going to be very difficult for us to leave soon. What remains is to trust in divine will, which has always been our hope.

Actually I could not do exercises standing up, but I did arm and abdominal exercises. I think the chess set for Daniel will be ready tomorrow. The official and sub-officials have been going to see television these nights: today, for some reason, they did not let us see it.

Good night, mi vida.

**Friday and Saturday, August 23 and 24:** My love, good morning. Today you did not send a message, but yesterday we heard your speech after talking with the president. I felt very optimistic, in contrast to the news of the FARC.

It doesn't occur to me that you do not know of the communication, so I believe the meeting with the president had this effect. Today we heard the president in the Assembly of the ANDI [National Association of Industries], who minimized the importance of the communication of the FARC and maintains that the UN will conduct the negotiations. Also, he reiterated that the fumigation of coca and poppy cultivations will continue.

I miss you so much. Here I'm making a sort of post-graduate program in nonviolence, also something about our history, on the violence that has always scourged us. I'm also surprised at how little is necessary to feed a person and how one can adapt to living without conveniences.

My soul continues being sad because of your absence and how I miss my other loved ones. That emptiness cannot be filled with anything.

Yesterday the armed forces succeeded in recapturing nine kidnapped persons in the state of Cesar. The good news has to do with the speeches of Andrés Uriel Gallego promising the necessary resources to finish the tunnel of the west in August 2003.

It is important that Luis Alberto García works on the book. I hope that these advances do not let them believe that they should do the same thing in the east, in which case there would be no objection to translating the responsibility to the nation, if that is what they want.

Love, today we are going to be watching for the formation of liberty. There are good declarations of President Uribe about the possibility of authorizing regional dialogues of peace, always and only when there is good orientation and it does not constitute joint initiatives.

This opens options to initiatives like that of the east and our proposal on nonviolence. Love, today I mixed the reports of these two days. I'll stop, since it is bath time. Love, after lunch Gilberto and I were called to meet with two of the commanders who watch us. It was a calm meeting, in which we discussed the reasons for unease on both sides, and I think we are on the way to overcoming it.

Several things I liked: one, a showing of the possibility that some commander come, possibly Iván Márquez. If this happens, it seems to me the opportunity that we have been waiting for to talk of nonviolence and to take the unrest and our proposal to the secretariat. Also, they mentioned to us that the video with the stories on nonviolence has been sent to the secretariat of the FARC.

Finally, I was convinced that in the FARC there continues the will and the desire of humanitarian dialogue. Love, we just finished listening to parts of the activity in the stadium. I confess that even though there appears to be some disorder, that's understandable. I was saddened, and also very happy.

I hope that the conscience in every town will continue growing so that they can express themselves with liberty and nonviolence. Love, in the early morning you gave me a pleasant surprise with that spectacular message, full of optimism and happiness. You shared information about all the families, expressing yourself with great eloquence and clarity—all that I needed to hear. You charged Gilberto and me and the military officers with positive energy and hope.

Also, I felt so proud to have such a special wife.

**Sunday, August 25**: Love: Today I woke up like new, thanks to the beautiful message at daybreak. The chess set for Daniel is almost ready. Now I have to think hard about gifts to Papo and Matthew. I really liked the day in which you told me he had visited the horses.

Today the military officers invited us to watch television. Besides the boa that the fighters got, and after they let it go, the day went on without major events. The gospel for today spoke about St. Peter as the head of the church and coincidently, in the newscast at night, we saw the Holy Father, who has been very active these past few weeks.

Our skaters in Belgium continue doing well and put the country on a high level.

**Monday, August 26**: Today you did not send a message. Something happened here that is not frequent nor is it the first time: Lieutenant Ledesma lost his spoon and Aranguren for the second time lost his tooth paste. They presented the complaint to the chief of guards. This generated various reflections: on the one hand, the reaction of the chief, who tried to imply that we had done it; on the other hand, the very irritated way the lieutenant reacted before this contrast with religion and the preaching of nonviolence, letting me understand the enormous difficulties that we must face.

Lastly, I ask myself what the attitude should be that society/the establishment shows before their prisoners. From this last point, the idea has been born in me to stay a week in the jail at Bellavista to try to evade the injustices of these circumstances.

Gilberto continues very seriously on his essay on a new education system, which he began several days ago. Close to our conversation with the commanders here, I got the idea that soon we will receive a visit from some high ranking commander, which obligates me too seriously and with precision to prepare a proposal of applying nonviolence, making Antioquia a laboratory.

President Álvaro Uribe today strongly called to the attention of General Rodríguez in a Council of Security in Urabá a complaint of the archbishop regarding insecure travel above La Llorona. Well, mi vida, this is all for today, kisses and receive all my love.

**Tuesday, August 27**: Love, good morning. Today I received your beautiful message; it comforts me a great deal to hear you. In one way or another, we have tried to clarify that "mediation" is very different from negotiation and that the role of the UN should be neutral.

We believe that both families and public opinion have mutual interest in the humanitarian/exchange accord and having the FARC get their troops out of the jails.

Here at daybreak it was raining; everything indicates that the rainy season is beginning.

I'm thinking that the gift for Papo could be an Indian blow-gun or some article of cowhide; we'll see how it goes with this idea. We have been able to continue a type of dyke, piling up stones, and we succeeded in raising the level twenty or twenty-five inches. Today the topic of Uribe continues red hot, and they also made announcements about the new hierarchy of the police.

Well, mi vida, receive my kisses and my love.

**Wednesday, August 28**: My love: Good morning. Today it looks like it's going to be a good morning, since the sun came out early. Also, last night I dreamt about you. It's too bad that the censor does not permit me to write the topic of the dream. I can only say that it was really pleasant to again "see you."

You haven't told me anything about Mafer and Papo, how has it been with them? Actually it was a good morning, but now in the afternoon, it doesn't stop raining. I'm going to the English class; now they have learned more than a thousand words and we're going to begin construction; I'll return later, my love.

What joy: Today in the news on television I could see you and listen to your speech about the Commissioner of Peace to the mayors of the East. Also, the announcement was made of the new video with statements from several congressmen. Tomorrow President Uribe meets with the families of the kidnapped victims. We'll wait and see the results. Again it feels like the environment for prompt release is growing.

**Thursday, August 29**: My sweet love: We listened to Martha Inés, Lina, and Camila. I'm waiting for your message. Today I got up at 5:30 a.m. Last night's news and having seen you are excellent motivators and only your message for today is missing.

Before 8 a.m. they informed us that we should get our letters up to date, since soon they're coming to collect them. All day long I have dedicated myself to this. I wrote a letter for you and for Daniel and Matthew.

**Friday, August 30**: Mi vida: Today I am also writing. Today you did not send a message either. Everything indicates that they will receive the letters of the military officers tomorrow. As yet they have not clarified the rules. They don't want the FARC to know that the military officers and Gilberto and I are together.

They have given the order to eliminate mention of us in the letters of the military officers. God willing, soon we will be able to have our news arrive to you.

**Saturday, August 31**: Love, good morning. Very early this morning they collected the letters of the military officers. You should have seen last night in the early morning hours, the fighters frantically writing. Peña sent sixty letters. In short, all were very well behaved, and they still lacked time.

# Part II
## IN NOTEBOOK RECOVERED BY THE AUTHORITIES AND GIVEN BY THE ATTORNEY GENERAL OF HUMAN RIGHTS TO YOLANDA PINTO DE GAVIRIA, WIDOW OF GUILLERMO GAVIRIA CORREA, IN MARCH OF 2005

*These writings, spanning September 1 to December 31, 2002, are Guillermo Gaviria Correa's notes. These and other notes of similar style served as the basis for the diary that the governor kept. The authorities found them in the place of the rescue operation; his wife only received them in March 2005. Sadly, the diary corresponding to these writings has not been found. The original style is retrieved in the third and fourth parts.*

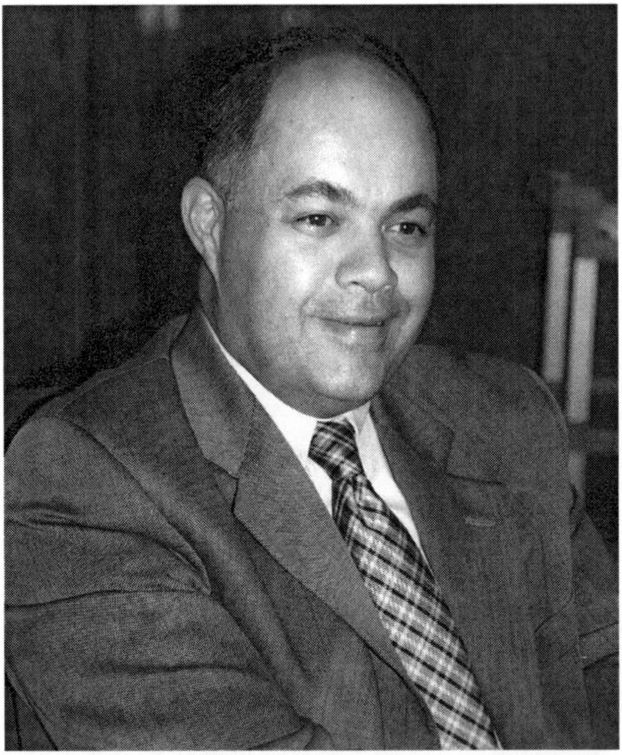

# 2002

**Sunday, 1; Monday, 2; Tuesday, 3; Wednesday, 4; Thursday, 5, September:** I've stayed away from the logbook because I've been worried about the absence of messages from Yolanda. Since yesterday we have heard her again. Last night there was an attack that the journalists have said was directed against my father. There were neither victims nor injured, only damages. Yolanda today gave speeches on Caracol. *El Colombiano* daily registers our absence.

The FARC issued a communication asking President Álvaro Uribe to give up the time of "grace" of seven years stipulated by Pastrana in the accord of the Court of Rome. The ELN also communicated that, despite the attitude of war of the government, it wants to continue the peace process, beginning with the National Convention. The proposals of Roberto Hoyos about soccer in Colombia has generated very good comments, and I'm happy for their triumphs.

General [Jorge Enrique] Mora reported that they killed 100 fighters in combat in Meta [La Uribe]. Here we continue working on paving the surroundings with stones to avoid swamps and the mosquitoes. A scandal around [Germán] Bula leaving the embassy in Venezuela.

**Friday 6, Saturday 7, and Sunday 8 of September:** Friday and Sunday at daybreak I heard Yolanda. The Antioquenian Fair was a great success, with nearly one hundred municipalities participating. Jaime Fajardo [Landaeta] gave very good statements on *The Personality of the Week*. Also, Yolanda mentioned that she will be attending the meeting in Neiva of the families of kidnapped persons. There are statements by Castaño in which he declares that he is prepared to surrender to the United States. Also, it was announced that the AUC is again unified. President Álvaro Uribe was in Medellín. He expressed his support for the offer of Luis Pérez to mediate the demobilization, and I don't know what his position on the subway has been.

**Monday 9, and Tuesday 10 of September:** Only today, Tuesday, did I hear Yolanda. Now Sofía [Guillermo's sister] had her daughter Helena. Carlos Castaño declared his adherence to the norms regarding the International Human Rights. Today I heard the statements of Minister Londoño on Radio Caracol, in which he was rude in his answer on the topic of the kidnapped persons and freeing prisoners, which is considered the end of a serious process of peace. He did not speak of exchange either. His position seems to be different from that of the president, in connection with the reactions of our families, which reflects optimism about the intentions expressed by the first mandate.

There is hope about the preparations in the United States to commemorate last year's attack on New York. Among the more than thirty-six countries that had victims in the attack, Colombia had eighteen or nineteen.

**Wednesday, September 11**: President Uribe traveled to New York, and Minister Londoño is in charge of presidential functions. Criticism is stronger on the reforms and the decisions about the budget, Human Rights and ICBF,[16] and the government on emphasizing the critical fiscal situation because of the debt.

Today we got acquainted with the pink macana[17] palm. Yesterday we brought provisions from the river's mouth and were able to pick some guavas.

**Thursday, September 12**: Today we heard Martha Inés, Lina, and Camila. You have said that you will leave for Neiva.[18] It was announced that the government initiated contacts with the ELN for the purpose of a peace process. The ELN seems to be willing to accept the mediation of the UN. There was the kidnapping of a child in Ocaña;[19] everything indicates that it was the ELN. I haven't been able to find news about the event in Neiva. There was very little coverage and none mentioned the government or the church.

**Friday, September 13**: Today I saw the news on television, including the statements of Alfonso Cano and the reactions against the entire establishment, which I interpret as threatening. I saw you for an instant in the first row in Neiva. Bush's strong words against Iraq dominated the international scene. Five of us went for provisions.

**Saturday, September 14**: Today the families of the officials and sub-officials received letters. The army retrieved Kenia (the girl kidnapped in Ocaña) in North Santander. They killed the fighters who killed the group of indigenists and captured others in the hierarchy, including someone in Medellín who it is believed ordered the kidnappings.

**Sunday, September 15**: Today we listened to the messages of all the families on *The Voices of the Kidnapping*. There are important aspects, like mentioning Yolanda concerning the apparent acceptance of the FARC in the mediation, or at least to have already made contact with the UN. Yolanda says that they have initiated conversations and that Lucas Gualdrón and Antonio Rojas (who we were with in Switzerland, along with Gloria Marín and Marcos Calarcá) are going to participate at this stage.

She mentioned the message that I sent to the FARC, but I don't know which it referred to; it can be one of two: the proposed nonviolence research lab/center which we sent by letter, or the intention I stated in Switzerland to make contact with the FARC in eastern Antioquia, which was hindered by the rupture in dialogue in Pastrana's government. She told me that she will go to Cuba with Sergio Trujillo; it seemed to me that she said with Aníbal, but Gilberto is sure that no other person was talked about.

She talked to me of a special place, but the radio static did not permit me to know what she referred to; a place to remember and to think of being (returning) together there; I suppose that in my case it will be the province of Guanentina. Last night I dreamt of chocolates . . . [a line missing].

Yolanda will return September 21. She leaves this Tuesday 17; hopefully she can talk with the Castros, since I believe it would be an excellent channel for the FARC.

The convergence of the announcement of Alfonso Cano and the sending of the letters make me think that the FARC is deciding to initiate a humanitarian accord. This is confirmed in the statements of the journalist on Radio Caracol that announced the video of [Alfonso] Cano which showed that Gilberto and I spoke and that Cano mentioned the accord. We believe that it is the section which they cut from the original video in which we made mention of the mediation at the UN.

**Saturday, September 21**: On the weekly program of the state government I heard important decisions: $5,000 million from the state for credit to small business in agreement with the national government. Book Fair. Seduca, a fund of $2,500 million for texts, of which $90 is million for the northeast. Administrative contract for $7,600 million for La Cortada-Yolombó.

Campaign of SSSA[20] to determine how to buy unrefined brown sugar. Agriculture: improving 50 hectares for sheep for $145 million. Infrastructure gives discounts in Pajarito and San Pedro for early payment (15 percent); the payment in advance goes at 30 percent. MANÁ,[21] 54,000 children (total 255 thousand children with nutritional problems, 15 percent of the school population under age 14).

**Sunday, September 22**: Ex-president López again wrote about the humanitarian accord. Surely tomorrow, Monday, there will be responses. Thursday the representatives of the State of Valle del Cauca met with President Uribe and their comments were very optimistic. Tomorrow, Monday, all the politicians of Valle will meet to analyze and press for an accord for the kidnapped representatives.

There is a good feeling around the humanitarian accord. Additionally, the fact of the news in past days in which Mono Jojoy asked the managers for the list of guerrilla prisoners to advance indicates that the topic is moving inside the FARC.

**Monday, September 23**: Yesterday there was a "No aggression accord" made among 500 young people in four gangs in Medellín, which proves that yes, it is possible to take apart this machine of violence. The representatives of the Valle del Cauca meet today with the Commission of the Senate to speak about kidnappings. There is a meeting of the Secretaries of Agriculture in Antioquia, which means to say that, as a consequence, Sergio and Yolanda are already here.

We heard that Isabel Cristina was elected International Banana Queen. Today no one from either family was on the air.

**Tuesday and Wednesday, September 24 and 25**: The absence of Yolanda has removed all my motivation to maintain this diary.

The statements of Londoño are very discouraging. The FARC has also suffered losses and important captures (a supposed block commander and a head of finances). It is Eugenio's birthday today.

**Thursday, September 26**: Yolanda was not on the air.

**Friday, September 27**: Finally I have heard Yolanda again. She tells me that again next week she will go, this time with Anibal. The FARC issued statements expressing little faith in the delivery of Castaño.[22] They classified it as "a business among three partners": the United States, Colombia, and Castaño. Yesterday President Uribe gave statements when he was leaving for the UN saying that the negotiations "are going in a good way." There we put our hopes.

**Saturday and Sunday, September 28 and 29**: Saturday we felt the army close. In the afternoon the commander returned. Today things are more calm. Santiago Botero [cyclist] and Juan Pablo Montoya [race car driver] each arrived in fourth place; in my opinion good actions. Yesterday Desmond Tutu (Nobel Peace Prize laureate) wrote offering to participate in a commission to work for our liberation. We heard it on *The Voice of Antioquia*, but we haven't heard anything more.

**Monday, September 30 and Tuesday, October 1**: Unemployment numbers: 16.2 percent national and under-employment 36.5 percent. Today we heard Martha Inés, Lina, and Yolanda; messages of love and optimism. Monday on RCN we again heard the news of Desmond Tutu (Nobel Peace Prize), on a national level. The expectations with respect to unemployment are no better. In Bogotá it has risen to nineteen percent, and everything indicates that it will continue to rise rapidly, until what Peñalosa began is finished.

Yesterday the contract with HP (Hewlett-Packard) for the universalizing of the Internet, 200 thousand computers and the installation of a factory here in Colombia [Rionegro] was appropriated. Two different figures have been given. The news speaks of US $125 million and the mayor Luis Perez of $500 million. Eugenio spoke of the project of the budget. I hope that in the future, on being approved, the figures allotted for key programs are mentioned. About 6 p.m. they told us that we will be leaving at daybreak.

**Wednesday, October 2**: We have packed and we were ready to leave around 7:30 a.m. Then, Gilberto and I went in a little dug-out to "the pier." The officials and sub-officials arrived there about 3 p.m. Here we spent the night and were here Thursday and Friday. We left again on Saturday at 3 a.m. We arrived at the new camp around 7 a.m. I had to walk and Gilberto went on a mule.

We have baptized this camp "Swampville." It rained almost the whole day, and we are literally among swamps. Saturday, Sunday, and Monday we have been working on settling into our camps. Tuesday, now settled, we spent almost the whole day inside the camps because of the rain and the mud prohibited any activity.

**Wednesday, October 9**: I'm writing on my new table, built by Negrete. The help of the officials and sub-officials to Gilberto and me is a gift of God. All of them try their best to make it easier for us here and to make us happy. The news revolves around the difficulties in Commune 13, the operatives in all the country, and the reforms. We listened to the great news that the UN is willing to assign its leadership to Nelson Mandela and the second option to the current president of Brazil, who turns over his responsibilities in January 2003.

[James] Lemoyne has had contacts with the FARC, President Uribe hardens his position before the congressmen who obstructed his reforms with the usual arguments, sophistic and narrow-minded. Juan Gossain editorialized in favor of Uribe today. Congress put on the shelf for today the law of "interchange," finding it possibly "obstructive and even counterproductive."

We are in agreement; it is clear then that it only requires the "political will" of the government and the FARC, as others, among them various ex-presidents, have sustained. Gilberto and I are very concerned about the situation in the twenty neighborhoods that form Commune 13 in Medellín, and we do not perceive any emphasis on solutions other than by force.

**Thursday, Friday and Saturday, October 10, 11, 12**: They announced that our letters could leave; Gilberto and I are anxiously waiting. The schedule for bathing has been increased by an hour. They have been delivering the "other medicines" sent by Yolanda and M. Ines more quickly.

**Sunday, October 13**: In the beginning of the week: Cecilia M. Vélez W., two percent educational coverage and seventeen percent coverage in superior education; World Bank, credit to subsidize one hundred million university quotas for stratums one and two. They look to eliminate regulations, the section is overregulated.

**Monday, Tuesday, Wednesday, October 14, 15, 16**: The referendum has been approved, but Congress did not approve the extension. The problems in Commune 13 are today an example of the gravity that the conflict is becoming. The humanitarian accord came with great force and support. Everything indicates that it is woven around the proposal of López. There still is no news about our letters leaving.

**Thursday, October 17**: President Uribe spoke before the governors; he said that the topic has all his approval and will be given by his government to obtain the accord of humanitarian exchange in the shortest possible time and that it continues in the hands of the UN. His statements were later supplemented with proposals of the Commission of Peace of Congress, where they showed that also Congress is interested in the exchange and supports it.

Today they gave me a letter from you from July 12. I think it should have arrived with the second shipment. Also, they gave us books about the biography of Uribe. In your very beautiful letter you tell us of some medicines that never arrived to us. Fortunately I have been able to maintain the fungus on my feet within reason, and the cholesterol has not bothered me. What does bother me is the fungus in the groin, which I have been taking care of, nevertheless it continues to advance. The president announced his willingness to submit again for consideration in Congress the call to extend term-limits for governors and mayors.

**Friday, Saturday, and Sunday, October 18, 19, 20**: The positive feeling continues. We heard messages from Yolanda only Sunday; Friday night she gave very positive statements from the summit in Manizales, where she could speak with the president. Sunday's message was very positive and the father of Quique Márquez finished with a list of what happened during the week and closed with the meeting of the FARC and the government in Spain (Luis Carlos Restrepo, Calarcá, Leyva and others. . . ).

The feeling among the fighters also clearly shows their interest and optimism. This optimism I see as the reason for lack of interest in changing camps for a healthier one and with less risk. Here, in the short time we've been here, ten poisonous snakes have been killed and there are two fighters with pito[23] rash. In Commune 13 they have announced 120 arrests and seventeen kidnapped persons recovered—five hostages and a family of twelve.

**Monday, October 21:** Today we complete six months. There will be a mass at 4:30 celebrated in the Cathedral. Roy Chaderton [Venezuelan chancellor] confirmed that his government is progressing in efforts for the liberation of Ingrid Betancourt. He seems to reenforce what France is doing after his interview last week with the president of that country. It appears that they have authorized the urban dialogues in Medellín to advance the processes in Commune 13. Luis Pérez decreed a curfew for ten days from 10 p.m. until 5 a.m. in various neighborhoods in Commune 13. The educational knowledge test will be done in Antioquia on October 24.

**Tuesday, October 22:** We heard Yolanda. She spoke of her trip to Rhode Island and Atlanta. She will attend a vigil in my honor (also Gilberto and other kidnapped persons) and later will go to Atlanta to the Martin Luther King Jr. Foundation. There was an attack on the police barracks (attempted) in Bogotá and there is also a conflict in Siloé (Cali). First day of the curfew in Commune 13.

**Wednesday, October 23:** Yolanda is in Providence, Rhode Island, for United Nations Day in my honor with the governor of the state and the president of the university. I heard her message. The mayors of the East insist on converting the zone into a peace laboratory. In Moscow, a group of Chechen rebels took over a theater and held prisoners in hopes that the liberation of Chechnya would be accepted. Today begins the construction of the new camp for us here.

**Thursday, October 24:** I did not hear Yolanda. There is news that the FARC hopes for the liberation of "all its prisoners" to free eighty-four political prisoners. The radio stations speculate that it involves more than 3,000 fighters. Nevertheless, the commander here calmed us saying that "that is not true, the FARC does not have more than 400 prisoners and they will not intercede for those who can leave for good conduct." Confusion reigns and we'll have to wait to get to the bottom of this issue. In Madrid they captured Alvaro Leyva Duran, and therefore if it were certain that he participated in conversations with the government and the FARC, this also is going to tangle things. In summary, one has to wait. In the United States two persons were arrested who were "the D.C. sniper."

**Friday, Saturday, Sunday, October 25, 26, 27**: Our new move has taken place; a lot of heavy and dirty work. At daybreak on Sunday we heard the families. Yolanda's message was marvelous. Her contacts with Andrew Young, the nonviolence leaders in the world, the contacts with the bishop to get to Nelson Mandela, and the well-intended and calm words for the fellow citizen of the FARC I really liked. Your love was felt in each phrase and your energy brought calm and hope to all of us. Giovanni Córdoba died. I would like to take a floral arrangement to the tomb of Carepa Gaviria when I return.

**Monday, October 28**: Today I did not hear Yolanda's message. The most important news had to do with the peace workshop in the East which began with two thematic lines: the first on "living together and citizen security" and the second for developing the "model of development" for that sub-region. The vice president attended, but it seems that the commissioner of peace, Luis Carlos Restrepo, didn't attend. Sergio Trujillo made a brave accusation about importation and about corruption in the importation of milk. Alberto Uribe, rector of the University of Antioquia greeted us. There is progress in the referendum on the topic of reelection, and the extension of the period seems to have been removed.

**Tuesday, October 29**: Carlos Wolff greeted us. Today begins the debate in the Senate on political reform. Eleven of the forty-eight articles were approved. Yolanda sent me a message. There were attacks against various bridges, among them those of Dabeiba, before La Llorona, Río Blanco. At night there were not eleven articles approved, but only four. Today I also heard a message for Bernardo Ernesto Vélez. I have thought a lot about him and his family these days.

**Sunday, November 3**: $700 million for roads. Letter of indicators. Attention to Guadalupe. $12 thousand million for the agriculture and cattle section. More than $2,200 million in agreement with Ecopetrol. Caravan to Andes and to the southwest. Invias[24] opens bids for Antioquia: Occidente-Liborina bridge. Zaragoza-Caucasia; Sonsón-Nariño; Angostura-Yarumal.

**Wednesday, November 6**: I heard Yolanda and I could see her in the news on television, at noon and at night. Today was the second *Meeting of Families of Kidnapped Persons* in Bogotá, with López and the commissioner attending. The government ratified its desire to reach an agreement, and the prisoners of the FARC sent a message saying that there would not be proofs of survivors until their treatment in the jails is improved.

At daybreak the secretariat sent an e-mail saying that the negotiations will be in Colombia, that an area has to be demilitarized, that the security of its negotiators is guaranteed, and that all their prisoners must be freed. They also mentioned the kidnapped persons considered political prisoners and subjects of an exchange.

**Thursday, November 7 to Tuesday, November 19**: The principal topic has been the humanitarian accord. There are discussions and debates at all levels. The kidnapping of Monsignor [Jorge Enrique] Jiménez introduced the perception that we kidnapped persons can be rescued, and even Monsignor [Pedro] Rubiano asked the families to help in this way, which I consider a wrong position of the church and inappropriate. The polls show seventy-eight percent in favor and thirty-two percent against a military rescue being attempted.

The FARC considers mediation by the UN unnecessary for a humanitarian accord, a position that has been interpreted by the news media as a rejection of the participation of the UN.

On November 16 we filmed the video for the families, and on the seventeenth at 6 a.m. they left with our letters. I lost my wedding ring after the filming. Love, the next day I found it in the river; a real miracle.

**Wednesday November 20–Tuesday, November 26**: There is news about conversations in Venezuela, with mediation of the FARC, between the government and the FARC for an accord of humanitarian exchange. There is an offer of the AUC to make a unilateral truce at Christmas. This would open up the possibility to arrive at a "peace process" with them. The ELN freed five kidnapped persons from Utría after having freed two last week. There is a Mass in the Bolivariana University for us and there will be a serenade tomorrow for my fortieth birthday.

Such advances as the processing of the referendum, the pension and fiscal reforms, and others prompted by the government—it seems good that Congress has been making up. Ex-President López spoke today about the statements of President Álvaro Uribe, and he said that the AUC should submit itself to respect the International Human Rights.

Serpa resigned from the National Liberal Direction and left a transition leadership (until the convention in March 2003) formed by ten persons, which has generated controversy and discouragement. In my opinion, they will do anything except lead the Liberal Party.

**Wednesday, November 27**: Today was my birthday, number forty. I was given many greetings and in the night I could see Yolanda, my mother, and Aníbal. The concert at night was very beautiful and we were able to see it in the newscast. Today we met with the commander.

**Thursday and Friday, November 28 and 29**: The AUC, in communication by Internet, informed that December 1 they start a "cessation of hostilities" to begin the peace process. The French chancellor gave speeches calling the FARC to assume its responsibilities.

**Saturday, November 30**: The principal news continues being the "cease fire" of the AUC. There is no answer from the government. On the other hand, there was communication from Cuba between the government and the ELN signaling that they will continue talking.

**Sunday, Monday, Tuesday, and Wednesday, December 1, 2, 3, 4**: A civic strike began in Venezuela. Tuesday Colin Powell arrived. On his agenda is the humanitarian accord. The European Parliament expressed, via five representatives, their support of the politics of President Uribe.

**Saturday, December 28**: At mid-day, the tribute of RCN[25] to Eusebio Medina. Interview with Martha Inés and Yolanda. Message of support of Yolanda and Martha Inés. *I love her because I love her. Very Antioquenian, Little tiple[26] guitar, give me a melody, There is in my life a great love.* Conversations with President Uribe, and I received gifts. *The Absent.* Diomedes. Very loving good-bye from Jorge Eusebio Medina.

## 2003

**Friday, January 3**: Our things arrived.

**Saturday, January 4**: Program *Caracol Personality*, State of Antioquia. Hurrah, Josué. We met the housing goals. For that, a good response is to resolve the access to credit. Antioquia now has a long term housing policy. Proposed for Antioquia is a new equitable plan for the distribution of resources for housing at the national level

**Sunday through Tuesday, January 5–14**: Today, Tuesday, the most important topics are the campaign around the referendum, the interview of President Álvaro Uribe last night on RCN, and the announcement of the national government about the social funding. It will be $3.5 billion for nine million poor people. This last announcement is a satisfying example of the capacity of the president to adjust and that finally the critics of Serpa and the Liberal Party are being paid attention to.

**Wednesday, January 15**: Martha Inés, Lina, Yolanda, and Sergio Trujillo greeted us on *How Medellín Woke Up*. Now it seems that of the $3.5 billion for social funding, there is only $1 billion. They are studying the possibility of budgeting $2 billion for that purpose. It is thought impossible to sign an accord with the IMF[27] to reduce public expenses, and at the same time they are thinking of budgeting for social funding.

# Part III
RETRIEVED BY THE ARMY
ON THE DAY OF THE DEATH OF
GUILLERMO GAVIRIA CORREA
AND GIVEN TO HIS WIFE BY
THE PUBLIC PROSECUTOR
OF ANTIOQUIA, A WEEK
AFTER THE FAILED
RESCUE ATTEMPT

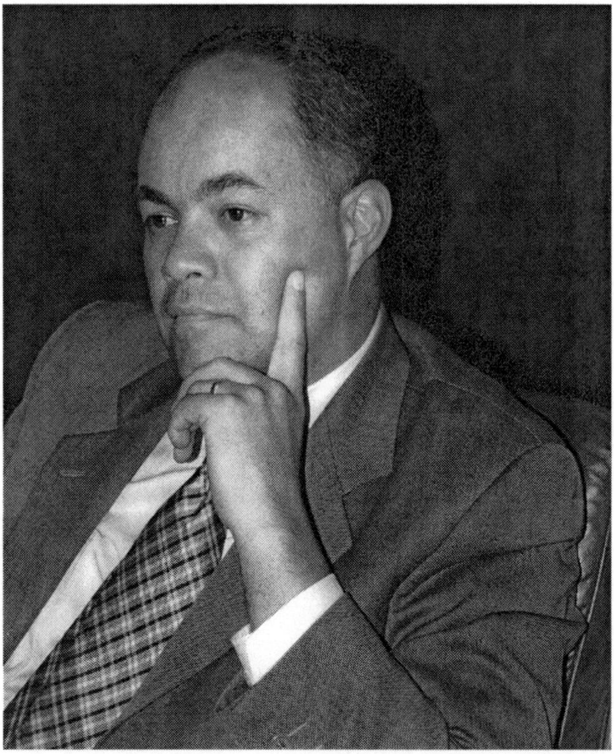

**Monday, January 20**: I hung your photo and that way I can see your face when I go to bed before I fall asleep and when I wake up and while I wait for your messages. Also when I feel your absence the hardest, I only have to "close my self up" and I'm with you again. On the outside, I put the other five photos of the children: on a little pole with cracks the laminated ones of Daniel and Papo, and with nylon the two of Matthew, so they are on the back of the reading chair. These I can see anytime of the day by only turning my head when I read or write.

Well mi vida, today has been simple; the only thing is that last night we could see the news on television, then we came to suffer in the soccer game between Colombia and Brazil for the under-twenty championship. Half asleep, I realized the loss. I love you, mi vida, receive my kisses and love.

**Tuesday, January 21**: Love, good morning. Today I am listening to your message while contemplating how beautiful and happy you are. Now I understand what happened Sunday at daybreak. On hearing Lina yesterday she explained to us that all night she tried to communicate, but she could not. I think the same thing could have happened to those at home and happened to you, and that is why it was so hard for you to communicate, and you came on late. In short, I hope that you feel encouraged and try during the week.

Love, today I began the book by Luis Carlos Restrepo *Beyond Terror* (Más Allá Del Terror), so far very interesting and I identify a lot with his analysis of history and what he does as far as I have read. We'll see if the resemblance continues, and what is more important, if his performance corresponds with his writings. On the news I perceive an intensification of attacks by the FARC against the population in different regions of the country.

It only rained one day. The rest of this first month has been marvelously sunny; the sun all day and the nights clear, despite the fact that the view of the stars is very limited because of the tree tops and the interference of small clouds at night. Nevertheless, I remember Saturn and (I believe that is what I saw when we were coming to this camp, I think that you can confirm this with Aníbal and my father) at least two of its satellites.

It was a beautiful image in the hours before daybreak. If you confirm this, it means that I no longer have 20/20 vision—but that I have improved, since Saturn, when it is closest to us, is at 1,276 million kilometers!

**Wednesday, January 22**: Love, good morning, mi vida. Today again I listened to your beautiful voice and when *How Medellín Woke Up* finished, the news came that we will be leaving in the early morning. Immediately we began taking down everything and we spent the whole day packing. It's strange, but the fewer things one brings, the more careful one is in packing. And our baggage, despite everything, adds up.

For this occasion, I packed two backpacks; one was practically all books, and Gilberto three backpacks and a little handbag. At 3 a.m. we got up to finish getting ready and we left at 4 a.m., after breakfast and packing lunch.

**Thursday, January 23**: Love: I am writing this today Friday. Gilberto and I go, he on a mule and I on a horse. I think it is a cross of a Percheron and a Creole. We traveled the first hours with a beautiful view of what I think is Saturn. Since there was a waning moon, but very clear, the sky was covered and the constellations could not be distinguished. It seemed to me we saw another planet which I suppose could be Venus, but between the tree tops and walking, one cannot be certain.

At dawn we were marching. Thank God the way was very good, without a lot of swamp for the summer days, and because after a certain time we always walk on the edge of a pair of deep river valleys. Halfway into the march we could hear the thunder of a great waterfall, but we were not lucky enough to see it.

We rested at the end of the descent, on the banks of a beautiful river, and there I loaned the horse to Lucuara, who was coming down with some problems due to a pain in his knee and bursitis in a shoulder. I helped him carry his backpack. There was a short distance yet, but for me very pleasant, since I could pick guavas before arriving at the spot where we stopped to rest.

Despite the effort of the officials and the sub-officials and our tiredness, I really liked the journey, I think above everything for the beauty of the waters. Here I have seen orchids that I was surprised we hadn't found on the whole trip. At night they gave us a marvelous meal: fried shad with fried plantains and rice. I was so happy that to celebrate it I lit a cigar and, together with Marín and Aranguren, finished about a third of it. The rest, for the next celebration.

The only sad thing was we had to miss the messages of the morning of the twenty-third. At night we knew that we were going to rest the next day, so we "put up the antenna" to be able to hear you both.

**Friday, January 24**: Sweet princess: Today we could hear you very well. I also listened to news about PCS.[28] I hope they do not succeed in making Aníbal too excited; it is crucial where he is now.

Now, more rested, we have been able to unpack a little and get out a notebook and these pages to write. It seems that we will be here a couple of days to later continue to our next destination. I would really like to stay here, above all for the river to be able to fish a little, despite the many gnats.

Today the fighters brought me very large and healthy guavas. I cut them in half and there was enough for everyone. We just finished lunch and they gave us crisp bacon rind, but very hard. The treatment of Gilberto was not done this time.

Love, I was thinking of asking you that the next time you send a pair of snorkel masks for diving and that you also send some sinkers (the kind that coils) and fishing reels and leaders; also, some medium fish hooks between the yellow ones (very large) and the little ones.

**Saturday, January 25**: Love, good morning. We still continue here and by the movement of provisions it seems that this will be our dwelling for the next days. We have eaten good fish and plantains, and they also killed a pig. Today we bathed in a beautiful well that made me think of your childhood days in Blue Pool [*Pozo Azul*], when probably the creek was still clean.

Later I read a beautiful poem by José Asunción Silva entitled "Infancy," in which he remembers the times as a child when he went to collect moss for the manger scene. It made me return to the memories of some days ago, and precisely Silva speaks of "how it is sweet in hours of bitterness to direct the look to the past and call up your memories."

Love, today Navarrete gave me this bracelet (he calls it a manacle) for you. I'm going to include it in these letters and I hope it reaches you. Negrete gave me three more some time ago: for you, Matthew and Daniel, and I'm going to send them also. The one without letters is what Navarrete made for you. Tonight I will be waiting for your message.

**Sunday, January 26**: Love, good morning. Your message was very beautiful. Too bad they cut it. I'm going to read the letters of Saint Paul (I have it here; letter to the Romans 8:37-39). Mi vida: today they informed us, in quite an unexpected way, that again we would be changing places, so we are rapidly packing to leave. We're going to leave.

Tomorrow, or when we arrive, I'll return to these lines. Good afternoon, mi vida.

**Monday, January 27** (Pardon this lapse).

**Tuesday, January 28**: Yesterday, Monday at 11 a.m., was when they informed us of the change. These quick moves are very traumatic and this one in particular was more so.

Yesterday I listened to your message, mi vida, and the best is that today we thought that the march would last all night and that we were going to miss the message of the morning. But we arrived at this place at 6:45 a.m. and I got out your little radio (which is the strongest one here) and we picked up *How Medellín Woke Up*, right there we put up the antenna and in the middle of the jungle and bathed in sweat we listened to messages from you and from Martha Inés and Lina.

Around us the jungle was being transformed into a new camp, which I will name "Gnatville," to make these little "flying piranhas" stand out. Fortunately, Gilberto and I have a good dosage of repellent. To the former camp I want to call it with the name "Small Mouth Villa," since we could eat so much of that type of fish that for some it tasted so awful, like a bull's horn.

Gilberto and I have grievously increased our baggage. I have two knapsacks and Gilberto three knapsacks and a handbag, and between the two of us we got a seventh package with sleeping mattresses. In this last march, which we began walking, we both had to carry a knapsack and leave the rest. I thought we were going to lose those things; among them the books that recently arrived and some clothes and personal hygiene things.

When we stopped to eat, they gave us a mule and a horse, and we could do the major part of the trip on horseback. Riding with a knapsack is not comfortable, but the alternative of leaving mine was not acceptable. We arrived at a site where we could lay down a few hours before doing the last stretch.

After arriving, we dedicated ourselves to set up the camps in pairs. The majority of the officials and sub-officials are preparing their hammocks. We prepared "beds" over forked poles and then waited for them to bring the mattresses, which arrived in the night with Gilberto's knapsacks. Mine they left because of weight. I thought I had lost it forever.

In connection with the hammocks, I want to ask you to send us two, but love, they have to be from the military. Juan Manuel Restrepo can get them with the people of the brigade, which have a mosquito net, the lightest and finest possible. They are for Gilberto and me.

Good night, mi vida; I say good-bye from our new dwelling in "Gnats Villa" and without baggage.

**Wednesday, January 29**: Love, good morning. Today we heard you, and the message about the statements of the FARC front about their willingness to move forward in the humanitarian accord which make us feel renewed hope. Today I have a temperament of demons. I think because of the anxiety of losing things, especially a pair of T-shirts and the books. Those of astronomy and history interest me most. I hope to take astronomy when I return.

It is very hot and humid, but all is not bad. The camp is in a comfortable place, and I think that soon we'll win the battle with the gnats. Here the meals have greatly improved. We tried the Carve. I believe it is a product of Noel; I liked it a lot. I think you could have it in mind for the campaign on childhood nutrition.

Today in the afternoon there was a dispute between Alejandro and Viellard. I had to intervene along with Gilberto to avoid their getting into it with fists. But after calming them down, and patiently listening to the complaints of each one, they returned to conversing and it was all over.

Both share the camp at this time and I suppose that, as with everybody, the intensity of living together is overwhelming them. Fortunately, everything is over now and harmony again reigns.

I am reading Luis Carlos; I believe I mentioned that. I like it a lot and I hope he can mold all this knowledge into his work. Oh, I almost forgot to tell you that in the afternoon they brought me the knapsack, and with it, courage.

Good night, love. Receive my kisses and heart.

**Thursday, January 30**: Love, your message today is very clear and comforting. I confess that I have opted to not hold many illusions and rather to wait for "the definitive moment." But at any rate, I see that the three aspects that you point out are truly important and signal a real clearing of the way toward the humanitarian accord.

Love, in case I haven't said it before, I love you immensely. I think of you all day (and when I wake up at night). I miss you and I feel so fortunate and proud to be your husband. I send you my kisses, and I'm going to pack the chess set and pack the letters, since we're going to turn them over after lunch to try to leave soon. The opportunity to record a tape has come up, and Gilberto and I are going to do it, one on each side. I hope that you get these also.

**Thursday, February 6**: My sweet love. I listened to your message in which you tell me that you returned to Medellín and that you are going to meet with the Facilitating Commission. I was reading and finishing the editing of your letters all day.

Now it's soon going to be 6 p.m., and we just heard the little airplane in which Juan Luis Londoño traveled did not arrive at its destination [Popayán], and they do not know where it is. It is possible that something has happened. God willing, no.

Again today we turned in the packages with letters and the chess set to the commander and rest in the hope that in two or three weeks they will be in your hands.

Good night mi vida. Receive my kisses and love.

**Friday, February 7**: My sweet princess. I listened to you early, and today I was happy to hear Father Yépez, who sent a message for all the kidnapped persons. Then we listened to your statements on *How Medellín Woke Up* about the meeting of the families with the Facilitating Commission. You will tell us what is important Saturday.

We are concerned about the loss of Minister Juan Luis Londoño, and we have heard the news flash. Now we have to wait for the quick arrival of the rescue teams with hope that all are alive and well. This puts in relief how precarious our "worlds" are. Here or there things can happen that in a moment change all our setting and life itself.

As I go deeper in the reading of Luis Carlos Restrepo, more and more I like the character. Now I see that my intuitions in the beginning about his role in the Mandate for Peace were justified. And even more, I was pleased to know in more detail about the civil development in Mogotes and all the drive that his roots in the diocese of San Gil-Socorro created as well as the work in citizens participation led by bishop Leonardo Gómez Serna. Toward the end was a brief mention of the constituency of Tarso and the efforts of the mayors of the East and their communities.

The day today began very sunny and that improved the spirits of all of us. I send you a big kiss, my love.

During the night an atrocious crime shook the country again. The explosion of a car bomb in the El Nogal Club in Bogotá caused twenty deaths and left 160 injured. At the same time, the shock and sadness about the disappearance of the plane of the minister and his committee makes one think of a possible kidnapping. I continue asking God for his well-being and freedom, hoping that soon they will be found.

**Saturday, February 8**: Love, it's going to be 8 a.m. and we have listened to your statements and those of Martha Inés and the wife of Lizcano regarding the interview with the Facilitating Commission. Your optimistic tone pleases me, as well as Gilberto.

I listened with great satisfaction that our helicopter helped in the work of search and rescue.

Love, I have thought a lot about the Internet and I think that you should take advantage of the option of EPM.[29] If after analyzing it with the help of some specialist you don't like it, I think you should look for someone who could do it. It seems important to me that you learn to navigate and manage in-depth electronic mail. That way when I arrive, you can get me up to date and teach me all that I lack. Take advantage of the time that you can free up for this. I know that you will not be sorry.

It's lamentable that the FARC chooses the way of terror to try to advance in its struggle. Each day they lose more territory, and everything indicates that they are prisoners of the narcotic trafficker and not the contrary. Each time their actions are more similar to the narco ringleaders.

With sadness I remember some unfortunate statements of Mayor Mockus, in which he boasted that his city never would be the prisoner epicenter of the violence like that existing in Medellín.

It seems there is much of this fanfare attitude by many authorities and persons who feel "in a privileged way," isolated from the painful circumstances that affect other regions of the country. This absence of solidarity ends up costing the community highly.

This early morning I was listening, while unable to sleep, to the other program of Herbin Hoyos: *Colombia Universal.*

While I listened I thought of you, and my mind roamed among a multitude of remembrances: Moments in Monserrate, Europe, our home, the Antioquenian villages, etc. Our friend Maruja, the professional friends of Bogotá, the Ivias family. In short, millions of things that compose our life in common and which makes me want freedom even more.

I want to hug you and kiss you so that you can feel how much I love and need you. I will keep in my soul the intensity of those moments, which at the same time is sad and happy, painful and sweet. I anxiously hope that night will come to again hear your voice.

Yesterday I began reading *The Divine Comedy.* I've already accompanied the poet and Virgil through hell and now we are entering purgatory.

Love, you know the desire that I have always had to visit Italy. Someday I hope I can dedicate some months to travel that land that, like yours, holds a great attraction to me.

At this time, reflecting on what happened to the minister, I more strongly believe that it is a kidnapping. It seems strange to me that, to date, they have not found the remains of an accident. And if there was one and there were survivors, it's certain that they are prisoners of the FARC. The statements of the authorities, like the Ministry of Transportation, seem inadequate to me.

They have said, for example, "We have rejected a kidnapping," and "The airplane did not cross the western side of the mountain range," which are really conjectures that can be contradicted by the obvious facts. Also, their earlier experiences do not seem to have left dividends.

Gilberto has begun the book of Luis Carlos Restrepo and has some criticism of it. Some in the way other writings are quoted and some are regarding his chronology of the actions mentioned from the time of *La Violencia*.[30] I however, am and continue to be, very impressed by the book. Mi vida, soon we are going to eat, and we will go to bed to wake up in the middle of the night and listen to you.

**Sunday, February 9**: My love, good morning: Your message gladdened my life so much, the news of your exams as well as Daniel's. Thanks to your mother for her constant solidarity. You can be sure that here I don't do anything but strengthen myself to make you more happy, once I can return to your side.

I hope we will be successful in having them listen to us, and that they permit us to play a useful role. But in the meantime, although we continue trying, we do not see any signs of an opening.

Love, we continue waiting for news about the minister Juan Luis Londoño and those accompanying him. Tomorrow is the forty-first wedding anniversary of Gilberto and Martha Inés. Imagine when we complete forty-one years of marriage. I imagine you will be a very beautiful "little old lady." We're going to be very happy, and by then I hope we can share our dream of living in a house in the country.

Love, today something happened here that makes us fear we will have to move soon. I'm not going to enter into details, since I don't think that would be wise.

I send you my kisses and love. Good night, mi vida.

**Monday, February 10**: Today we got up with a great breakfast of rice and beans. Then I could hear your beautiful voice, and your message again filled me with joy. Later in the morning, Gilberto showed me the anniversary letter that he wrote to Martha Inés. It was very beautiful and really reflects a home built with exemplary love and patriotism.

In the area of communication, a multitude of opinions were aired demanding ways to cease hostilities with the terrorists. I understand the pain and the rage that they feel, but I do not sense the solidarity that can protect the society from these acts of violence.

I also feel that, because it happened in Bogotá, perhaps there is greater awareness about how repulsive and criminal acts like these are. It seems greatly influential how the mayor tries to move the conscience of the Bogotan society, so lacking in compassion for other regions of the country.

Also, in these hard times centralization favors the inhabitants of Bogotá. In a communication by the FARC (in *La Luciérnaga* insinuates that it was Alfonso Cano), it points out that in the club El Nogal, paramilitaries met with other members of society and some of the state. The FARC did not carry out the act nor deny that it was executed.

We heard statements of Father [Darío] Echeverri and Bishop Castro which were very focused. We also heard parts of the speech by President Uribe and, although very fragmented, it made us realize that he continues being a calm and prudent person. In the afternoon we heard that the search for a humanitarian accord continues.

This afternoon they brought us peach-palm.[31] It made me remember the Valle del Cauca and our friend Germán Jaramillo. Night is coming, and there was no clear news about the whereabouts of Juan Luis Londoño.

Love, the cigars are almost gone, now I'm going to light up the last half. I hope that you will think to send me another four or five in the next shipment.

**Tuesday, February 11**: My sweet love. Today you did not send a message. We listened carefully since early morning, but the FARC sent a communication with respect to the humanitarian accord. As in other situations, we are forming a precarious idea based on the opinions of the journalists, who interpret what the message contains, and with the few pieces that one or another radio station deigns to read in written form.

Even when there are mixed sentiments, I think that it constitutes a step forward and gives basis for the national government to name its negotiators and demand from the FARC the names of those who will do so on the part of the fighters.

I do not think this is the moment to be bottled up in details like who will be freed, or what lines will be used, since these are precisely objects of the work of the negotiators.

I did not hear your statements, but the newscasts have given good coverage. A good proposal; nevertheless, I do not believe the government processes things so quickly. I also consider it convenient that it does not disappear. On the contrary, I believe it is going to be very beneficial and necessary to get it going and support the negotiations.

I do not believe that it would be acceptable for the position of the facilitator to end up converted into negotiator for one of the parties. I also believe that to have facilitators is simply advisable.

Lastly, neither does it seem to me that the church should assume the role of negotiator for the government. Finally, the FARC has taken its step; now it is fit to wait for the national government.

Amid so many deprivations, there are also some luxuries that become feasts, despite their simplicity. Such is the case of the peach-palms which we ate yesterday afternoon or the delicious banana juice which they gave us today at mid-morning. I believe that I am not mistaken in saying that it is the first time in these eleven months that something like this has happened.

In the afternoon we could also eat some popcorn that you sent. It is a small pleasure to enjoy and share with my companions in captivity while I read, thinking of how you would enjoy them if you could do so with me.

I just finished the two volumes of Arturo Echeverri. The stories of Belchite and Antares I really liked; they were rescued from the forgotten coffers of my memory, along with some remembrances and dreams of childhood.

Finally, being 5 p.m. the news was broadcast about finding the airplane of the minister. There is also news about a cassette that arrived for the family in which the ELN announces that they have them and all are alive but in poor health. Considering the options, it seems the best possible news. We wait for further development in the next hours.

**Wednesday, February 12**: Love: I heard your voice and I was pleased amid the sadness that covers us. In all the garbage that we have heard about the causes and speculations, before I went to sleep, I heard some parts of the speeches of President Uribe in Panamá. His words give the impression of putting any process of opening a dialogue with the FARC in doubt. Now is when I feel the Facilitating Commission could demonstrate its worth.

I believe that this commission should function to help avoid the obstacles that arise on one side or the other. These statements give more certainty to my gratitude of yesterday.

In the morning I also listened to Fabiola Perdomo and now to Angelino Garzón. I knew of his statements and also that last night the guerrillas saw him on the newscast on television. It's disquieting to Gilberto to determine what was tried in the topics of the zone or territory, if they are asking to negotiate or to surrender.

From here it is clear that the majority of the commentaries made about the communication of the FARC are by journalists or staff or directors who do not know, nor have they studied those communications. This makes the commentaries influenced by the circumstances around the journalists at the moment and sifted through the curiosities of the interviewer. It is not surprising, then, what distortions end up accompanying these supposed explanations and explorations of opinion.

We, in Antioquia, I hope can derive some practical teachings from these mistakes. Today we had a meeting with the commander and long conversations in which he expressed his displeasure about our diverse commentaries and attitudes, which he does not approve of. After the conversations and the explanations, corrections, and our unloading, the environment was better, and we were invited to watch the newscast on television.

We could share the pain that grips the country at the tragic death of Juan Luis Londoño, although I feel that in Antioquia the pain is more intense. I hope you will be able to take my word of condolences to María Zulema and her daughters and to Doña Lucía de la Cuesta.

His abrupt departure makes me reflect on the precariousness of our lives and how futile our efforts are when they are not directed at bettering the conditions of the lives of our fellow citizens, when these efforts are not dedicated to the building of equality and justice for our people.

The reaction of the country to the fact of his death, which we share from here, shows not only the current nature and importance of his actual efforts, but also the recognition of his services and past successes and his charisma and dedication. Without a doubt, María Zulema was correct when she expressed, with satisfaction, her joy for the solidarity and recognition that all the Colombians gave her and her children.

Love, I continue making progress in reading *The Divine Comedy*, and each page increases my surprise and admiration for this work and also touches the most profound strings of my religious thought. I constantly want to know what the impact it generated among his fellow citizens when it was written and known. It should have generated some sort of catastrophe. At the same time, the hardness of the infernal images is surprising. It shakes the poetic sweetness of its allusions of love, and the loved object or person, and catches the philosophical depth of his explanations about the mysteries and anxieties common in all epochs of humanity. Well, I send you my kisses and love.

**Thursday, February 13**: Love, good morning. I heard your words and I know that you will travel to Bogotá to be with the family of Juan Luis Londoño. I knew also, although I did not listen to it, that Father Yépez sent a message to us. I lament that I have lost it. Anyhow, we trust that we will hear yours and Martha Inés's and we think that there will not be more.

Today you used a phrase that is almost word for word in Song 27 of Dante (Purgatory), when he, at the invitation of Virgil, comes into the flames that give way to paradise. He regains valor "on hearing the name that is always on my mind."

That's just what happens to me with you. Even when I have other thoughts, or I talk with some companion, or I read, you are always on my mind. So many refrains, so many sayings and theories could have been inspired in the reading of these pages. How many poems and songs could be nourished by the beauty and imagination of this work?

I would like to see what my father's work is about. There is another very beautiful reference later on, in Song 7 of Paradise, when Dante describes a gesture of Beatriz saying, " . . . and radiating over me a smile that would make a man in the flames happy, she began to tell me. . . . "

This book is like a majestic symphony in which each passage surpasses in magnificence the one before and at the same time, from the first passage, one believes to have arrived at the apex and does not see how it can be surpassed in the following. And nevertheless Dante, apparently without much effort, does so with all naturalness.

I have a good supply of books that I do not want to leave behind. I see the dilemma coming of which ones to choose when those about nonviolence arrive. I hope to have the opportunity to read them all thoroughly or only keep those that are really indispensable or which would be difficult to replace. That is why I indicated to you the best option would be to send photocopies.

We continue not knowing how the national government will answer the FARC and what will become of the humanitarian accord. The headlines and many questions from the journalists seem to me to be unfortunate and damaging.

Love, I ask that from now on, you make the communications complete, and you read them to us with much care or try to have them read by *The Voices of the Kidnapping*. This way we'll know for certain what the FARC said, since for us, by way of the radio journalists it is impossible. We hope that the Facilitator Commission manages to lower the forceful intentions of the government and the step toward negotiations is taken.

I think that the government could offer to negotiate publicly, facing the people, with all the cards on the table, and in this way remove many obstacles. Clearly at the time other aspects arise, like the interrupting and superfluous opinions of so many participants.

But transparency is reached and flexibility is fixed in one's mind. At the same time, it avoids manipulation, hesitation, wavering, and displays of "pride" by the participants. It also resolves the need of "grounds" upon which to negotiate, since all participants make a proposal and counterproposal from their position.

Love, speaking on another topic, I ask that Sergio compile for me all the information he can about the *stevia* (sweetener plant). I want to have it for when I return, to know who produces it, markets, prices and costs, future perspectives, etc. He should research all that he can find out with scientific rigor.

I would also like to know about the sweetener industry and in particular about the low calories. Toné [Guillermo's brother], this information can complement it in technical terms. Do not send it; it is for when I return.

I understand that in Planeta Rica there is a person who cultivates it, and also Gilberto tells me that the Japanese, in the past have shown interest in it. Lina can also be useful for these explorations. Hopefully they will compile documents and not just verbal information for me.

Love, another job for Toné: to research seeds to study the possibility of producing high-quality seeds for better productivity and eventually to think of exporting seeds.

**Friday, February 14**: My sweet love. I listened to you early, and I am aware of the difficulties that began around the accord and in general the difficult circumstances the country is passing through.

Today we wrote and delivered to the commander here a new letter, seeking to open the possibility of our meeting together. Former efforts have been fruitless. Monsignor Castro already expressed that they will continue their work and corrected those who misinterpreted that the FARC rejected some of his communication. It is a good sign.

Furthermore. his correction points out, as I also have been writing, the superficiality of media comments on these topics.

The country and Neiva mourn another act of violence. You make known to Juan [Hernández, then governor of Huila] and his people my voice of solidarity. Fifteen families are mortal victims and scores of injured. (At this moment I'm listening to *Santanderian*

*Countrywoman*, which they put on the fighters' equipment but is heard in the whole camp. I love you.) It was explained that it was set to detonate at the moment the presidential airplane landed.

Without a doubt, these acts are going to radicalize the president more, and it is very probable that this will also occur among the general sentiments of the people. In fact, already one can begin feeling the mood in Congress when it speaks of building a legislative barrier against terrorism. And undoubtedly the mood is leaning toward the selection of Vargas Lleras as president of Congress.

My love, I ask you to send my words of gratitude to Miguel Ángel Bermúdez and to the people of the state of Boyacá for these magnificent demonstrations of solidarity and embrace of our nonviolence thesis.

I also ask you to send my words of congratulations to the people of the Plains for their soccer success. Rogelio Gómez has been very excited, and I do not doubt that he has a lot to do with it.

We have really enjoyed the triumphs of Centauros. I approve of his selection of music, and I use this opportunity to tell you to not send electric or electronic apparatuses since they keep them for reasons of security. This, according to how the commander here explained to me, is what happened with the Discman. At any rate, tell [Alfonso] Alvarado that I take it as received and, as you see, we are listening to the music that arrived to us, literally, from the other bank.

What contrasts. While we Colombians debate between life and war, the world prepares for a multi-million copy release of *Harry Potter*, and the United States looks for ways to make war in Iraq. How does one attain the convictions and passion that nonviolence generates in us while subjects of the same world frenzy for the magic of Potter?

For a moment I thought they were going to play the Plains song that you like so much, but after listening to probably a whole disc of Plains music, I remain only with the desire. Well, my love, the day is coming to its end and I prepare to receive the most desired day of the week. Good night, my love.

**Saturday, February 15**: My love, good morning. Yesterday was Camila's birthday, and Gilberto always suffers a little at not being able to be with her. Aside from this, she also told him in the last messages that his presence was the only gift she wanted. Send our congratulations to her.

Amid the difficulties, the proposal of the president of Brazil before the UN arises, offering his help with mediation of a peace process.

Although I don't think it has any connection with the humanitarian accord, we see it as a door that could open for the FARC. This should not be considered a small thing, since the perceived tendency sums up a good part of the international community, in contrast to the "warlike" activities attributed to the FARC in the last few days.

Also, some unknowns are raised around the development of the events related to the *gringos* injured and the "kidnapping." Love, in these last few days they killed a small animal which the officials and sub-officials call "mother snake." In reality, it looks like a small lizard, only it has a thicker head and a much shorter tail than the small lizards. They classified it with a deadly capacity equal to that of the serpents and some nice "traits."

For example, they say that after it bites its victim it goes to the sand and with its mouth upward laughs to itself until the victim dies. Obviously I'm not going to test this thesis, but it does surprise me. Like this, there are other very particular beliefs that I can tell about witches, minerals, trees, etc.

I heard that Father Yépez was the central figure in an event in San Ignacio, and it surprised me that the entrance costs twelve thousand pesos. I hope that they were able to completely fill it.

Well, princess, we are getting ourselves ready for dinner, then I will go to bed early to be fresh when it's time to hear you. I hope that the commander again loans me the tape recorder, since your messages are jam-packed.

**Sunday, February 16**: My love, good morning. I listened to your words and was very pleased with the news about your children. It wasn't clear to me if Aníbal and my father are going to Bogotá or if you will travel to Medellín.

The day has been very boring and slow. I suppose that the circumstances contribute to the gloomy state of my soul. I know, princess, that I cannot permit sadness to dominate me, but there are times in which it is impossible to maintain a level of optimism.

Some days back I thought that the world turned its back on the topic of Iraq. How wrong I was! Thank God the wisdom of humanity shows it is an enemy of this new war, proposed in an obstinate way by President Bush. The fact that millions of persons are seen as partisan for rejecting the war reinforces the convictions of nonviolence.

Also, in the world context, and perhaps there to a greater degree, those that have me as a prisoner here are assumed valid.

It seems that tonight will be a full moon; however I'm not going to enjoy it. Good night mi vida, receive my love and thoughts.

**Monday, February 17**: It has been raining hard since early morning. The little creek that supplies us with water has grown, and now it's almost midday and still raining, but it's beginning to let up.

We heard the news that the president of Ecuador offered his help to President Álvaro Uribe, but he indicated that his country will not participate militarily in the Colombian conflict. I feel that the proposal of the president of Brazil has had little exposure and not been commented on in depth. I hope that in the next few days more interest develops. I believe it has merit.

Yesterday, at dusk, we enjoyed a group of monkeys that passed by the tops of the trees over our dwelling. With a good dose of curiosity they stopped and looked at us, then after some brief moments, like we would look at the monkey cage at a zoo, they marched on.

Negrete already read the book that Sofía sent. His comments are superlatives. He says that it is the best that he has read. Tapias agrees and then Gilberto along that line. I continue intensely focused on *The Divine Comedy*, and I have to recognize that there is a lot that is incomprehensible to me despite sensing the beauty and the immense merit of this work.

I'm also progressing in reading of the history of Colombia, and I finished the Luis Carlos Restrepo book. This last book fills me with joy. I hope that you have been able to read it, and hopefully the cabinet will do so. I especially recommended it for Governor Eugenio, Luis Javier [Botero], and the people of the Consistent Peace Plan.[32]

**Tuesday, February 18**: My love. Today I heard you talk of school supplies and the next financial statement that they are preparing for the next month of March.

Today has been a gray and cold day. At midday I was dedicated to the construction of the bench to do situps and the bar for chest flexes on the floor. As usual, Negrete helped me a lot.

Today I have not felt well. I have a slight headache and my spirits are on the floor. Really, for several days I have been melancholic. The news affects me as much for the Colombian people as for what it signifies in terms of the future of our captivity.

Yesterday in the afternoon I listened to *La Luciérnaga* to try to make me happy and I remembered how it made you laugh. I confess that it made me a little happy, and I could go to bed less anguished.

On *How Medellín Woke Up* they made very positive comments about the accomplishments of VIVA. They especially pointed out that the contributions of the nation to the programs with respect to last year [2001] had quadrupled.

On the government newscast, I heard that Álvaro González had been chosen coordinator of the "commissioned" of the States of Peace of the country, and that this constituted recognition of the Consistent Peace Plan. I'm glad to know also that it begins to spread this among the other states. Good night, mi vida.

**Wednesday, February 19**: Good morning, mi vida. I heard your beautiful message with all the care and attention that you give to encourage my optimism which has been suffering from a painful weakness, as you can see. Today at least it was not raining at dawn, but the day is gray and sad.

I stayed awake and dedicated myself to thinking about the topic of rural housing. Like I told you previously, I think a great initiative could be given to rural dwellings with these pilot projects to teach carpentry to the rural people. I thought of a name like "Rural Training Centers" or "Regional" or "Service."

Perhaps they could be dedicated to training rural people in different jobs, in addition to everything related to carpentry and improving housing. I think that it could be structured on a barter basis. I also think they can be established on banks of tools that can, again by way of bartering, be sold, exchanged, or rented for work. When I speak of work, it can also be produce from the farmers.

This Rural Training Service (RTS) would be connected with the schools, and they could enable the students to gain experience in different tasks, according to their interest. The Polytechnic and the University of Antioquia could have, with the help of VIVA, a team of researchers dedicated to evaluating the results and to research and developing new improvements: things like improving the materials, how to treat and strengthen them, and to study new applications, taking advantage of regional products.

Along this line, housing designs can be made which are very superior; with all the conveniences and securities. And above all, design the restroom area and the kitchen to offer better and more sustainable hygiene.

The RTS could also provide loans to develop anything related to solar energy and water treatment. The designs can be explained in simple brochures, some like the carpenters' furniture manuals, where the amount of materials and an estimate of man hours of work are stated.

The RTS can function on the basis of tables of equivalence to appraise the cost of all its activities accessibly for the rural people. Before I said that the RTS would be banks of tools. I forgot to say "and materials." The RTS can produce modular elements for the houses, and also furniture, based on the work that the rural persons offer.

These finished products are sold or bartered to the rural folk without interest in acquiring them, or state programs of improving rural houses. In this way, the RTS is in a permanent capacity to offer work to the rural people, obviously so they improve and increase their abilities, through different training that is offered them.

Love, I believe also that the RTS can incorporate the system of recycling which we saw at Adelaida's [Guillermo's sister]. This is to take advantage of the coming together of the rural folk at their site. The university team, besides keeping the coordinators of RTS up to date, should be permanently renovated.

The job of keeping the coordinators up to date implies the preparation of courses and activities such as nutrition, farming concerns, something about veterinary medicine, the topic of energy and health, as well as exhaustive training in the tasks in relation to which the coordinator will teach the rural people.

The program should begin with an extended dialogue with the rural people and be supported with long-term follow up of their inquiries. It should be based on the analysis of their points of views of and wishes for development of an RTS structure of activities. What is put into action should be completely apolitical to avoid setting up military targets for the participants in the armed conflict. Their work can be managed by the same policies that manage the Air Program of Health.

Now that I mention it, it occurs to me that it can be the temporary headquarters of activities for APH, and in some way it can take care of the rural population between helicopter trips. All the analysis is separate from how important the selection of the coordinator of RTS is. As in all enterprises, here the human being is the key to success.

I think that someone from the community should be selected with the direction of the state, giving him adequate training and accompanying him until he passes the testing period.

From then on, the coordinator himself should make sure the candidates are prepared so they can replace him. The task should not be difficult for someone who is in ongoing contact with the community. One of the most important administrative responsibilities of the coordinator, if not the principal one, is to keep account of his transactions. Nothing should be done for free. Everything should be appraised and its equivalent value established and recognized.

The payment for the RTS activities, such as courses, rents, sales, etc., are precisely established for each reason according to the circumstances, and are published in tables permanently displayed in the same establishment. In this way, the flagship programs can benefit the most isolated communities, which rarely receive services from the state. And when the state does intervene, it creates more terror than well-being.

Well, mi vida, these are the reflections of the sleepless one. I love and miss you.

**Thursday, February 20**: My love, good morning. My spirit is slowly improving. The book about *Divine Readings* helped me, as well as Dante that my father sent and which I have finished.

Your words about RIA[33] are really comforting, as well as what I have studied about education in Eugenio's financial statements. The series on Teleantioquia I could not watch. What irony: we can see international networks but not the network of the state.

I also heard the beautiful message of Father Yépez. What joy to know that he will be sending weekly messages. The position of Brazil, although it appears to have bothered Senators Enrique Gómez, Manuel Ramírez, and the minister of defense, constitutes perhaps the only door open to the FARC and to us.

The government has decided that the resources collected for the war are not sufficient. Congress begins to pressure for results, and the attacks are causing anxiety and desperation in volatile public opinion. If they asked me, I would say that what the government has done is to harden its tongue. Do they think that by throwing around aggressive talk they can achieve military successes that have been elusive in the military history of the past forty years?

Yesterday I heard that the economic analysts estimated the money received by the drug traffickers at five billion dollars. If a significant fraction of these resources are diverted in the war on the part of subversion, and additionally other resources of diverse groups, and finally those of the state; according to that mentioned by the minister yesterday in Congress, it is over ten billion pesos.

We are talking about figures which can easily surpass the poverty, marginalization, and underdevelopment of large portions of the population. Why is it so hard for us to recognize this reality and correct it? With half of these resources it would be equivalent to a major social revolution in four or five years.

The nonviolence view in this context is not a utopia, it is a necessity impossible to postpone. What riches and opportunities have been destroyed in Colombia in only the past ten years? I referred to these unknowns when I thought of the need to create indicators on the cost of the conflict. I would love to work these figures in depth, not only for Antioquia but also for Colombia.

Love, our activities here have diminished notably. We practically do nothing but wait. Fortunately the books fill a great void for us. Last night I was also a little sleepless.

Today is one year since the dialogues broke down. We hope that there will not be more attacks, since these are the activities that the FARC are accustomed to using to celebrate anniversaries.

We heard about the controversy between the mayor and the

EPM. I hope they overcome it. I have a lot of hope in RIA. I hope Gonzalo [Bernal] and his team begins to demonstrate the success that this initiative—what we conceived for the purpose of routing Antioquia toward its true vocation—can have.

In Venezuela, the Chávez government has hardened against the opposition.

**Friday, February 21**: My love, good morning. I listened to your beautiful message. Ten months of separation have managed to strengthen our love. As Neruda so beautifully says: "The tempests were not able to tear her from me, nor could the distance that separated us fill in the spaces of the love we had conquered." Your "presence" goes with me each moment of the day.

Now Saturday is drawing near with your sweet gift of love and company. I believe that when I leave, I'm going to miss these "*Dawns in America.*" Last night we saw a program on television in which they did an interview with Marín's family. It was very satisfying for him, and his excitement was contagious to all of us.

Yesterday there was a persistent announcement, spoken by some French "diplomat." According to it, Ingrid [Betancourt] was about to be freed, or she was, up until last week. We all received this news with joy, except for Salem the Jew from whom we are accustomed to hearing diatribes shot against what is done to benefit anyone who is not exclusively him. We understand his pain!

Love, some days ago we turned over the letters and the chess set to the commander. I hope any minute they that tell us the good news that you received them.

My love, I heard some very short statements in which you announced a new march to Caicedo. I know that I had thought of it myself, and despite that, I am fearful. I hope that God and the Virgin, to whom we pray daily for your protection, does not let anything bad happen to you. It cannot be done with retaliation or obstinate persistence but rather as an example of the will for reconciliation to be firmly maintained, despite the pain.

When Bernard Lafayette asked me once if I saw someone capable of replacing me in nonviolence, I answered "yes," but I did not speak of the persons I believed could do it. Now I can tell you that I thought of you and of Aníbal.

I believe that both of you have the strength of spirit that is required, and you also have your "emotional intelligence," and that political predisposition that makes you even more integral to continue trying to plant this new culture.

It is crucial to try to situate yourself, know and strengthen the bonds with other persons in the country and outside the country, who share the convictions of nonviolence. If examined in detail, we see with humility that we are not the first and that on the contrary, and fortunately, there are many highly esteemed people making serious and peaceful efforts to better the conditions of our fellow citizens.

I believe that it is important to push the "National Meeting of Nonviolent Initiatives," to invite those who want to share their experiences, hopefully duly documented, and those who can help from the intellectual and the academic community.

The government of the United States expressed in a threatening way its rejection of the crime of the North Americans and the kidnapping of the other three crew members of its aircraft. A new chapter begins to develop, inasmuch as I believe that the FARC has made the future known and even desirous, to explore or sound this string.

Bush has been finding opposition and very strong rejection of his campaign against Iraq, and now he receives this challenge in what has ironically been called "our own back yard." It would not be unusual that he feels blocked on one side and tries to vent his impotency on the other. The question is: On which side do you think we are going to be?

I am reviewing the analysis of the report of negotiations, and with satisfaction I find that the principle topics are advancing, with the notable exception of the program of computers for the schools. I feel like some of the officials and sub-officials here, like the father who did not attend the birth of his four sons: MANÁ, RIA, VIVA, and the Trusteeship of Antioquia.

In my case, they will be the sons of my beloved Antioquia, since yours will have to wait until I return. Kisses and good night.

**Saturday, February 22**: Love, good morning. The morning has been uncontrolled with news about the statements of Minister Londoño and the United States. The statements were apparently overcome with the "reprimand" of the president and the removal of the endorsement of the president and the chancellor. Nevertheless, I think that the episode leaves communication less clear and more worrisome the actual attitude of the government about the handling of the conflict and the possibilities of bringing about a dialogue.

The church has not made a statement, and I believe it should make a complaint, since with his mockery, the minister has injured the spirituality of the great majority of the Colombian people.

It seems that after six months of trying to contain his big-mouth temper, he will now begin to show his true way of doing things. Arrogance and cynicism, which he had managed to tone down, have flowered and begin to be considered deeds of the present government. Personal qualities should, without a doubt, be decisive elements for the selection of our companions on the team.

In the evening, before going to bed, we were invited to watch television. We could watch *Happy Saturdays* and the newscast. The first one impacted me in a very unfavorable way; the sad level to which our people are being accustomed to humorous topics.

On the newscast, Juanes filled me with joy with his freshness, his love for Colombia. Without a doubt, he is a great ambassador for Antioquia and for Colombia. I hope you will let him know of my sincere congratulations. His music also makes us experience moments of satisfaction and Antioquenian pride.

The fighters prepared a bag and a half of popcorn, and we could enjoy this delight with them, especially now that it has been a long time since tasting corn. Presently, our basic nutrition are lentils with spaghetti, a little rice, and the inseparable little sweet bananas. On rare occasions, a few beans and sugarcane water.

I think we eat really well under the circumstances. I continued right on, without sleeping, until the hour to wake up for the program and listen to your beautiful word with some interruptions, since without realizing it the signal had been lost. I recorded and transcribed your message the best I could early Sunday morning.

The moon was not visible here, but I substituted for it my memories of other days, and I send you my kisses and love.

If I understand correctly the initiative of Mr. [Glenn] Paige, it is the greatest honor that has been offered to me in my life, and I don't feel I merit such recognition; nevertheless I hope this serves Colombia. Like you say, the Lord works in mysterious ways.

An example can be the option of Brazil to help in the process of dialogue that very sadly for Minister Londoño, but precisely for his positions, could end up being acceptable for the FARC.

Lastly, I continue without news of the boys, but I am pleased and calmed that Papo is accompanying you. I did not understand your mention of the state of Santander. It seems that you have been there, and you have not mentioned it in the last few days, and I overlooked it. I have to force myself to resume the exercises. I think that is why I'm not sleeping lately.

Well, mi vida, until tomorrow. Sweet dreams.

**Sunday, February 23**: Love, good morning. I slept until almost 10 a.m., the hour for Mass. Today there was nothing special; only that I'm playing a little more chess. Today I beat Negrete in a game, which doesn't happen often, since I'm more of a beginner than he. Yim and Aranguren are the most enthusiastic.

I'm also sleepless today, and I decided to write you, so now it is about 10 p.m. Everything is dark. Only the kerosene lamp that we have in the shelter is lit, which I am using for light.

Today in the morning, on Radio Caracol, there was a program about kidnapping, motivated by the first anniversary of the captivity of Ingrid, excellently led by Guillermo Rodríguez according to what Gilberto tells me. In the program, María Teresa Uribe de Hincapié participated and made a good statement about the need to look for "unarmed leaders." I really liked it.

I believe that you could talk with her (keep in mind that she is a leftist intellectual). She is a wonderful person.

Love, I confess that I have a lot of fear related to the march that you planned for Caicedo. What I wrote has a different reading, once I am permitted to return.

Also, I believe that there is a lot of work to do among the Antioquenian society, in terms of priorities. We should guide them in nonviolence to transform many situations of injustice and neglect that require your presence, conviction, and leadership. The attitude of society facing its problems should be our priority, now that we can do something in that respect from the government.

MANÁ, for example; I feel that it lacks strength and economic conviction. The goals that I read are very uninspiring. I think that we should cover 100 percent of those less than five years of age in the Sisbén 1 and 2. Also, one has to think of the adults who suffer from hunger, and we should be able to involve more integrally the more powerful sections of the Antioquenian community.

In VIVA we are passing through a critical time, and the same in reforestation. Your presence there is crucial, and, if that were not enough, I don't think I could resist your going through that Calvary and running the risks it involves.

All the efforts we have made for nonviolence need a tough, persevering spirit like yours to keep the flame alive and to make it grow. I'm thinking all this, but I don't believe you will be able to know it since I don't see any possibility of sending these lines in time for you to have them before the anniversary. I am asking the Most Holy Virgin to dissuade you.

I think about Matthew and Daniel and about your children. How I would like to play soccer with them, go with them to their music classes or basketball, to their painting or horseback riding; to be at their side or to be there to help with their homework, to control television.

By the way, you have to restrict television for the boys. Please, I ask you to control Matthew so that he learns to take advantage, better than I, of his time, and above all that he is not submitted to that "daily shower of violence." Nonviolence begins in the home.

How it pains my soul to know that I am not within their reach. I always had my parents right at hand. I can't remember even one opportunity when they were not there. I, on the contrary, believe that I am the opposite example, and now even more so.

Another thing I ask of you, love. One has to see the way to help correct Matthew's "bad disposition" and, please, one has to teach him to be generous. I suffer, thinking that he can end up being miserly or envious. Daniel, on the other hand, has a much gentler temperament and I remain more tranquil about his human qualities.

I believe that Irene, Adelaida, Seth, and Duncan [Guillermo's sisters and brothers-in-law] are the best substitute parents in the universe. Of course, again my conscience bothers me knowing that I cannot be closer to them.

Well, my love, I'll try to go to bed again; I send you my love and kisses. Good night.

**Monday, February 24**: Love, good morning. Your message was very beautiful but I feel you are sad, and I understand why you feel like that. You have good reason. The situation of the country bothers us too, and each day it seems to get worse. We keep faith in God and the Virgin. The messages of Father Yépez also are comforting. I anticipate the one for this week.

I have begun to resolve debates about the "Gringo invasion" and the competencies to grant the authorizations. I still worry more about the form than the depth. Furthermore, the hypocritical attitude of our leaders, and at this stage, duly assimilated and incorporated by the community, is a true constant in our republican history. This debate, and the mutual insults between peoples who among themselves call each other brothers, has occupied the minds and all the newscast airwaves in the country. Whoever chose the cóndor for the coat of arms made no mistake.

**Tuesday, February 25**: My love, good morning. Today I note you seemed happier and that is enough to make my life happier. Additionally, Father Yépez sent a beautiful message about Ecclesiastes.

Today I spent almost the whole day polishing my abilities as a chess player. I played with Negrete, Aranguren, Lucuara, and Yim. All together we played series: a series is three games, whoever wins two, wins the series.

The truth is that I didn't do well. I won the series with Lucuara and one game with Aranguren. I lost all the rest. But despite that, I have hopes of getting better, and tomorrow will be the day of revenge.

Gilberto remains strong and very mindful of the national events. Now, despite the critical situation, he feels soon there will be a change in the humanitarian accord. I hope that he has "luck" in his reasoning.

I am less optimistic, but I'm also less gloomy than last night, and more confident, like Jesus, in the potential of human beings to incline toward the good. Yes, God made man. He was willing to suffer and to give his life for us. I see in this truth a great confidence in the human race.

These are guideposts which should guide us in the way we act, and not the verbal skirmishes with which, with frequency and obsessive tenacity, the leadership class tends to tie itself up and which the people follow with a morbid curiosity.

Well, mi vida, as you can see, we also have small battles here between optimism and pessimism. But, for the time being, faith and hope are winning.

**Wednesday, February 26**: My love, good morning. I heard you giving speeches and then your message. Sincerely, princess, I'm concerned. I noted a lot of anxiety in your voice. I suffer so much, perceiving your sadness.

I want you to receive this kiss that I send you with all my love, and hopefully it gives you a little comfort. I hope that on the weekend you will be able to distract yourself and enjoy yourself a little. I well know that Papo always makes you very happy. Give him a big hug from me.

Today they are interviewing the minister of transportation on Radio Caracol. Without a doubt he is a man of quality, and he speaks well.

It still is hard for me to get to sleep early. Gilberto says that it can be stress, although I do not feel any evidence of that if I reflect on the anxiety of our situation and how much you all suffer there. I'm going to try to relax a little more.

I have been thinking of the possibilities of having a campaign of citizen participation. I think that it could outline a competition between the municipalities of Antioquia with some 124 prizes, which would be given on the basis of various criteria: citizen participation in the design and execution, contribution to better the conditions of equity, and finally, that they help transform the social reality of the municipality.

The prize could be up to one billion pesos to finance the cattle projects. A jury that works with enormous responsibility, transparency, and objectivity has to be selected. Certainly there would be problems, like methods and resources, but I think that it can be a project to be in effect in four years. And the educational result can be more valuable than many of the efforts we make from the administration.

There must be simple but comprehensive rules and regulations, and given a good distribution. I think of it as a process to invite citizen participation and tie citizens to local development, obviously within the framework of the priorities of our plan for development or the results of the Consistent Peace Plan.

It implies transferring the capacity for decision-making and prodding the creativity of our communities, such as their ability to work as a team. The result should leave, besides the finished project, the notion of the value of participation. I would give it the name "Participate in the Future."

Well, mi vida, later I will give more details. Now I'm going to read the Bible. I'm interested in Nebuchadnezzar, and I'll also page through the gospel this week (book of Matthew, I believe follows, for Sunday, March 2). I also want to re-read Ecclesiastes, which is what Father Yépez read yesterday.

I'm a little beat, since I began sit-ups again.

**Thursday, February 27**: My love. I heard your news about Matthew and his passing school (you spoke of change, but I think you wanted to say from kindergarten to elementary school). How I would like to embrace him and share a little with him of this stage of his life. Daniel still hasn't sent your message to *The Voices of the Kidnapping*.

Love, I have read some of Ecclesiastes in the Old Testament based on the message of Father Yépez and I find it very comforting. It is also a very revealing book about the advances that humanity has achieved. Topics that previously seemed reserved to the knowledge of God today are elemental information accessible to a child. Likewise, topics that we consider inaccessible today will soon be studied and understood more precisely.

It also makes one think about why other topics, like war and the ease with which we resort to violence, continue being bulging tumors in the organism of society.

These days, there has been a lot of debate about the confrontation between EPM and the mayor, and Iván's [Correa] remark. Now the centrism of some ministers begins to show itself in criticism of the mayor, and he reverts to angry outbursts, as if this were the only audible way to answer.

Edith Cecilia [Urrego] I like a lot, and she has begun with very moderate statements. I wish her the best. I question what Ivan's aspirations are and if his "group" will not have some occupation prepared beforehand in Bogotá.

Love. You, Eugene, and Aníbal could think of Ivan, since I consider him a good executive. I leave with you all this consideration. At the root of the interview of Andrés Uriel [Gallago], I have thought, a little with remorse, that I could have been less stingy with him.

Now I think with more conviction and certainty that we only learn from our errors when we reflect on them and correct the attitudes that brought us to commit them. (It sounds easy but extremely devilish to correct. Even minimal attitudes have roots that we do not suspect). Neither do I forget that I was very generous with him when I could, and he made great efforts to avoid public criticism about what I consider his errors.

Mi vida, the solidarity of Miguel Ángel Bermúdez and the Boyacan people has left me perplexed. In the last few days I have frequently listened to all the spreading out that they have done. I would like to embrace them and express appreciation for so much generosity and honest expressions of solidarity.

Please share with him, his family, his town, and our friends there my gratitude and that of Gilberto. I was very pleased when I learned of his judicial triumph, and even more so for the "compensation" that constituted the order imparted by the then-president, who by his attitude left clear what his intentions were.

I was happy that you opened the way for Operation Smile. I congratulate you, mi vida. I believe there is a chain of restrictions and blockages that hinder these efforts of structural and external solidarity to lend their support in Antioquia, which we should eradicate. You have begun to overcome these barriers. One has to wait and see what other activities can program themselves. Without a doubt, I would like to be part in some stage.

By the way, I have thought of the need to fortify the Air Program of Health. For example, I would really like us to succeed in duplicating or triplicating its achievements. I know it is an expensive service, but I believe some economies on scale can be obtained. Very surely Juan Gonzalo López can help us and leave a great institutional commitment of the nation shaped by consent with Antioquia. I believe it has to advance rapidly to achieve results.

Something has been rolling around in my head: the restriction of medications. What sense does that make? On what basis does the state justify that? How can we Antioquenians accept that medications be denied a compatriot? How is the morale of the troops maintained?

Questions like these and others like them we should answer on the basis of seeking practices congruent with the ethics we preach and with constitutional standards. The support and the solidarity of the citizens should incline itself toward those who have as standards of conduct equity and justice and demonstrate this congruency.

We cannot combat hatred with hatred. Thanks to the enraged declarations of our generals, we are getting ourselves used to believing that to reject the violent actions of the guerrillas, and insult them, and stigmatize them, is the same thing. This is a serious error we have been making for a long, long time.

There is sad news about the death of twenty-three soldiers in a helicopter accident. The numbers of dead soldiers and fallen or shot-down army helicopters are hard. Well, mi vida, the rest of the day I dedicated to chess and exercise. (The truth is, more chess than all the rest).

**Friday, February 28**: My love, good morning. I listened to your message with joy and enthusiasm. Yesterday, you mentioned that I should not worry about your moments of sadness. Now I am happy that you have overcome them.

It is a good day, for Operation Smile as well as the concert and activities of the Boyacans in surveys by Radio Caracol about the popularity of the president (sixty-nine percent approve and thirty-one percent feel defrauded) and that of the RCN about Londoño (fifty-three percent that he stays, thirty-five percent that he steps down, and the rest DK/NR).

I can only say that this last one seems to me to be very favorable to Londoño and I believe that, at least in part, can be dragging down President Uribe himself.

Love, to continue with supporting the Air Program of Health which I began yesterday, I also think we should evaluate well the needs of the state and then study the possibility of assisting (the service) at a reasonable cost in the other states. In this way the fixed costs under the direction of the state can be reduced.

The helicopters are very expensive tools and they must be used 100 percent. I think that buying a new helicopter for the Air Program of Health is justified. A big one like that of the state or look for the contribution of another government. If it is structured well it can (why I say can, should) be free of the cost and simply increase its coverage. I ask you to talk with Eugenio, with the secretary of health, and with Juan Gonzalo López, since I am sure that it contributes to the public welfare.

On the topic of the language that the establishment uses, via generals, teachers, leaders, businessmen, and rulers, they should dedicate more attention to Juan Camilo Jaramillo and hopefully, Bernardo Toro (we were with him in the beginning). It is a very complex and definite topic, which doesn't arouse much enthusiasm in the people since it is not very visible, but I consider it important and strategic.

These last reflections have to do with the humanization of the war, which is a form of nonviolence. Restrictions should be eliminated. PAS[34] and the sub-topic of public communication should be extended and supported, to work seriously in disarming the language and attitudes, at the same time eliminating the carrying of weapons.

Now I see more clearly that the way of nonviolence is similar to a ladder. The direction must be carefully selected, then at the same time, we must climb each step. I believe that many steps must be climbed among the Antioquenian and also Colombian societies, then the actors of the conflict.

Also, in terms of implementing it, it is wiser to direct oneself to 40 million than to a specific group. Whoever accustoms himself to being aggressive with a specific group ends up doing the same thing in the moment of confronting another group.

I think of the scars that they are causing in the spirit every time the conflict becomes more cruel. Perhaps the worst of luck is that, different from physical scars, which are converted to evidence of the pain suffered; and even in a certain way of errors we commit, those scars each Colombian carries in the soul we do not see. If we could see them, it would terrify us because of the way we have been "resolving our conflicts."

**Saturday, March 1**: Love, good morning. Yesterday I talked to you about the similarity between a ladder and nonviolence. Today, to reinforce, I take the idea of *The Divine Comedy* in which Dante sought in principle "to descend" through the different circles of hell until the center of the Earth, then "to ascend" through a purgatory and the heavens until the divinity, to God.

Today I heard with much excitement your statements for Radio Todelar about the campaign of Operation Smile, about the notebooks and school supplies, and about MANÁ (about 100 thousand children in ninety municipalities). And finally, your words about nonviolence, our kidnapping and other comments. You were magnificent, and I noted that you were more enthusiastic. Additionally, today I anxiously wait to hear you. Your words are my manna, and I believe they ease the pains of many kidnapped persons and their families. Regrettably, tonight we could not use the tape recorder.

Good night, my love.

**Sunday, March 2**: Sweet princess, good morning. I just finished the Sunday account by Diana Uribe about history in the Babylonian epoch. Coincidentally, I am reading the *Book of Daniel* which speaks of the persecution of the Jews, and in particular I was impressed by the reference to the nonviolent answers of the Hasidim before the impositions on their culture and religion. The Hasidim were the Jews who were part of the "party of the pious" and during the persecution frequently arrived at martyrdom rather than violate their sacred norms. Nevertheless, after suffering in a nonviolent way, they took arms. Diana Uribe, on her part, explained where Antioquia came from (in Syria).

Antiochus was the father of one of the four generals that inherited the empire of Alexander the Great: Seleuch. He gave the name to a region of territory that he received in honor of his father.

There's another interesting fact: Saint Matthew, the evangelist, was born in Antioch, and thinking of him I chose that name for my son. Today, when I write these words, I believe the gospel is precisely on the book of Matthew.

Love, I am sorry that Nelson [Osorio] and Adriana [Colmenares, state officials] are withdrawing. I would like you to not lose contact with them. We should visit them both when I return.

I continue asking God that a verdict against Carlos [Wolff] not be rendered. I don't believe that his conduct, if accidental through some error in procedure, can be censured. The big pitfall of our legal system is to assure immunity to the real criminals as well as to threaten and block the honest dedicated officials.

All the attitude and activities displayed by Miguel Ángel [Bermúdez] and the Boyacan people deserves a separate chapter. I am short on words. I only want to tell you that in addition to the gratitude I feel for the facts, I especially value the respect coming from him; a man who has suffered in his own flesh infamous persecution and whose mandate was usurped by mandate with the implied approval of the then-president of the republic.

**Monday, March 3**: Love: I heard your message sent from Bogotá. Today will be the meeting with those in solitary confinement for peace and relatives of those kidnapped. We also heard the message of Martha Inés on *La Carrilera (The Railroad Track)* on RCN. I was half asleep.

I have begun to read the materials about Bolivar that you sent me. Here it seems that more books have arrived, but we don't know anything. I am anxious that they are the ones about nonviolence. The meals have become monotonous since for several days they have been soup made of rice and plantain.

Several days have passed, and we know nothing of the letters and the chess set that we sent. I'm very happy to know that MANÁ reached the figure of 100 thousand children daily. Now efforts must be made to cover all those five years and under in Sisbén 1 and 2.

They just arrived with a cow, undoubtedly to kill it today, which signifies two or three days of meat. February was a very hard month for the country. We hope March brings better news. Today the officials and sub-officials woke up excited, and they are bringing sand to adapt the floor around the shelter. Now we have a good gymnasium in the yard.

The book of philosophy, *The World of Sophia,* has caused sensation. Negrete has read it, Tapias, and now Gilberto. I'm next.

Today begins the financial statements. Here Tele-Antioquia does not reach and the two radio stations do not reach at this hour of the night. We are hoping, but I greatly fear, that if the Frontino station does not repeat it at another hour we cannot hear anything.

Good night, mi vida.

**Tuesday, March 4**: Love, good morning. I heard you tell about the meeting in the House of the Valley with the former commissioners and their commitment to the humanitarian accord. In fact, it was impossible to hear some of the financial reports. The news about the Idea has continued getting better. It was announced that it grew more than 300 percent.

The positive news is about the findings of Ecopetrol. Now they talk about a well of 200 million barrels. Everything indicates that the exploration was a success, but a lot is still lacking to verify the reserves and measure them with certainty. They speak of another 150 million dollars in exploration work.

Here a group of fighters prepare to definitely leave. Some have come to say good-bye. Soon their replacements will arrive and a new period of adjustment will begin.

**Wednesday, March 5**: Love, good morning. We have listened to you as well as Martha Inés and Lina. The painful news about Carlos Wolff caused me much sadness and concern. I think it is a scandal of the attorney's office, and I do not swallow that he has committed some error in the process of buying a car.

The few things that have been said show that the investigation refers to buying a car and some kickback related to the headquarters. This decision of the attorney causes me a great lack of confidence, and I believe that Carlos should look for and apply all the possible options.

Today Lent begins, and with it the invitation of the Holy Father to fast and pray for the peace of the world, and that of the bishops here, to do that for the liberty of those kidnapped. I'm going to do both. I began fasting this morning and praying the rosary, and I'll do it at mid-day. I'm going to offer other little sacrifices so that the will of Our Lord will incline toward peace and our freedom.

The words of Monsignor Jiménez, the bishop whom the army freed, may help to "force" the humanitarian accord. The national and international public pressure also is an element that can help toward a conclusion soon.

We continue waiting patiently, studying and reflecting a lot. I miss you immensely, as well as our children and families (the Antioquenian and the Santanderian). Also our good friends and the government team.

I have not been able to know anything about the financial statements, nor could I hear the message last night that you mentioned. At this hour, practically 6 p.m., the Frontino radio station is lost and here the one from Urrao does not reach.

So my pain is doubled: I cannot be there, nor can I hear what is presented to the Antioquenian people. From the reports that you sent me, I know that the projects are moving along and I'm very pleased, especially about MANÁ.

Love. Today I found that two pairs of my socks had disappeared, the only ones left, since the others we shared with the officials and sub-officials. Fortunately, I still have the old white ones that you sent me in the first shipment; they are really darned, but they still give good service. That happened Monday night or Tuesday.

The pattern is repeated—they take advantage of the departure of one of the contingents. Well, I'm not going to permit my soul to get upset. Here is where I should apply the nonviolence and most especially the theory of the followers of Gandhi.

Love, now it is afternoon. The concern about the socks was a false alarm; they have appeared.

The book about Bolivar has a very Venezuelan focus, and it also concentrates on the battles and strategies of war, which for me is quite monotonous. The narratives and assertions do constitute a very valuable document to consult.

**Thursday, March 6**: Love, good morning. Today I could feel in your message a special confidence in the progress of the Facilitating Commission—very satisfying at the present moment in which only the hardening of positions by everyone is seen.

In particular, it seems to us that the words of President Uribe regarding the attack in Cúcuta show a change in his attitude, which removes the possibility for dialogue. Ben Sirach (Eccl.) says "There is no medicine to cure the illness of the arrogant."

The most serious attitude of the president is that he is generating a chorus of echoes that end up making one believe that this is the only way. In his remarks, the president makes fun of those of us who believe in dialogue, similar to what he has done in relation to my position on nonviolence when campaigning.

Nonviolence is not trying to make conflict disappear. Its true role is to transform the attitude of society—a society possessed by ignorance and taught to resort to violence to resolve the most trivial and daily matter. A society that has accepted the marginalization and poverty of millions and refuses giving up some of its excessive privileges to achieve better equity and justice.

Father Luis Fernando Restrepo, Gilberto's nephew, read in a recent message some portions of Isaiah, and I myself find that eight centuries before Christ, already the prophets had the mission of nonviolence: to struggle against injustices, corruption, and violence: "Learn to do good, look for that which is just, help the widow."

Especially that part (Isa. 5:8) about orphans and widows makes me think of those displaced by war and of the mothers who are the head of their families. It also speaks of the excessive wealth of some: "Woe to those who add houses to houses and join fields to fields until it occupies the whole place, and they are the only owners of the country!"

So these problems have their trajectory. To eradicate them would be a huge task and full of obstacles. I believe that we have begun well with Manna and the programs of VIVA, RIA, education, and the Consistent Peace Plan. They are a good synthesis of the first steps for this voyage.

The more I think about it, the more I am convinced that these five standard tasks must be emphasized to leave them well consolidated and positioned in the minds of the leaders and of the people.

**Friday, March 7**: Love, good morning. Your sweet words and those of Father Yépez gladdened and comforted my heart. Coincidently, I am following Lent; I do not eat meat during these forty days, and the words of Father Yépez have come to complement my efforts to dominate rage and diverse manifestations of pride.

Yesterday the three women [cousins of Viellard], accompanied by two men arrived. The repellent Nopikex [a soap in a black box] that they sent is really the best that we have had and very effective. In the future, if they again send a package, hopefully it will be this.

With longing I think of Daniel and Matthew. I imagine Matthew has grown a lot and I wonder how life is for my sons. What is Daniel thinking about for his profession, and what new things is Matthew learning?

Viellard it seems, was bitten in the forehead by the skin disorder called "pito" (ie *leishmaniasis*). For three weeks he's had an infected sore on his forehead. He seems like a blind donkey. We have begun to cure it with home-made remedies that are here. Earlier they have served here for one sore that Negrete had on an ear, and before that for Cote on his arm. Yesterday they treated him with herbs, prayers, and washing with hot water.

Love, I frequently think of the suffering of my parents, especially my mother, since my father has always been strong as an oak. I know that she also is strong and has her faith as a refuge and finds comfort. Nevertheless, I want to ask that you be very conscious of her and try to accompany her to the extent that is possible for you.

In the correspondence that we sent (second package), there was a letter for my father. I'm very happy to receive the two books that he sent with the promise to send the study on *The Divine Comedy*.

I ask myself about the basis of this special interest of my father in art and astronomy. In short, I am sure that it would be very instructive to examine under a magnifying glass. It is a surprising book, deep and of great courage, able to criticize with unrivaled toughness the most powerful of his epoch. I imagine how his reading in Italian is.

Since last night we heard of the fire in the community neighborhoods. Hopefully the conditions of these families will improve. It can seem contradictory, but perhaps a tragedy like this serves them so that authorities of the city, state, and nation, as well as the citizens themselves, do something concrete and specific in this respect.

Yesterday afternoon they gave us delicious *guanábana* juice. I thought of you and the juices at Planeta Rica and what they sell in little bottles in the southern area of Cesar on the main route.

I'm glad that at least today Carlos Wolff can give his complete report of his conduct. This way Antioquia will know what excellent work he has been doing.

Love, in his letter he speaks very well of your and our Antioquenian family. It is a really beautiful letter and full of nobleness and generosity. Like you refer to him in your letters, a soul that is truly a friend is perceived, and I would really like you to read the letter that I sent him before you deliver it to him.

Give them all my affection and gratitude. Now begins a critical moment. My father, who knows his loyalty and capacities, can offer him the support that he's going to need.

**Saturday, March 8**: My love. Receive a first kiss this morning to celebrate your day. Thankfully I could hear your beautiful message that you usually don't do on Saturdays. It was a great surprise.

In the past few days, an intense sorrow has taken over my spirit which doesn't want to leave me, even though I am very conscious of the harm it causes me. Added to this sadness is what is accompanied by my reading the history of Bolívar; full of treason, lack of understanding, and slander.

Ecuador has expressed that it will not intervene in the internal conflict of Colombia, declaring the FARC terrorists. On the other hand, Brazil expressed, according to the news reports, its support of the Colombian struggle against terrorism and drug traffic. Chile also has pronounced itself to be of the same sentiment.

Everything indicates that the international camp has also hardened its position, and that will undoubtedly contribute to the situation of the kidnapped ones, making it more complicated, and there is no indication of a short-term conclusion.

Sweet princess, I hope that today you receive the love of all our friends, and that you have a happy spirit. From here, on a very sunny day, with fall breezes that filter through the tree tops, I send you my love, the love of my heart who I miss and always remember.

I'm concerned that yesterday they diagnosed Marín with another case of the skin disorder called "pito" (i.e. *leishmaniasis*). There are two more with Viellard, although it seems that this last one does not have it. They are doing daily treatments which we hope will be successful.

We two, as well as the officials and sub-officials, have very good health. Gilberto regularly takes his prostate pills, and he has that aspect very controlled. He suffers a lot because of loss of vision. It's difficult for him to read. He needs stronger glasses than the ones sent to him. Reading is crucial to him and to me.

I'm anxiously awaiting the arrival of the books on nonviolence, although I have not finished reading those I have here. Today I will begin reading García Márquez.

**Sunday, March 9**: My love, what a message, so filled with good news. What meant the most concerning our captivity is that of the progress of conversations between the FARC and the Facilitating Commission, which we understand is already taking place.

News about Matthew and his birthday, the house of Antioquia, the clear accounting and the very calming effect of the expressed and efficient management of the tragedy caused by the fire being put in "the hands of God." You are very right in thinking that it would really please me if I could celebrate this very special date and demonstrate my love, which will last as long as I live and my heart beats, since you are the soul of my soul.

We could not record, but I took very good notes, since I was awake from the beginning of Montoya's race in Albert Park. I imagine Anibal would have really enjoyed it, since he likes it so much and it was really moving.

Usually here, on waking up Sundays, it is very calm although sleepless. On the one hand, your messages and those of the families; and on the other hand, the stories of Diana Uribe, which are mixed with my reading the Bible (Old Testament).

The day began with the sun trying to shine, another one of a long series of beautiful summer days, without rain, which are predictable when winter begins, and it does so without consideration.

Last night among the messages there were two that caused us great joy for the acknowledgment that was made of your labor on behalf of the kidnapped ones. One was the father of Quique Márquez, and the other, toward the end of the program, a lady we could not identify. But in both, their valuable and wise efforts were acknowledged. I congratulate you and I'm proud of you.

Love, I continue studying the third report of negotiations that you sent me. In general, the progress can be perceived, but it must be pointed out that the report still has too many errors which lamentably show that the secretaries do not conscientiously revise them.

It is important that each one understands and assumes the responsibility that is his in the precision and tidiness of the figures under his authority. The errors make the reader entirely lose confidence in the document. The report is without a doubt a valuable effort, and I am sure that it will yield great benefits.

For me, a very concrete report with indicators on the flag programs would be desirable. From now on, until the end of the government, we all must hammer on these six topics to leave the indicators and successes formed in the minds of the Antioquenian people.

Of course, there are many other topics of great importance that can and should be presented to the public opinion when there are achievements. Each secretary has this responsibility. I only want the whole team to have them in mind and help to disclose them at any time to be able to imprint them in the imagination of the people.

**Monday, March 10**: My sweet love: As usual, the day began with your sweet words. Today promises to be filled with happenings: the controversies of the minister with the military commanders and with the chancellor of Venezuela, the issue raised by the secretary of the United States toward France, and the communication of the FARC denying their participation in the act against El Nogal.

While courage warms up the spirits, and the news media achieve their objective to elevate ratings, I think about the folly of the furious declarations of our public officials and the military.

Our history is full of verbal, boastful threats that, at the same time, unleash heated actions and decisions that frustrate the good intentions of the government leaders. They lose direction and permit their fellow team members to fall into the trap of backbiting.

The pattern is repeated time and time again, amplified and distorted by the interventions of the journalists and media directors who at the same time add what fits their interests or criteria. "Flies do not enter a closed mouth" seems to be the most forgotten refrain, and how good that would be for our public life.

I do not understand why a people who copy everything have not adopted a sensible practice of avoiding heated (improvised) statements to express well-prepared communications through intermediate authorized spokesmen.

That is, in the case of the military, even more incomprehensible. Before a microphone each one is converted into a talkative commentator on his strategies, accomplishments, plans, and methods.

A spy would be unable to gather this information that the officials themselves divulge, apparently without evaluating the consequences. The other aspect relevant to this "mouthing off" is the credit given for speaking. Many officials believe that to say something is enough to make it happen. With uttering a decree or expressing a solution, the problem is solved.

There is little commitment to the execution of orders or plans on the part of the heads responsible. Little is dedicated to designing the method and the way to do the tasks. Superficial commands, military or public, fulfilled by saying, declaring, decreeing, or ordering—without any consideration of its feasibility and reality of execution, especially in terms of resources required.

Here we have been able to learn how many commanders of the army behave and how frequently they are corrupt in daily management of the troops. Corruption is a virus, slow in the human species, and it is the head of the institutions who have to provide a remedy and watch that they do not gain ground for the organism that they orientate. Like a virus, corruption is cowardly and flees at the first indication of an antidote or honest desire to face it.

My love, yesterday the first pages of the book by García Márquez were nothing less than my own return trip to childhood, so satiated with memories of liberty and love, of the country and friends, of nature and traditions, of adventures and spirituality, of fish, cows, dogs, animals, and family.

What sweet nostalgia fills my head, and that at a distance in a childhood very similar to that of so many fellow citizens. When can the future generations enjoy this simple peace that so generously can be offered in the Colombian territory to their children?

Nevertheless, the words are so powerful that it is for its cause that we are killing each other. Each one looks in his knapsack for "quotations" that will justify his new actions against his brother. Facing the howl of a threat of war, the innumerable shouts of peace of millions seem to lose their strength, but later, when the arms cease, humanity will judge, and it is there where again the value of the word of the nonviolent person is recovered.

If we achieve a nonviolent culture, I believe the obvious results will be to invest the principles and to be committed to the solutions without violence for the capacity of crushing any other system.

What up to now is considered mere historic record could shape the daily realities for the well-being of millions, for the sake of true justice.

I am wondering, love: How is the planning going for the Global Center for Nonviolence that I proposed for Medellín? I should ask Eugenio through your channels for the support decided for this initiative, and make use of all the help our friends in the rest of the world can offer us. I am willing to continue working to that end, even after my period as governor ends.

Love, today they read a beautiful letter from the people of Granada for me. According to Gilberto, who heard it, they were thankful for and praised the participation of the state in the reconstruction and acknowledged my support. Hopefully you can get me a copy, since I would like to read it and answer it when I return.

At any rate, express my gratitude and support so that the recuperation of civic spirit and the enjoyment of this beautiful and vigorous municipality are achieved.

Love, I continue waiting for more clarity about the proposal of [Glenn] Paige. You mentioned it in the next to the last version of *The Voices of the Kidnapping*, but I have heard nothing more.

Actually, I have not been able to continue the financial statements nor the Saturday programs. I hope that it will be possible to soon read the fourth report and hopefully it can arrive with the books on nonviolence.

Love, in your messages, I am concerned that you insist on coming. I beg of you not to do so, since it would be fatal for me to see you in these circumstances.

Your work there, in all areas, keeps me optimistic, and also there are your children. The activities for nonviolence could not bear your absence, and all the sacrifices that we have made would be in vain. Please, get those ideas out of your head.

**Tuesday, March 11:** I heard your words from Bogotá; the recounting of your difficulties in arriving—and the final return by land. These references brought back so many trips that I made with you over our roads, seeing them changed to what they are today.

With interest we await the march that you announced, which we understand will be toward the end of the month. We believe it will be the collaboration among all the resources to again dedicate a day to the relatives and the kidnapped ones.

I also will be waiting today if something transpires in your interviews. In the morning we also listened to the "fashionable controversy" between Pedro Juan (Moreno) and Fabio Echeverri.

I return to thinking on a campaign to prohibit the carrying of arms. "Antioquia without arms, invincible." Gilberto tells me that he, like the Ministry of Defense, authorized the prohibition for Bogotá prompted by Mockus, Bromberg, and Father Alirio López—a very valuable person in the whole process. Also, it suits Gilberto that ahead of time, we talk in depth with general Campo about this.

Today on the radio was the news of the death of Patricia Medina, kidnapped for almost thirty months by the ELN with a son of seven and a daughter of four. She was killed by her captors after twenty-one months of there being no proof of her survival.

Love, I continue remembering my childhood and the memory gives way to the conviction about the importance of offering this opportunity to our children. These years perhaps are as decisive as the studies themselves.

Our lives are a succession of living experiences converted into active and passive, in lessons that form the human being. I have a notebook with cows on the cover (from Colanta), and I remember the happiness that I experienced when we got up to milk before dawn. I'm remembering Tamerlán and Acero, who produced fear in us but would entice us to risk petting their heads over the brick wall ruined by their horns.

These memories are interrupted by the statements of Angelino Garzón about the contacts with the FARC for the task of facilitators. He points out that messages have been sent and received but nothing is direct, and they will continue with their mission of negotiating the approach.

So, I continue thinking of how to ensure that our children live a childhood with positive experiences and that love of nature, nonviolent feelings, brotherhood, and patriotism are planted in them.

The day finished without major events. I forgot to tell you that, a couple of nights ago, I stayed awake listening to Guardino's story. He told me the whole process of his dating and of the difficulties with his wife which caused them to separate a year later, and he became coupled with Isabel, his present companion and mother of his daughter Yeridza.

Synthesis of the *machismo* present in our people and the uncertainties they live for lack of education. Yim finally has made the decision to read the autobiography of Gandhi. This reading interrupts a surprising inactivity that only was interrupted to play chess.

Well, I hope it goes very well with the re-inauguration of the House of Antioquia. Please, be careful not to drink too much liquor.

Kisses, love, and good night.

**Wednesday, March 12**: My love, good morning. This morning I missed your message. I have offered to the Lord this sadness that I believe was derived from the party last night. I'm going to begin reading the story of Sofía, which has made a great impression on those who read it, among those Gilberto.

Today, according to what I heard, the retirement of Carlos Wolff will be determined since the time has passed for the attorney to grant it. I think I can see what will happen: destitution, suing by Carlos—which he will surely win, work stopped, then repetition of the state against the attorney and after four or five years, everyone loses. Nevertheless the associates of the attorney impeccably wash their hands.

Today, like an echo of the somersaults of our justice, the Ministry of Defense repeated against the Dian in a process that was lost at a cost of 850 million, which was drawn in the adaptation of a confiscated airplane of the narcotic traffickers.

Yesterday a dilemma developed in relation to the *tagua* (ivory nut) and the gourd tree. The cone is the size of the pit of an avocado and extremely hard. In the beginning, with Negrete we identified it as a gourd, but later one of the fighters told me it was an ivory nut and another confirmed that. This made me wonder if the famous "vegetable ivory" is really this tropical nut after it hardens.

It seems unlikely that a wood would be called fruit, but I would like to clarify this doubt. Toné could do it in the twinkling of an eye. Love, they just called us to the classroom for a meeting with the commander; later I'll tell you what I can. A kiss, princess.

Love, now we have finished and the event was not important. I love you and miss you. Kisses. It seems that Eugenio had a bad experience with the Ministerial Cabinet. How the centralization hurts. It seems like all the blah-blah-blah of the national government begins to show how much of it is really committed to decentralization.

**Thursday, March 13**: Love, good morning. I finally listened to your message at the end of the program. I note you are losing your voice, and it seems to me to be occurring with some frequency. You should see a doctor because I'm concerned that you could have some chronic infection or something dangerous that we should take care of as soon as possible.

Last night Shakira offered a wonderful show to Colombia from Bogotá. Now she will do it in Barranquilla,[35] where she will surpass it for love of her little country. It's wonderful to see the love that she professes publicly for her country.

The survey of Radio Caracol about the extension of the mandate of the governors and mayors gave forty-seven percent in favor and fifty-three percent against. They seem to me to be very encouraging results, since the campaign has not yet begun, and surely the vote against will be related to personal sentiment about the mandate at the time in respect to territorial entity.

We need to wait and see what the general sentiment is in the case of Antioquia. I believe that the real reform is that which opens the possibility to re-elect any leader immediately.

The other news that caught my attention this week was that of the custody of three magistrates in the first International Court (six women and six men). Without a doubt this mechanism constitutes an important step in the transformation of the world toward a greater respect for the rights of humanity.

One hindrance, which each time will be more effective, is to bridle the abuses of the strongest in the international context. That also will serve to help in judging criminals of all classes in the world.

The first great challenge will be the development of the matter of Iraq. I can't believe that the United States can calmly usurp the right to declare war on whoever it believes is convenient, and if it does so against the stipulations of the Security Council, it not only will be assassinating Iraqis but dealing a fatal blow to the UN.

The International Court cannot remain a simple spectator in such a case. Equally, Great Britain and Spain should share the responsibility that the court assigns them. The change, then, consists of shifting decisions from being based on the political strength and interested vote of some nations to decisions based on respect for judicial laws and international human rights.

About the meeting yesterday, you should remind me to share with you some important reflections. The story of Susana, Daniel, Joachim, and the judges of the Old Testament. Monsignor Augusto Castro gave statements to Radio Caracol this morning that seem to me to be prudent and very wise. For us, they are also bearers of optimism and hope.

Samper has proposed the creation of a kind of Andean NATO; a body formed by countries of the region to confront terrorism.

Today also, through statements from Raúl Reyes to the French Press, we heard that Ingrid is in good physical health, and they add that she cannot be so in spirit knowing the unwillingness of President Uribe to advance the humanitarian accord. A good sign, since it shows a desire.

We now know that the march about the kidnapping is scheduled for the twenty-seventh, still two weeks away, but the topic is taking on color again. In the meeting yesterday, the commander told us that two weeks ago they introduced our recommendations, also those of the officials and sub-officials.

He is waiting for the orders to get them and give them to us. I suppose that it is in regard to the books on nonviolence and by chance some candy.

I send you my love and my thoughts, which are always for you.

**Friday, March 14**: My sweet love. Your message today was very beautiful, and I'm happy to know of the progress regarding the topic of quality standards. According to my calculations, we have already succeeded in Tele-Antioquia, the Idea, the Liquor Factory of Antioquia, Pensions of Antioquia. In short, I'm glad that all the state administration is entering into the custom of standards of quality; the secretaries should do the same.

Your reading about the statements of yesterday coincide with ours here. And the words of Father Yépez about the importance and excellence of prayer I have in mind and will always.

A few days ago something happened that I interpret as a message from the Lord. I was reading in a book of the Bible, in Daniel. For curiosity I was reading it to clarify something that Lucuara had said about the madness that Nebuchadnezzar, King of Babylon, suffered for several years.

Later in the meeting with the commander the topic came up that brought to my mind the story that you mentioned, and at night reflecting on it I accused myself for not doing anything. Gilberto thinks I did well in not speaking. He advocates not stirring up the waters. I feel that I was inferior at that moment and that I did so out of fear of consequences. Of course in my mind the reasons were disguised as convenience and good judgment.

Love, when I read the poems of Neruda or some others, or the most beautiful sections of *The Divine Comedy*, those in which Dante speaks of his love for Beatriz or other accounts of love, I feel they are lukewarm compared to the sweetness that your words distill and that your messages produce.

It is interesting how the distance and the separation have served to strengthen the confidence of our love and pulls out the weeds that choke out the growth of our love together. Today I see a quiet way, full of mutual confidence and respect; of desires to share everything, and of indestructible unity.

This love will be capable of destroying the obstacles that can continue existing and others that arise. I do not envision the moment of again contemplating the joy in your eyes and hearing your adorable laugh. I love you and will love you forever, mi vida.

Love, it is important that you do a routine of exercises, not for looks but for health. Also, I think it necessary for our parents to do daily exercises. I suggest walking. It is a family priority, and with the help of Aníbal they can (also with Baltasar and the people of Indeportes) design the routines and follow them.

It is not a whim, but a piece of discipline that certainly will improve the quality of daily life for all. I think that Jorge Luis can expound arguments in favor of this proposal.

Yesterday we killed a coral snake that passed through the surroundings of the camp. It makes me think of Gandhi and his ashram, where, despite the snakes being a latent danger for adults and minors, he prohibited hurting them. It seems absurd to be more fearful of a snake than of an armed human being who has declared us an enemy to our death.

These are the impressions of teachings that we assimilate; many times uncertain or false events arise and unconsciously we incorporate them. There is much we do not know about animal behavior, about insects, fish, reptiles, birds, even about dogs and pigs. "All I know is that I know nothing," Socrates said, perhaps the philosopher of greatest influence in Western culture. That is so true, and at the same time how far we are from this reality.

**Saturday, March 15**: My love, good morning. Yesterday afternoon we again experienced the happiness that you all felt upon receiving proof of our surviving. We still do not have all the details, but up to now it seems that they joined those of ex-Minister Araújo with ours. They are those of November 16, 2002; that is, the video that we mentioned and sent with the letters that you received in December 2002.

We heard you, and also MI and Lina, who seems to me to be correct in her statements. Last night, after we heard the news at 5 p.m., this seemed to be a news center. All the radios were turned on to different stations. When news appeared on some station, the person responsible shouted and everyone tuned in to that station. So we were first in Radio Todelar, then RCN, Caracol, Múnera Eastman. In short, a complete mix that lasted until about 10 p.m.

At that time it began to rain very hard and continued until 8 a.m. this morning. With this storm, we believe the rainy season has begun, which here is very heavy. All night long the air felt overloaded and the lightening and thunder could be heard in the background.

Now, while I write, Viellard is fishing in a little creek that passes in front of our shelter. Yesterday in the afternoon he caught a *mojarra* which they prepared, and they gave it to me. That was my supper. Today, with the creek rising in the night, he's having better luck and now we have three little animals and a *mojarra* that escaped when he pulled it.

Now the replacement has arrived and again the slow and painful process of knowing us and understanding us from a distance. Tonight, surely the messages will reflect the joy of having seen the images and also the frustrations of knowing that they were taken four months ago. At any rate, the fact that they were received reflects a desire of the FARC.

# Part IV
RECOVERED IN THE RAID
BY THE ATTORNEY GENERAL'S
OFFICE AND GIVEN
TO YOLANDA PINTO DE GAVIRIA
ON MAY 3, 2003 BY
THE DISTRICT ATTORNEY OF
ANTIOQUIA

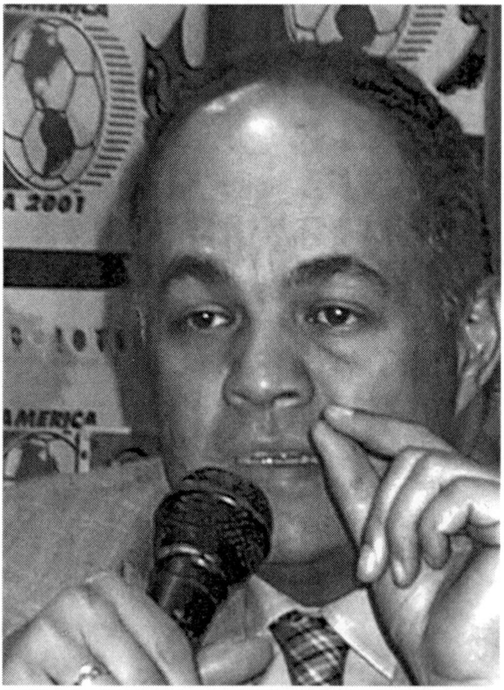

**Continuation, Saturday, March 15**: My love: I have finished this marathon of preparing the application and the letters of yesterday ( I am writing this Sunday sixteenth). Receiving what you and Martha Inés sent made the day shorter. The commander called me and I had a long conversation with him, which ended with his authorizing me to send you the application and our letters, which overlapped my lunch and bath. I hurried to finish writing by 6:30 p.m. and I'm sure I left a lot out.

What pains me the most is that I did not have time to write my mother. The other letters I answered I had been writing with the certainty that I could dedicate the necessary time for my mother's before the next shipment. In short, I hope God lets us, in the same way as he did now, again send news as soon as possible. The excitement of the day kept me from sleeping, despite going to bed with the desire to rest for the program *The Voices of the Kidnapped*. Good night, my love; what joy fills me to get your news and I send you these lines.

**Sunday, March 16**: Good morning, my love. Yesterday your message was very beautiful and democratic; everyone loved it. Here I have learned how frequently I am mistaken in judging what others want or hope for. Your insistence on the need to trust in the progress of the process of the International Humanitarian Accord, which you explained in detail in your magnificent letter of February 26, 2003, is being understood little by little here, and it sustains us and fills us with optimism.

Today I will work on calmly reading all the documents and letters that you sent, since yesterday I only had time to skim through them. Yesterday was really a wonderful day, and the most wonderful of all is that besides the letters that we sent you, I think that very soon you will be receiving the letters and the chess game of the second shipment. Yesterday's was the third shipment, and now I'm beginning to prepare the fourth.

Love, it's almost 9 p.m.; I'm sleepless because the last two days have brought me so much happiness. There has been so much that I have not had time to write; I could only read and write the application. Only today could I read your wonderful letter. Actually you have flooded me with love with your sincerity and the intensity of your suffering.

It was a long letter, unlike you ever wrote before and full of your pain and thoughts, of your loneliness. All that you mention in it is now motive for joy and optimism for me, although I believe that changes and sorrows will lead to good things. I feel a strange and very high state of spiritual well-being.

At the same time along with all the reasons you, the center of my existence, give me, there are others. They are very numerous and have joined together on this beautiful night of a "waxing moon" (according to the Bristol, the full moon will be the eighteenth) to make me feel happy and hopeful, optimistic that the future holds even more than just a humanitarian accord.

There are reasons for me to feel good and proud, like the news about the progress of Daniel and Matthew, the very significant fact of "our" nomination (for the Nobel Peace Prize), sent to Stockholm by Dr. Paige. (Love, what really fills me is that we are both nominated, that is understanding the strength that it gives to this purpose to be prompted by a couple. I well know, personally, how much support I needed and got from you so I could trust my early palpitations, my first and imperfect incursions into nonviolence and its application to our land.)

Dr. Paige's explanations in the paperwork are sufficient reasons to fill me with pride and energy to strengthen my commitment and my convictions. Another great thing is the letter he wrote to the FARC-EP secretariat. I do not have illusions about a conclusion, but I do know for sure that it was written and encouraged by its author's sincere conviction that frankness and transparency can contribute to opening doors so that our message of nonviolence at least is heard.

To this reflection I am also moved by the last paragraph of Lafayette's letter, in which he speaks about the role that nonviolence will play in this century and the changes that the country will see and in which, I believe, the FARC-EP (EP = *Ejército del Pueblo* or People's Army) will be participants. He elaborates on his vision of nonviolence in the future of Colombia and the world. They are voices of authority in the international context, and they fill me with hope that FARC-EP could feel motivated to at least hear us. Later they can evaluate how feasible our proposals may be and how concerned they should be about opening a space for these proposals.

In this respect, the most notable and encouraging event happened today, and it is a slight chance of getting to speak with the commander of the front. This is related to the petition that I sent you, and I cherish the hope that it can lead to other possibilities of teamwork or nonviolent cooperation.

As if that were little, today I saw the video that you sent in which, besides SEDUCA's[36] program for promoting the nonviolent dialogue among our boys and girls, you, my mother, my father, Aníbal, Claudia, Martha Inés, and Lina are there in the homage that Boyacá (lead by Miguel Ángel [Bermúdez]) offered. A small "proof of survival" for us, the same as for you, fills our soul with joy and love. They all look well and Gilberto and I feel very, but very, good. I have not finished reading the letters and I am thinking of how to end the story for Matthew and of Papo and Mafer that you briefly mention to us in the letter.

By the way, I am eating a Cocosette of those that Papo sent me; give him my thanks, as well as to all whom with their generosity have been our delight. But there are even other reasons. Each day I feel with the support of our Lord God and the Most Holy Virgin stronger and more frequently; each act makes me understand better the mysterious ways of the Lord, I also believe that in a very special way in these last days he has given me all the elements to choose the correct way, and he is clearing the way of obstacles.

Love, I want to tell you that I perceive a change of attitude among our captors which can, with a little divine help, mean an opening to take up the conversation of nonviolence with them. I told you a few weeks ago that I believed God hoped that I would learn something in this captivity, something special; I believe, I can't say that I am absolutely sure, that I am ready to leave. It can sound absurd, but in earlier opportunities, when we have believed that the inexorable hour of liberation was approaching, I came to feel that I still had something to learn. Now I feel differently.

It could be that the pain of this separation is pressuring me to feel that I have already learned what is necessary, that it has fulfilled its purpose, and that really I am not ready yet; nevertheless, I calmly feel that something is happening around this, and it is something very positive. I give thanks to God and the Most Holy Virgin and the whole multitude of people who are permanently praying for us. Please, don't forget to tell them.

I also hope, my, love, that as you wrote in your letter, you can feel the enormous and wonderful strength that I am feeling. I send it with all my love. It is so extraordinary what happened that I believe that even our Yolandita can be a reality in the way that you state in your letter. I have asked for the authorization and I am awaiting the miracle. Do you see the mysterious ways of the Lord? Separate us to have our daughter!

Without a doubt, my love, if the miracles are not as I believe, there is one or the other. You mention the concern for my health and if I have medicine. Never in my life have I been so surrounded by more medicine than now, and never have I been in such an unbreakable condition of good health.

I'm only concerned for the health of Gilberto; he is very thankful for the medicine received, but at his age I believe he should not be running the risks that we run here. Provisionally he is like an oak, he misses stronger eyeglasses, but I will try to get our captors to understand his vulnerability and to return him to freedom soon.

**Sunday, March 16**: Don't worry Martha Inés, on the contrary, the greatest risk to Gilberto's health is that something will happen to Martha Inés; including his only suffering is, as it is for me, an enormous and painful burden. On the other hand, I aspire that the FARC-EP understand that Gilberto can and without a doubt will be more productive and useful to the proposition of the humanitarian accord there than here.

My love, you can always tell me your sorrows. I hope that you do so with ease and with all your spontaneity. Don't be afraid to do so, because for that "I'm at your side," I'm your husband, who supports you; weep and laugh on my shoulder. When I say that you should be strong, I really mean to urge that you have confidence in our love, and that it will withstand all these tests and even harder ones, if there could be harder ones.

Don't hide your sorrows, tell them to me, write them so that, although it sounds strange, this will permit them to leave. When I receive them, I really receive your manifestation of confidence and love, your tenderness and the meaning of your sacrifices. All this gives me life and strengthens my love. Love, I'm going to try to sleep a little; good night. I'm sending you love and kisses.

**Monday, March 17**: Love, good morning. I just finished listening to your message in which you tell me that after returning from the west you heard the *boleros* program; that means that at the same time I was sitting here, enjoying the moon and writing you with a heart full of hope. For breakfast, we all polished off one-eighth of a cheese and the last cocoa. What a wonderful idea, that cocoa. One would think that here it would be easy to obtain but it is impossible.

The edible ants we enjoy at night, imagine, some had never tasted them; what irony, come to try them amid captivity, precisely where it is most difficult to get food.

Today everything in the world centers on the imminence of war against Iraq. The United States is going to deal the blow of thanks to the UN and will make clear that the rule in the future is the law of the strongest and that it is willing to defend its power to take control of the oil in Iraq.

In South America the Bolivarian countries, with the exception of Venezuela, supported the United States, among them Colombia, which rushed to support Bush before he had even made his case. Large countries like Brazil, Argentina, Chile, Mexico, showed their independence and character. Our rulers, who think their conduct will win them friends, do not delay in siding with force when only a few weeks ago they pretended to be neutral and objective, and even the president himself prided himself as being a companion and guarantor for UN peace process which he contributed to undermining now.

Yet from here it seems that those who wanted the war and those who opposed it did so according to their economic interests and distance from Iraq. On the playing table of the great economies there is little interest in millions who want peace, and this reality is argued among the smallest countries. Even then, nonviolence will prevail and our job is to not let down the bar. An age full of uncertainty for humanity is just beginning. Good night, my love.

**Tuesday, March 18**: Good morning, my love. I listened to your message about English classes and the summons to the radio station for the twenty-seventh between 8 and 9 a.m. Later I heard your message, which you seemed to have recorded in conditions that were a little sad. Your public statements sounded more enthusiastic and happy. Very soon, my love, in less than a week, you will receive the letters of the third shipment and the special petition, and then I think that will help you to raise your spirit.

A few days ago I heard a news that bothered me; it had to do with the declarations of the CREG (Commission on Regulations of Energy and Gas) in which they announced a lowering of the tariffs on energy at the order of six percent until Ramiro Valencia Cossio claimed that that was achieved thanks to his negotiations with the minister of mines and energy. What is irritating is that a week ago the present minister criticized the attitude of Luis Pérez in favor of freezing the tariff and if I remember well, at the beginning of the administration when he presented it for the first time as mayor, also the private secretary of Pastrana, Eduardo Pizano, considered it a mortal blow to EMP and a week later Ramiro Valencia himself, as minister, announced a reduction of ten percent in the tariffs.

Give my congratulations to Luis. Ask him to verify if the reductions boasted by the two national governments have become a reality, since I do not believe that this should have been done. In the magazines that you sent there is an article by Alejandro Santos Rubino. It was very interesting that finally the Santos house is opening its eyes to the reality of the country and their being responsible for allowing that reality to become what it is for helping the country emerge from the crisis.

But not only should they understand it and assume the commitment to struggle to correct so many errors in our society, we should achieve a critical mass capable of pushing, without violence, the real changes, social transformations that depart from a new attitude facing life in the community, which I call the culture of nonviolence. At the root of this, I have been thinking a lot about young people's camps of nonviolence.

Love, I believe that you should try to increase the number of camps you do each year. I listened to your message that you were preparing it in Santafé de Antioquia. Yesterday (Monday) you said that you arrived late from the west. I interpret that now it has taken place and I cannot have any more news.

I think that with the help of Eugenio and the whole cabinet, as well as our foreign friends and looking to continue other commitments with nonviolence or other forms of pacifism (Mockus, Father De Roux, etc.), you can carry out various camps and prepare and consolidate a group that, coordinated by you, is dedicated to prepare its members with the necessary rigor.

Love, I'm thinking of a very ambitious goal of five camps a year. Of course, surely it will be impossible to reach five this year, but I think we can achieve two or up to three. And everything should be planned for five for 2004 (with extension of the period or without it). I am referring to creating the structure that guarantees the continuation of this wonderful effort. Looking at the first part of the video with the effort of the Secretariat of Education to help our boys and girls discover the magic, the richness, and the power of the word, and to tie this discovery to the culture of nonviolence, I really get excited. I hope, my love, that this idea draws your attention.

Love, what do you think? I just finished reading the letters that came in the last shipment and I found in one from Liz [Elizabeth Ramírez Herrera, friend of Guillermo and Yolanda] a mention about the plan this year to have four children's camps of nonviolence, just like the topic I wrote until our captors invited us to play volleyball.

What a coincidence and what great joy to know that you all are already working on this wonderful effort. Yes, there is telepathy and connection between our souls. I love you, my love, you give me much joy. I would only add that the goal of 500 children can be increased to at least a thousand, without damaging the quality of what is going to be taught. But of course you have more elements to make the decision which seems best to you. Well, good night, my love.

**Wednesday, March 19**: My princess, good morning. I loved the news yesterday about your conversation with Matthew. I'm pleased that he can come without fear to a person so wonderful like you. After the message this morning also I felt warm and very calm. Paige's documents are excellent and his proposals honor me greatly and fill me with great joy, above all because they do not refer exclusively to me but to both.

It makes me a little sad that in the petition for liberation, they only talk of me and do not include Gilberto, who all his life has struggled with civic valor for the peace and equality in Colombia and that in this has so much solidarity. In the most remote eventuality that the FARC-EP were disposed to accept his arguments, the only thing I could do is yield the option to Gilberto.

I believe, although with pain, that you understand this. If Paige's arguments about me are true, I cannot accept gaining my freedom and leaving him here; on the contrary, my most fervent desire is that the FARC-EP anticipate the liberation of Gilberto.

My love, I spoke of the topic of Yolandita with the commander who cares for us here; we should wait until he consults with his superiors. I know that there is little probability, but I do not lose faith that the Lord and the Virgin will do this miracle; your faith takes me by the hand and I feel the joy that is born with hope. I will tell you at the first opportunity. You, in the meantime, get all the preparations ready; this shipment I will personally have to give to the doctor of the Air Program of Health (Jaime, I believe is his name; I'm accustomed to calling him doctor).

I believe that the jar will go from my hands to the doctor's and from his to yours. If they authorize it like that, we can coordinate it so that I deliver it during one of his visits to the zone. Or better yet, you can come and receive it personally. How do you like this miracle? Maybe it is too preposterous to think that God would do us this personal miracle, but nevertheless I continue hoping. Also, the doctor could come with you and to run fewer risks, if that were possible, to make the mixture in the place of meeting; in short, you can determine the details with the doctors.

**Thursday, March 20**: My love, good morning. Your loving message filled me with love and sweetness. Since last night nothing else is heard but the war of the United States against Iraq. On this topic it is not only the absence of nonviolence, it is the dominion that the United States assumes to attack whatever nation on the basis of accusations of terrorism, including crushing the authority of the UN, constructed on the basis of world consensus and, which is even worse, with great influence of the United States itself.

The double standard is exposed without any modesty at all. The events that will be produced immediately after will leave exposed even more the real intentions of Bush, and therefore the North American people.

I believe that then the need of nonviolence will be seen, then we will talk again, but if "punishing" the United States is not achieved (I do not refer to military punishment) and assure that in the future it will submit to the will of the UN in a way that the rest of the world can believe, then the law of the strongest will reign, and the space for nonviolence will be reduced, or perhaps it will be the great opportunity for nonviolence to defeat weapons.

The recent judicial complaint of the Colombian indigenous people against the European conquerors has prompted me to think about our lawsuits against the tobacco companies, and in light of so many multimillion dollar verdicts against them, it could make something similar against the arms producers.

If a company that sells cigarettes is responsible for the cancer that this produces in the consumers, why not think that the producers of arms are equally responsible for the deaths they cause? Add to this the schemes and dirty negotiations that precede the orders to buy and even the crimes carried out to justify the conflicts and all the support that, in secret, some nations lend to others against their common enemies and the terrible effects on millions of human beings. Then we harshly see that this lucrative business is, as no other, cemented in the pain and misery of many, some of whom are not even consumers of arms.

It is ironic that the countries with the ability to veto in the Security Council are at the same time the greatest producers of arms in the world. It is similar to what occurs in Colombia, where the army, which boasts a monopoly in the production of arms, opposes disarmament, or rather, permitting restrictions on carrying arms.

You mention that former President Samper will be in Medellín and hold a meeting. I have expectations about what will be discussed and also about the results of the meeting that President Uribe had with [James] Lemoyne and Luis Carlos Restrepo a couple days ago and where the topic of the humanitarian accord was discussed. I suppose that during these days the petition has arrived that we sent you six days ago (March 15).

**Friday, March 21**: Love, good morning. We listened to your messages and both Gilberto and I were surprised by the absence of references to the dinner with former President Samper. About him, the only thing we know is the news of his backing Luis Pérez's management of the EPM.

Love, I believe that the changes in the cabinet were well done; I heard that "the new way of doing politics" is unsatisfactory, I would have liked them to pay attention to this team, and they well deserve it. In earlier letters you mentioned it, as well as my interest in taking care of some requests of his father.

Regarding Juan Fernando Meza, I believe they made a very good decision, also I like that of Baltasar (Medina) and in general I think that, although my information is incomplete, they have accomplished a lot with a lot of tact.

The news about the departure of Lucía González came as a surprise to me, with her and Carlos Wolff's leaving I fear that the matter of decentralization can suffer a delay if Eugenio himself does not raise it with a complete decision.

Here we continue in good spirits and reading everything thanks to the good allotment that they have sent. I hoped for and am still hoping for more literature on nonviolence. I received Mario López's document and Glenn D. Paige's book (*Nonkilling Global Political Science*),[37] but I should take advantage to to read as much of this literature as I can. I feel very well, thanks to your love, which I receive in each message through your statements to the media and in an intense way in your correspondence and shipments.

Every day I thank God for allowing us this wonderful communication. Also I'm encouraged by the many opportunities that seem to open up, especially the very remote opportunity for us to have an interview with the commander of the front to speak about nonviolence.

Yesterday I incorporated the luminous mysteries to my daily rosary, thanks to the guide that you sent in the last package. Tomorrow at the time of the program Montoya will cross the race in Malaysia; I hope that you can send your message and hopefully you have received the third package and can with all discretion let us know. Yesterday we played volleyball again.

Last night I fell asleep listening to the speech of President Uribe, so I did not heard his call for solidarity with the United States. Today we have heard that there will be a announcement in Medellin of our nomination for the Nobel; however, we have not heard anything more concrete in this respect.

Herberto is showing me how to make bread, of course, pure theory because there is no way of practicing here. I think I would really like to learn how to make good bread. Of course in our captivity, I realize how whimsical I am.

Also I would like to know about the cultivation of edible ants and of grapes, as well as about the production of wine. Some day, Lord willing, we will have the possibility of doing these three things in La Cristalina. I have not heard anything about the launching of our nomination, but in its place I did hear the declaration of a nonviolent jail at Bellavista. I'm very happy to know that they continue in this proposal and that it has advanced; nevertheless I hear nothing about advances of my project of a new jail or of the Liberty Farm.

Neither in the reports I have read nor in statements of any kind. I'm grieved to think that my commitments in this area have been abandoned. Good night, my love.

**Saturday, March 22**: Good morning, my love. Last night I received the good news, when we were ready to sleep, of the delivery of the third package. We could hear you as well as Martha Inés on Radio Todelar, RCN, and today the widely broadcast news on Radio Caracol. I continue thinking that in a very few days the second package, which has the chess, will arrive. According to my calculations, I hope we can receive what we asked you for by next Saturday at the latest. Also I hope the door is open for future shipments, in the conversation with the heads of the front, our proposition to conceive Yolandita and at least the liberation of Gilberto by the FARC-EP.

Love, I have just been interrupted to hear your statements on *How Medellín Woke Up* before leaving for Bogotá. I hope that Daniel Ernesto can enjoy the celebration of his birthday. I'm very pleased that our petition has been treated—your words confirm that. The war advances against Iraq and everything indicates that the military objectives are going to be achieved without much difficulty; the enormous military power of the United States makes itself felt.

The UN remains silent, in a dubious attitude that seems contrary to that which I hoped for, since its authority has been made fragments and its fundamental purpose to evade war is trampled on by its most powerful members. If it does not act with determination, with much difficulty it could it reclaim a role after the conflict is ended, since it will have yielded to the United States.

Groups in the civil society in all the world remain active, and they will be the ones who should carry out the analysis that can point the direction that guarantees peace in the future of humanity. There still remains a great unknown: What will the International Court do? Will it be that it can rescue itself in the search for world peace by legal means? I think that in the world crossroads, in Colombia, the most "marketable" effort, by all means, is to create a culture of nonviolence.

How good it would be to be able to remove all the false images many in our country have about "the power of the people" or "the strength of love." Paige's nominating us for the Nobel flies around in my mind; that alone constitutes sufficient prize for you and for me. What happens from now on depends on the will of the Lord, and I do not doubt that for Colombia it could become very constructive if it manages to advance some. Each time I think more of the necessity of studying literature about "Nonviolent Popular Defense."

Love, it is necessary that you send me literature about nonviolence. I've sent you notes about what I'm most interested in; nevertheless the best counselor would be Mario López Martínez. He has already recommended Giovannio Pontano to me, try to get something from him and send me photocopies. Look! Try to copy them on both sides to reduce the size.

Gilberto told me some news that really reveals the United States' soul: Despite investing daily almost 20 million dollars in propaganda for the war, the audience preferred a show called *Friends*. While its government launches a battle that it considers indispensable, the citizens are more interested in their daily entertainment.

Precisely, love, in the literature that you sent me from Mario López M. about nonviolent defense, I just read something about "the body of European civil peace," the white hard-hats and the civil peace corps. For several months, including before the kidnapping, I have thought that with time this will be my proposal to the Colombian people, to transform our armed forces into civil corps of peace or nonviolent brigades. An army without arms.

Of course I haven't really processed the topic; it's rough and needs a lot of study, reflection, and debate with those who know about this. Good night, my love. Receive my kisses and love.

**Sunday, March 23**: My sweet princess: Your message at dawn calmed my anxiety of the last few days a bit regarding the march to Caicedo. Also my energies were renewed to know about Matthew and his new school, about the paving of Andes-Tapartó, your incursion in the Internet, and what seems to be the acquisition of a computer. Of course, I'm enormously happy that Tuesday it will be delivered.

Your words of love accompany me amid the great loneliness that covers me and crushes my soul; just your spiritual presence alleviates it. Two things made me very happy: the news about the jail and the advances of nonviolence, despite the fact that I have not received news about the advancement of my project of new installations and the Liberty Farm.

Secondly, I am happy to know that you have been able to consult about the march. I understood that you had made them at the highest level [Secretariat] which is what, to my knowledge, could give a different order that would be unfortunate. God has been very generous in allowing this communication to reach you before the march.

In the second package there is a lot of information about this topic and instructions. I hope that they receive it soon even though opening this second delivery seems to have annoyed them. Never did we know that it should not be distributed, and for that reason we did not include instructions in this sense. It is lamentable that this indisposition could ruin some of the good expectations of the past week.

My love, we are coming to an end of the wonderful provision of candy and cheese that you sent; I have made the ants stretch, and they taste like heaven; I do not have much hope regarding new shipments, but it is possible that you have provided some.

I must confess that since Friday I have been very discouraged, I don't know what it is that affects me, but only your words help me; my thoughts are made worse by the fact of being conscious that, despite the captivity, they are treating us very well, and the Lord and the Virgin in many ways make me feel their protection.

I don't understand why in moments in which I have much and very good reasons to be happy and hopeful, this is when with more force the sadness of the captivity attacks me; on the other hand in the darkest moments my spirit seems indestructible and unmoved. I'm embarrassed to overwhelm you, but I feel so useless because of these chains, and I see myself condemned to bear this for even more time.

I greatly fear that the letters that we sent with the officials and sub-officials in what I call the second package, in which we included the chess (mine for Daniel), can be delayed more.

Gilberto and I continue very united and dedicated to read and to write them. We have been in this new camp (which I have named "Mosquito Land") for two months. I'm going to try to resume the English classes which we suspended because of moving. At the same time I hope to begin classes for the fighters (male and female) very soon.

With uneasiness I heard of the loss of Colanta. I hope it doesn't affect its strength or generate traumas; you know how I love that company and my conviction that this type of effort produces the best social benefits, with all its capacity for social transformation. The state government cannot permit that it suffer a calamity or that the circumstances of the country affect them. It should be their unconditional ally in whatever is necessary facing its concourse. There is no other enterprise that shares its benefits among almost 15,000 rural families.

Today the commander surprised us with Coca-Cola and then guava juice. For some days we have been eating *mazamorra* [boiled whole corn], you know how much I love it. If we add to that the candies, the cheeses, the ants, you're going to be envious of the banquets that we are relishing.

I began Paige's book, and reading his writings and documents that Mario López sent have been very useful to me. Well, my love; good night and sweet dreams.

**Monday, March 24**: My love, good morning. I did hear you on *How Medellín Woke Up*. I suppose that you took advantage of the holiday to sleep a little more, although I know when you are in Bogotá, you get up early. I imagine María getting you up with *tinto* [very strong coffee served in a small cup]. By the way, what happened with her pregnancy?

The war in Iraq continues and now it seems that it will not be as easy as thought in the beginning. The news talks of agreements made by [Saddam] Hussein with basis on the "lessons" learned in the Gulf war. To me, it gives me the impression that the army of Iraq will defend positions, but it's going in the direction of converting into a type of state guerrillas, a guerrilla army.

This morning I woke up thinking that the "Anglo-American" forces are capably conducted toward an ambush and this contributes to great arrogance and the conviction that such power (enormous) is enough to crush the enemy. What I have not been able to share nor accept is the silence of the UN. Each minute that passes without a clear position of energetic complaint and condemnation, I feel that it loses authority.

On the other hand, the Red Cross complains about the trampling of the rights of the prisoners/victims of the war, which were photographed and the images spread at international levels. What a contrast! While one organization raises its voice with photographs and these are transmitted to every corner of the planet, the other, which gathers all the nations and has a world delegation to maintain peace, remains silent before a war that crushes the entire framework of international humanitarian rights and juridical pacifism.

Love, last night I was listening to the program until I was overcome with sleep, that being at 9:30 p.m.; now I'm too accustomed to going to bed around 7 p.m. and sleeping around 8 p.m.; at any rate, I will be trying to "accompany you" every Sunday.

In my readings I discovered an interesting datum: The word *germinal* was used in the French Revolution to name the seventh month of the revolutionary calendar. This month corresponds to the period comprised between March 21 (day when I read it and we complete eleven months of being kidnapped) and April 19 (two days before the anniversary); this last date coincides with two important dates: April 19, 1970, when the election was held that, according to some, Pastrana robbed from Rojas Pinilla.

This fact, at the same time, was chosen by the leaders of M-19 to name its revolutionary movement. They said that they did so because they were ready to carry out what "the people should have done in this occasion and they did not." But also on April 19, 1810, independence was declared for Caracas, which later was taken as the date of independence for Venezuela.

Émile Zola, the French writer, titled one of his works with the word *germinal* in which he harshly criticizes the lack of social conscience and solidarity of the ruling management class of that time, at the time of reclamation of social justice and equality. If you are interested, it would be interesting if you could read it; I'm sure you will find interesting similarities to our present reality and the French people of the nineteenth century.

**Tuesday, March 25**: Love, good morning. I see that you have enjoyed your weekend in Bogotá, and I'm glad for that. The message from Lina leaves us with the impression that she will accept an outside offer. This news made Gilberto sad, and he's going to have to really put forth an effort to overcome it; the hardest part is that he sent a series of questions to "help her" in the decision, but these are in the second package, precisely the one delayed in leaving.

At times we professionals confuse ourselves and let the aspiration of a great professional success which also signifies stability and economic ease for the family pull us, only to realize later the price in terms of quality of life which we eventually pay together with our family. I believe that this is what most affects Gilberto, especially because he has always been able to enjoy a united family.

Love, I miss you a lot. I should concentrate on answering and writing a series of letters that I'm delaying doing, among them to my mother.

**Wednesday, March 26**: Love, good morning. Today we received several greetings, since besides yours, we were written to by Carlos Villegas and Martha, Gilberto's sister. Also we woke up with the good news of the statements of Luis Carlos Restrepo about the decision of the national government to maintain the exception for seven years to postpone the agreement of the International Court and its desire that the FARC-EP interpret it as an indication of the will of the government to reach peace and reconciliation.

Reading Paige an idea comes to me that at a university level their proposals could be adapted to structure a curriculum for a course called Nonviolent Political Science. Hopefully Eugenio could push this topic in the School of Government, with the help of the higher education system. I'm glad that Dr. Uribe Correa was chosen (as rector of the University of Antioquia) in such a forceful way; this gives him great backing to give continuity to all the good that came from pushing Jaime and to introduce all the good that is coming out of these proposals of the very worthy aspirants.

We must produce a good course on nonviolence and a good program to give structure to the education for nonviolence. I believe that specialists like Beatriz Restrepo Gallego and advisors like Mario López M. can give valuable support, and I am sure that Juan Camilo Ruiz could lend his enthusiasm and dynamism.

I'm losing hope in leaving before my term as governor ends. That is why I beg you all to do everything possible to leave educational material in nonviolence, at the university level as well as in basic education, everything that can guarantee it to continue.

Also, I believe we should do whatever is necessary to create the Global Nonviolence Center, to maximize the possibility that all our sacrifice will not be forgotten with the change of government. This effort should also be made with VIVA, RIA, and MANÁ since at this point I do not believe there is a lengthening of the period and it would be crucial that Eugenio, you, and each person responsible be set on this final stretch; on this will depend the ability of the programs to achieve and convert themselves into references for the communities they claim and support the programs in the future.

Lastly, there are the Consistent Peace Plan and the strategic projects of the Planeo [Strategic Plan of Antioquia]; in that area or field there are months of broadcasts and of popular consultation, referendum, or plebiscites—the figure that finally you all chose as the most appropriate.

This last step is crucial and the consultation and petition of the registrar should have already been done. We have to bear the expense of broadcasting the Consistent Peace Plan so that the Antioquenian people support it.

My love, I also ask you to dedicate extra effort to the final government report; a good synthesis of accomplishments is important for letting everyone see, educated or uneducated, friends or enemies, what progress was achieved; remember the format of our presentation before the World Bank in Washington.

Lastly, my love, I send you all my love, my heart, my dreams, all my being which only aspires to be able to embrace you again, look into your beautiful transparent eyes, and share your joys that, hopefully God willing, will not separate us more. I believe that it would give me great satisfaction if I could remove from nonviolence the connotations of utopia that it has and prevents its being taken seriously in our society.

**Thursday, March 27**: My love, good morning. The march that you organized for us was a wonderful avalanche of solidarity and tenderness. We could follow you from radio network to radio network. Meanwhile we were listening to the messages sent to us from various persons through other radio stations. They played my mother's message, recorded in Radio Todelar, several times. Irene's message, and of course, your many interviews by all the diverse stations still resounds in my hearing full of joy and melancholy.

To the whole team of the government, a thousand thanks for your enthusiasm and the mystique with which you have taken your responsibilities for the Antioquenian people.

My love, in addition to all these wonderful messages, the commander just gave me a package, or rather part of it, that you sent March 20. My love, you don't have to send grains, neither beans, nor peas, nor lentils; here they give us all these. Also here the food is so abundant that I have to make an effort not to get fat. What we really like is the candy and the books, like I indicated in the second package of instructions.

My love, today I could speak with the commander and it seems to me that the topic of Yolandita was proposed by him and accepted in principal by the next level, who will make the respective consultations. When I have more information, I'll send it to you. In the meantime, could you send me a letter with all the details and instructions about how it is done and how much time the semen can be in the jar without being ruined and at what temperature it should be maintained and if a thermos is necessary or what.

I believe that these instructions can come from the clinic itself, well detailed so I can talk with the commander about it and can plan everything for the moment when the FARC-EP authorizes it. I see that you sent some of my old clothes—very wise. In the meantime, I have more clothes than I can use; from now on, I think that the books, candy, and letters will be enough for me. (In the candies, I include of course the cheese and the ants, when that is possible.) Another crucial topic is discretion. In the next letters I will be indicating which you can announce to the public and which should stay within the family circle and not be passed on to the public as proof of survival. In this we should be very strict.

Don't worry about it. I will clearly mark if it is public or private. When you receive a private one, you will know that the public should not know, nor the news media, and you will let me know that you received it through *The Voices of the Kidnapped* or *How Medellín Woke Up*. You can use "Uncle Leonel came" to tell me that you received it or "Uncle Leonel left" to indicate that you sent what was asked for in this/these letter(s). The same instructions are valid for Martha Ines, and Gilberto should be sending them in our next package, which will be the fourth.

Love, Irene tells me that Daniel is sending messages each week, but they are not being read on *The Voices of the Kidnapped*. I ask you to get them and you try to read them; you can do so during the week, with yours, in *How Medellín Woke Up* so they can be answered.

It is late, and all the energy of the day has kept me from sleeping, I'm conversing with Gilberto. We don't understand why in this package there were no letters for him. I share half of all that arrives for us, except the clothes, but we both have more than enough clothes; love, here two changes is enough! I love you. Thanks for sending the red T-shirt.

**Friday, March 28**: My princess: We heard the messages of this morning; still in Radio Todelar we heard the mayor of Marinilla send us greetings in the name of the community, very warm and human. Besides that, the arrival of the things and the announcement that others are on the way is very encouraging. Today I listened to the good news about Batuta Chocó and the trip of the Youth Symphony of Medellín to Europe. I think that is wonderful. Too bad that they cannot take them to Urabá, but I'm glad that they can visit Europe and show this face of Antioquia.

I heard President Álvaro Uribe refer to us in the march of the Summit of the Governors and also the march that will take place in Medellín in April, in which they will send everyone from Antioquia to show their solidarity.

Love, I'm going to continue with the letters; between reading and exercise it seems as if we have all the time in the world and really for me it is short. Now we have finished the table to begin the classes of English, which we will do Monday. Until tomorrow, my love.

**Saturday, March 29**: My love, good morning. Today I was listening to Lafayette's statements on Radio Caracol when Gilberto called me to listen to your message. As you explain it in your last letter and you reiterate it in the message, we continue with faith and optimism, since we feel the topic is advancing, if we are conscious that it is not resolved on a short term.

Love, I continue content with the messages and examples of love that we receive thanks to your wonderful march. Also we have read with enthusiasm the magazines and in particular I really liked the articles by William Ospina; please give him our approval for his quality and tell him that I completely share his position about war.

I also read a very interesting article about Susan Sontag, a writer from the United States who is against Bush and the imperialistic policies of the United States; her latest novel, *In America*, would be good to read if you can get it. Even today the medicines have not arrived and they should have been here. I hope they will arrive very soon. I'm concerned about Viellard's sore in his right eyebrow, I hope that we receive the medicine to prevent the infection from getting worse and damaging his eye.

For Gilberto and me, love, don't be concerned. We are in perfectly good health and each day we get better; I feel that never in my life have I had such good health: only a cold when we were first taken and after that nothing, a few fungi which we control and one or two little headaches that are cured with Acetaminophen and a nap of a half hour.

Besides, I don't think there have been more than a total of ten. Or, my love, you're going to have this husband for a long time. Like Gandhi, I think I will last 130 years. It's not clear to me what the domestic calamity of Álvaro Gómez Jaramillo is; please get me out of this anxiety, what happened?

I'm very happy to know of the efforts of [the secretary of] agriculture to support the milk farmers in Urrao. The tank is very good news. Good night, my love, I was listening to you tonight.

**Sunday, March 30**: Love, good morning. Last night I couldn't sleep until after I heard you, I thought various things that I will include here and in the letters. Your message was less clear than at other times. Finally I understood that the communication cannot be read, that now they are done in direct contact between persons of the government and those of the FARC-EP around the humanitarian accord, and also that former President Lopez wrote about the topic again and marked guidelines to help and activate the humanitarian accord. We continue optimistic on this front.

My love, we have been receiving all that you mention in the lists that you include and that of Martha Inés for Gilberto. What you mentioned last night about the essay of the *Divine Comedy* has not reached me yet, and it seems strange since the Green Book with the documents of Mario López is almost finished.

My love, among the things I thought of last night are the following concerns. First, is it possible to check out the DNA of the little seeds I'm going to send you once it is authorized by the FARC-EP?

Second: Am I right that this checking out does not set up a delay which affects the quality of the seeds?

Third: Can you compare it with that of Adela or another member of the family?

Fourth: Does the receptacle that you sent let you know if after filling it and closing it, it has been opened again or could be contaminated or something like that? That is, is it guaranteed that the sample does not suffer any contamination or disturbance?

Love, I ask all this just in case they do not authorize me to give the sample to the pilot/doctor in person. I'm going to include in the envelope some of my hair. All this on the basis of the authorization of the FARC-EP.

Love, a book that I would like to receive is a good manual for meditation. I think the best is to inquire of someone who knows and can recommend one that isn't "to leave the mind blank"; what interests me is how to have better control over my body and my soul.

I read somewhere here that Samper has been practicing with a woman professor; maybe she can recommend something. For quite some time I have had this uneasiness; I remember that I even got two cassettes of yoga, but I think that obstacles have stopped me. Now I have the time and believe that it also could be useful for me here.

Love, I have enough clothes, at least for the next eight to twelve months, do not send me more—I repeat, only letters, books, and "sweet snacks," and if in some moment nothing of these can be sent, don't be concerned, your messages and your love fill my soul with joy and strength.

My love, how much pain I felt with the news of Ángela's illness, that of Jose Fernando Montoya; I would have liked to have known earlier, so I could have written a letter to Jose Fernando and one to her. I'm going to do so now, but it pains me for a person so sweet and generous, so valuable and full of solidarity, to leave us. My faith in eternal life comforts me a little, and I hope also that it will be a comfort for José Fernando and his adorable daughter, who I beg you to give them a big hug from me. Beginning today I will include her in my prayers each day.

I remember now on the march of the twenty-seventh, between so many messages, the word from Ruth [Guillermo's secretary]. Tell her that I send a great hug and a kiss and that I am pleased to know that she has recuperated and is healthy. Include Marinita also and all the wonderful people of the government who sent us messages that day or are waiting and entrust us to the Lord in their prayers.

I'm happy to know that there are some advances in the topic of decentralization and regionalization, but I hope that this doesn't let them lower their guard and that they continue the plan for a solidly justified proposal to achieve true autonomy.

At times a little dose of decentralization ends up being a blow against the autonomy because it partly and transitorily satisfies a desire that can be converting itself into a cohesive force, capable of achieving transcendental changes, and in this way interrupts and cools it. Watch it. It happens that the functions are decentralized and they give some resources that let them try it once or at most during the government's term and then become our "feed bag."

So the most convinced and enthusiastic decentralizers, for lack of clear structural and long-term objectives, end up mocking their own intentions. I want to alert Eugenio about this and insist on a multidisciplinary team (history, literature-culture, politics, judicial, economical, geographic) to form something that is worth "selling" as a proposal that unites and motivates the Antioquenian people to a new feat: that of regional autonomy.

Love, I also received the photos of December getting the gifts, very beautiful; the faces of so many Antioquenians fill me with pride and satisfaction; really the effort that I want to continue doing, if God permits, is to improve the conditions of our children, that each one can have a happy and formative infancy and childhood.

The topic of Childhood Camps of Nonviolence makes me enthusiastic, and I urge you to act to increase the number of participants, and hopefully more than four or five, although this can be the plan for next year. I repeat: The key is to develop a team that wants to continue the camps when we leave the government.

I'm going to listen to mass, my love. The father was very deferential. He mentioned us on two occasions and in the end he announced the financial report for the week that is beginning. Now I'm listening to María Teresa Uribe, who speaks about the history of the 200 years of the University of Antioquia.

Again, I ask you to give him a hug and try to introduce Eugenio in the team to decentralization/ regional autonomy, as I call it.

**Monday, March 31**: My sweet love: Today you did not send a message. I imagine that is due to some bad news, but I hope that is not the case. I heard the news of the first assembly of the RIA, and I'm very pleased that it is becoming a reality.

It is important for Gonzalo Bernal to keep in mind and understand well the faults that affected Corforestal—all the difficulties participation of the private sector generated. It is good to know the criticisms generated and how to avoid them; what was weak has to be converted into strength.

I am confident that we are initiating a true change of industrial vocation of the Antioquenian people. From the start, we need to get the academics to support vocational teaching. Each time the term *vocational academy* sounds better. Surely Juan Camilo Ruiz can give free rein to his enthusiasm, and in the framework of the efforts for the system of higher public education provide a good space for teaching the trades; the beginnings of social change and of its "macro-social" indicators are here.

How good it would be for Antioquia to lead the way, prompting a great turn toward dignifying the trades. I believe, now that I listen to the criticisms of the labor reform and the predictions that it will fail to create jobs, that the vocations can offer better and quicker results in employment than other reforms.

How good, then, that RIA goes ahead and consolidates. Now, ensuring that Gonzalo [Bernal] remains there for sufficient time must be sought, after the end of our government, to assure its consolidation, strengthening, and permanence.

Winter here has taken over; it's been raining for two days, but it really doesn't bother us, and with the vitamins that Gilberto and I are taking, I think that each day we are better in "nonviolent defenses." At any rate, after waking up with the rain, the sun came out with all its joy of nature. Yesterday a tree fell on the camp of one of the fighters; fortunately no one was injured.

I have a lot of hope that soon you will receive our second package of correspondence, since there are letters for Daniel, Mateo, Papo, and my father besides the diary and letters for you and Eugenio. Also the chess is for Daniel. There is a lot of reflection about the way the government goes, that with the passing of time, it's losing its urgency. I'm going to listen to the official report.

Love, what a beautiful surprise to hear you halfway through the official report. Also, I really liked the first program. Today they killed a pig, but I continue my fast for all of Lent. Also, we played a little volleyball. I send you my love.

**Tuesday, April 1**: Love, today I listened to you, and that made my day even better. It's not clear to me about the jail. I don't know how much we have advanced in this. First on the topic of the new jail, and second on the topic of the Liberty Farm.

Hopefully we can achieve both objectives before the end of this period. I heard the financial reports today. Your report greatly touched me, and the way many people who call and refer to us is very comforting. You haven't told me anything about the doctor's appointment for your throat.

I feel that soon it will be your birthday. I hope God will give you the best gift possible: a little tranquility. When I return, I will compensate. You can be thinking how you want to do it.

How good that you are conversing with Matthew and Daniel and can tell me about them. I get the impression that you did not read the letter Adelaida sent. I ask you in the future to please read all that you send me, and make copies so they are kept there. In the same way, I would like you to read all that I send and also make a copy to keep of what you send.

We should see that Noel and the Exito and others are connected to the program for Manna. Also, I would like Materia Gris to design a good sample of this and the other key programs, RIA and VIVA, if you haven't already done so; something that can be imprinted on the minds of each Antioquenian. I would really like it if they had a good campaign for Manna. It should be shown to the Antioquenian journalists and the rest of the country, mainly key people. I would suggest that you try to alert Alejandro Santos Rubino to it. He wrote an article in *Semana* that I believe I mentioned to you, "Cannons or Butter," which I like and makes me think that the integral focus of Manna could interest him.

**Wednesday, April 2**: Love, good morning. We heard your message along with those of Martha Inés, Lina, and Pirri. The Internet messages his wife sends to Gilberto are also being kept in *The Voices of the Kidnapped*. Like Daniel's we cannot hear them. It would be good if Martha Ines could do what I asked you to do with Daniel's.

From what I could hear, the antiterrorist laws already passed the last debate in Congress. From the brief comments and paragraphs read, everything feels like the freedom of everyone will begin to be restricted, especially those of us who do not think what the national government wants us to think (or don't swallow it hook, line, and sinker). Increased penalties for offense which currently already have a high level of impunity, and also threatening restrictions for free-speech "offenses"/ "violations" / "crimes." All these efforts make the government take on dictatorial traits.

The figures of the ninth day of war against Iraq show more than nine million bombs and missiles. That is a thousand daily. This should suggest something to us in relation to our conflict. We can at least make some observations in connection with what is happening there, and in the rest of the world.

Sometimes I think the UN received a fatal blow, but other times I think that it is the right moment for a radical transformation, which I believe should be toward a world organization of nonviolence. An organism that little by little is committing the world to nonviolence and supporting it with a decision of investigation and its applications. It would spread the history of nonviolence and develop and apply its methods to evade, resolve, and transform the conflicts of humanity.

When the UN suffers such a serious blow, perhaps what this signifies (at least I believe this) is that its actual focus is not correct. A true commitment to nonviolence probably would permit it to arise again. It is clear that it cannot confront the desire for war of the great powers, but it will oppose violence in all its forms on a world scale and promote transformations among all the nations to the extent that nonviolent methods and their applications and potentiality are developed and spread in all areas of human life.

Returning to the new antiterrorist statute, I feel that rather than disarm the language and attitudes, it lamentably will achieve the opposite.

**Thursday, April 3**: My love, good morning and congratulations on your birthday. Today we received many and very beautiful messages. First, I received that of Ana Rosa [Pinto], then I received yours, your mother's, and Aníbal's.

A few minutes before Father Yépez left, he recited a reading from the epistle of St. Paul to the Romans chapter 8. So I got up renewed and with enthusiasm for the celebration of your birthday.

I'm really concerned that the medicine has not arrived. I'm going to try to talk with the commander. Love, by the way, I would really like you to send me a good, complete Bible. Those from Ediciones Paulinas are very good, and above all I require that they include ample explanations about the books and the texts. It should have very thin pages and hopefully a good cover to avoid poor treatment and the humidity. The size should not be too big.

Love, also I am doubting that you sent the Glucantine I asked for in the first medicines.

To Gilberto, as usual; Lina, Camila, and also Zoraida [Gilberto's sister], and his niece Irma greeted him. Also Iván Echeverri.

Love, I heard that the mayors also are giving accounts. It pleases me so much to know that they are adopting this practice and that Teleantioquia is going to help them. Hopefully the Department of Planning and the state government will help and advise them.

We heard something about the events for celebrating a year of the kidnapping, and also that the governors and the president will go to work from Medellín in our honor. Please don't forget the rural people and the marginalized.

My love, there is a Banco de Colombia commercial on the radio that begins with a commitment to nonviolence. I ask you to call Dr. Jorge Londoño and express my congratulations, although he only used the term *nonviolence* once. In reality, all the commitments that the citizens voluntarily assume are commitments to nonviolence. I'm glad that this sector sees it execution in its real dimension.

Love, actually six boxes of cassettes arrived. The commander still has them. I believe that here it is impossible to hear them, so it is not necessary that you send more. In the future it is enough to send the clear financial reports at the same time that these are being given (10 a.m.-12 p.m.), and with the reports of the planning activities.

The good march of the government makes me think of the importance of a new leadership. Remember I talked about a collective leadership instead of a messianic-personal leadership? Well, here I see more clearly the importance of empowering the cabinet, and that the secretaries are dedicated to empowering their teams. At the same, time they will transmit this attitude to the leaders of communities so that, they in turn, do so with the citizens.

I feel that you play, and have always played, a very valuable role in maintaining the direction and orientation of the whole team. Although it may have seemed to you that I didn't notice, your presence and the power of your spirit, your emotional intelligence and political sense, have always been a monumental support for me.

Now they are, without a doubt, the element that cements together our ideas and commitments to all the team and helps maintain loyalty. But, my sweet loved one, you not only infuse spirit and rhythm to the government team but from here I feel how well you make our Antioquenian family feel in these unfortunate moments.

Aníbal, who has already written me, said it beautifully today in his message. The words from your mother also have been very good for me. I can imagine her with that face that shines with intelligence and spark as she spoke her words. Give her an embrace and my kisses, and also for Ana Rosa, Ricardo, and their children.

I spoke of leadership because I think, listening to the radio, that here we confuse leadership with reactivity. The media asked the leaders, "What is your opinion about. . . ?" Our "leaders" answered believing that thus they orient the people. In reality, they are generally reacting with negative leadership to actions of others. More of a leader is one who drags people with his actions, as in our case Mr. Marulanda.[38]

A change of attitude toward nonviolence requires that we understand that the people cannot continue hanging on the last car of a train that is leaving. He has dedicated himself to prosecuting a man who attacks him, because he wants to be the train's engineer. Leading signifies constructing solutions, and if it is nonviolent leadership it is very probable that this is more difficult and requires of him more creativity and valor when putting them into practice.

I conclude this oration saying that to lead is to take the step before others do. Doing it responsibly requires us to know where this will will take us.

Everything I said previously was an introduction to tell you thank you, my love, for being so wonderful. I send you thousands of kisses and a strong embrace. I love you and each time I miss you more.

**Friday, April 4**: My sweet love, good morning. Thank you for the beautiful message today. I'm pleased that you are well cared for and peaceful. It is God's gift to know that we have such good friends.

I imagine the homily of Father Yépez and the love of all these beautiful people. Also, it so happens that I am going to receive the gift of hearing you twice tomorrow. I feel equally obliged.

Love, yesterday you told me that Mafer will return in July. It occurs to me that perhaps you could convince her to spend a few days in Barcelona before returning and maybe you could spend a little week with her there and return together. (Note: I'm sure that already you have thought of something similar!) If you plan and figure out the time, it will be much more economical and you can coordinate something with Sofía.

Yesterday in the financial reports I heard the excellent plan that Eugenio gave to Jorge Eusebio Medina who insinuated bad management. It seems to me to be timely, perfect, and respectful; in sync, one hundred in grade. I hope they clarify for me from the district attorney's office with respect to the Licoantioquia[39] since by radio it is impossible to get a clear idea.

Last night the guards killed a warty snake about two meters long. I was already in bed, but it caused such a commotion. The fighters have a lot of respect for this type of snake.

I heard the complaints of the mayors of the east about the electrical rates. I am in full accord with them. Their municipalities should enjoy the lowest rates on the market. The silence of the mayor of Medellín and the EPM leaves me perplexed. This is indeed a just complaint and the upright attitude of Mayor Luis Pérez in other battles I miss now.

It is necessary that the state announce a decision and follow up the complaints of the mayors of the east. Please communicate my point of view to Eugenio and to the public.

The arguments that I heard today by the minister of energy are frankly fallacies. Not only should they grant the permit for the dam of San Carlos, but we should battle to guarantee them the best tariffs on the market.

Yesterday it rained all night but without consequences for us, with the exception of some leaks, which we immediately fixed.

This week pork was on the menu but I, faithful in my decision regarding Lent, have continued not eating meat. And like Navarrete, who is allergic to pig lard, the commander consented that they prepare separate plates. Little by little I am overcoming the dependence on meat. (Nevertheless I am sure that it will not be equally easy in front of a plate of our favorite recipe prepared by you.)

Heriberto has been working with climbing vines. It produces a fiber that Heriberto separates into thin straws. With that he makes all kinds of little baskets. He gave Gilberto and me some fans, and he is making Gilberto a soap dish.

Today they did a type of cauterization on Viellard in the sore that began to open above his right eyebrow.

The present debate/conflict is the struggle to destroy the "political reform" and begin to think of the referendum as lost ground that is irrecoverable. Today Radio Caracol mentioned that eighty-one percent of those interviewed were not interested in voting for it. Without a doubt, this would be an opportunity for President Álvaro Uribe to show his political ability and influence over Congress. I think that, in large part, Minister Londono contributes to the reticence being generated around the referendum.

**Saturday, April 5**: Love, good morning. I heard your words and felt that your throat has greatly improved. You sounded very optimistic about the possibilities of progress. We have accustomed ourselves to the rhythm of the FARC-EP, which is very much slower than our desires. At any rate, we are confident that you have information that permits you to have this positivism.

The texts for the class still have not arrived. Last night I thought a lot about the topic of tariffs for the east, and by extension, in the other municipalities' producers of electricity in Antioquia. A serious analysis of the information is necessary to prepare a nonviolent campaign. Juan Guillermo Gómez, the Antioquian Electric Company [Eade], should furnish it, but it has to be kept in mind that this entity is in charge of the topic.

Nevertheless, in my opinion, it should be EPM and eventually Isagen, which also generates electricity based on the resources of the region, which assume the costs of offering it to these municipalities at fair tariffs.

Keep in mind that Juan Guillermo belongs to the team of Dr. Prieto. On this topic, don't let them be convinced with artificial arguments. The objective is that they enjoy the lowest tariffs on the market and that they acquire, in the most favorable conditions, the Central de Calderas in San Carlos. This last item mentioned can convert itself into the generator of resources to attend to the social necessities of the east. Once the objectives are achieved, one has to begin to think of the rest of the municipalities of Antioquia.

Love, they should not permit the process of acquisition and the information study to be extended. I believe that in a week, at maximum, they should be ready for battle. The first stage should be to consolidate the teams with the mayors and the community. The second, to try to have those responsible understand the justice of the aspirations. And if they do not, only then go on the third stage, direct nonviolent action.

At some point you are going to be faced with the arguments of "rentability." I'm more interested in justice than in rentability. These are not to be confused. This is a struggle for decentralization and autonomy. Never lose respect for the opponents, and always offer the possibility for reconciliation and appropriate departure—negotiated in a transparent way and before the community.

**Sunday, April 6**: My love, good morning. In the early morning hours your words filled my spirit like raising the sails of a boat after a small calm. I'm glad to know of the visit of your sisters and their families. And you can imagine that the mention of pizza made me remember how much we shared in the apartment in Bogotá and what we ate in the restaurant near our (apartment) in Medellín. Often I have thought that it would be delicious to again eat there.

I'm also happy each time that you talk with Daniel and Matthew and you share with me their news. I enjoy hearing of Papo, Mafer, and your children. I think it would be better not to mention too frequently your meetings with Samper and López. I suggest that you speak of "Ernestico and Alfonsito, your brothers," and I will understand what that means.

In the program there was a lot of disorder. I understand that there are limitations, but this morning they passed six messages for Ingrid, all in two or more minutes, among them three repeated from her aunt in Miami. I don't complain, since I feel privileged to be able to hear you, even for a few seconds, since your love fills the words that you send me. Nevertheless, I believe that more organization could notably increase the possibilities of the messages.

In the last part of the program, from 3 to 4 a.m., the prerecorded ones generally repeat often, and some two or three times. I still have not been able to hear any message from Daniel. I believe it would be better if you made a copy and you read them or got them to me by *La Carrilera* (*The Railroad Tracks*), the program of RCN which originates in Cali and is heard from 5 to 6 a.m., Monday through Friday. There you can send them by fax and they read them. This is an alternative way in case you prefer not to do it yourself on *How Medellín Woke Up*.

Love, yesterday the rest of the large number of groceries that you sent arrived. Since the afternoon we have been able to enjoy milk, tuna, coffee, and vegetables. A thousand thanks, mi vida.

I suspended the mass. I insist it is not necessary for you to send grains (staples). It seems to me that in the matter of foodstuffs most convenient is to follow the instructions that I sent you in the second package. A brief list is as follows:

1. Cheese: The kind they have sent us and eventually that made by Colanta in the plant at San Pedro.

2. Chocolates: In a block: of milk, white and bitter (my mother's). The kind you bought for Papo.

3. Brown sugar blocks Copelia and from Urraeña: a good amount and well packed. Also include Quipitos Colanta and guavas El Caribe (with caramel dessert).

4. In candies, there are three types that I think are sufficient: toffees of coconut, supercoconuts, and *charaleños* [candy].

5. Colanta powdered milk and instant coffee. For now we have some but will need more in later situations.

This is in case the instructions of the second package did not reach you, and for some miracle, this arrives first.

As always, mi vida, keep in mind that what is really important are your letters and those of Martha Ines and our families, as well as some books. The rest are "luxuries." Love, I forgot the dried fruits and nuts. Like I wrote you somewhere, I want to experiment a little with nutrition.

**Monday, April 7**: Love, good morning. Today I heard your message, but just imagine, I did not write anything all day. These lines I'm writing today, Tuesday. In the morning I read a little, then I dedicated the rest of the morning to the English classes and exercises. For breakfast we enjoyed the chocolate that you sent us, then we went to play volleyball and to bathe. In the afternoon Lucuara and I played chess until it got dark.

I'm thinking about and structuring a story for Matthew. I love you, mi vida.

**Tuesday, April 8**: Love of my life, good morning. Today we woke up with the good news of the rescue in Bogotá of the child kidnapped in Villavicencio,[40] which generated the protest march Sunday in Bogotá. I heard some words from the child Andrea, who in solidarity offered to exchange places with the kidnapped boy.

It seems that Herbin Hoyos sent an extremely crude report about the excesses of the war of the United States against Iraq. The report that was made is terrible, denounces the indiscriminate way the United States attacks the civilian population, and says the Iraqis are not responding to the fire.

Love, today I did get up early to write you judiciously. Pardon the laziness of yesterday. In your message of today from Bogotá, in which you spoke of looking for ways to revolutionize the rules of the game, you indicated to me that there is a stumbling block.

Gilberto thinks that it could be that we are in a period before eventual progress. The experience has ended in our being used so that each time a pact of delivery is intended, they always have been at the point of capturing some commander and, of course, that messes everything up. I think it has to do with rhythm of the FARC-EP.

The news of the imminence of the Children's Camp for Nonviolence for April 22-24 in San Jerónimo and the twenty-nine amusement centers is wonderful. I congratulate you, my love, and I hope it is pure success. I understand 500 children of the region are invited but that you hope for 2,000 to attend. These are the number that I have always had in mind, and I see that we are synchronized.

Love, I have been thinking that an interesting way to stimulate participation and finance the camps is to give them some hundred computers to the most outstanding for their commitment and assimilation of nonviolence. Not for getting the best "grades," but because their own companions have recognized their nonviolent virtues and temperaments. That would be a hundred computers for each 2,000 participants.

In the end we will be distributing 400 computers for the program of 50,000. Obviously these figures can be looked at with Eugenio and modified according to your criteria, from above or from below.

Another idea that has been rolling around in my mind is the creation of a Secretariat of Nonviolence. In principle I am thinking that it would be to transform the secretariat and that under it would be three managements of equity.

Excuse me, in principle the two because I do not think of breaking the promise made to the women of Antioquia. Luis Javier Botero can be assessor of the secretary and be in charge of human rights and the Consistent Peace Plan. In sum, to struggle against the structural violence: inequity, poverty, attention to the victims of the violence while advocating respect for human rights.

It would be responsible for the culture of nonviolence, which means to say that, together with the Secretary of Education, they would structure the program of nonviolent education for nonviolence in which the universities should participate; that is, the system of superior education in Antioquia.

The idea comes to me from two sources: the conviction I've had about the necessity to create a Ministry of Peace; and then second, reading the book by Paige (p. 133). Remember how much I spoke in the campaign and later about the importance of some clear and forceful indicators of violence and its costs in all its manifestations? Well, this would be a fundamental responsibility of the Secretariat of Nonviolence.

Statistics about violence and its progress or, better, our progress to eradicate them: family violence (children, women, spouses, elders), homicides, suicides, criminal/delinquent violence, police violence, violence in prisons, school violence, violence in the workplace, violence in the media—how important that someone could dedicate himself to quantify this—violence in sports, economic violence, guerrilla-paramilitary and military violence, displacements and victims, and additionally that could quantify the costs.

This secretary would propose, in an open work with the participation of the UN and international organizations, alternative solutions and would assume the programming of the nonviolent campaigns. It could edit publications and convey the history of nonviolence in Colombia.

It would be in charge of making visible all the efforts of thousands of persons, in small isolated and uncoordinated ways, to build peace in Antioquia and Colombia. I am certain we could gain international support (above all "Nonviolent Thought and Assessment").

I am not sure if you are experiencing the same enthusiasm that I feel in thinking and writing these lines. I see in this secretary a way of assuring that the nonviolence in the state government is long lasting and gives "clients" and institutionalism to nonviolence. It's a way of openly recognizing the structural violence which rules our society and of assuming commitments at the highest level to confront it responsibly and creatively, in a peaceful manner.

Please, talk it over with Eugenio, and you already know that I am confident in your criteria. If I were there, I would do so right away. I think that improving this text could also serve for the exposition of motives for a statute, if that is required. This implies a delicate change in direction that can postpone it, and for the moment, I do not believe a certain incongruity between speaking of nonviolence and "coordination" with the military authorities will crop up.

This dilemma assails me permanently. I should confess that I still have not resolved it, but the more I read the more I'm convinced what is right is to walk toward a country that sets aside armed means for its defense and transforms the military system into a nonviolent one, the nonviolent social defense.

I am not naïve. This will take time, and what I believe is that one has to keep in mind that it should be understood in this chronological framework, and not in a simplistic manner. Already, everything or nothing! The creation of that secretariat implies a commitment to begin a radical process of transformation. On the one hand, in the interior of the government; and on the other, in society.

Here is also situated the institutional responsibility for the Nonviolence Camps for Children, the eventual conferences, and with more time I do not doubt that it can give way to institutes and bring about the creation of the Global Center of Nonviolence, with the help of the private sector.

Such institutes can have short lives, of a few years, created to implement a policy in relation to a specific program which deserves it. I hope this helps to determine what we understand by nonviolence for so many people who continue believing that nonviolence is to say passively "No to violence."

To struggle against violence we should be able to identify and unmask it in all its manifestations. We should "arm ourselves" with valor. I do not doubt that the exercise will cause some concepts that society should question to tremble and eventually to disintegrate.

**Wednesday, April 9**: My love, good morning. I listened to you very calmly and positively speak about the preparation of a proposal following your message of yesterday and the realization of a meeting that would count on the presence of President Álvaro Uribe and the high commands.

We anxiously await the reading that you told us about. Yesterday was the session in the Assembly and we do not know what happened. Except for some superficial and positive comments about the commitment assumed to prompt a humanitarian accord, we do not know who were on our side, who was cited. In short, it doesn't seem to have much transparency.

Yesterday after writing to you, I dedicated myself to reading a little, and to clarifying some doubts of my English students, to which I dedicated several hours due to their renewed interest, almost a frenzy, with those dedicated to read and understand texts in English.

The rest of the day I dedicated to chess. I played intensely with Yim and Lucuara. Today I remembered the death of Jorge Eliécer Gaitán. Fifty-five years ago he was assassinated, and without a doubt that produced a change in the direction of Colombian history. For me it is clear that the liberal people came to have much confidence.

Nevertheless, I believe that it is doubtful his discourse was really different from that of his competitors. I say that because there are in many paragraphs the aggressiveness and the passionate bitterness that lamentably have been converted in the application of the watchword "Divide and you will conquer."

From these reflections is born my revived interest in promoting a shared leadership. A collective product of nonviolent empowerment of the population of Antioquia. The proof that it functions is the government of Antioquia. Committed and shared tools, and team leadership of the team, guarantees continuity and achievements.

At night we listened to the opening session of the Constituent State Assembly to consolidate the results of the Consistent Peace Plan of and the mention of the letter that you announced and that they presented to President Álvaro Uribe.

We listened to you on the program *La Luciérnaga,* and Gilberto and I remain a little concerned with the mention by Hernán Peláez of the supposed rejection of the FARC-EP to the Facilitating Commission. We do not want it thought that this interpretation of the media was guaranteed by the families and much less when now it can be thought that the families also reject it—when neither the one nor the other is true. Good night, mi vida.

**Thursday, April 10**: My love, good morning. Receive my kisses and all my heart. As usual, I am thinking about you and missing you so much.

Today your message about the Constituent State Assembly and the letter were very clear and together with that of Martha Inés helped us clarify some doubts that we had. We will be listening for the complete reading of the letter, but we understand that the fourth point is the kernel, the substance.

We are going to increase the English classes to one hour daily, since the students are diligently working and have many questions. I hope that the document I asked you for arrives soon. Yesterday the news began by pointing to the defeat of Hussein by the troops of the United States and Great Britain. It is interesting that while this happens between the international media, Bush and Blair still say that it is premature.

I have abandoned reading a bit. I'm going to intensify it, play chess less, and concentrate on the story for Matthew.

**Friday, April 11**: My love, good morning. The message was very clear, and we begin to understand the whole message contained in President Álvaro Uribe's letter, also from Martha Inés and Lina. Yesterday after listening to you, I went out to the *chonto* (a hole that serves as a septic tank), and I did not hear the message of Father Yépez. However, I could read the Bible of Lieutenant Ledesma. I hope you can send me one soon. I insist that it should have abundant historical and exegetical explanations.

Today, Lina asked herself a question. If some of us are learning to resolve peacefully our interpersonal conflicts, and those in the heart or bosom of the family, why doesn't society change? What impedes the change? The answer would demand a treatise, but I also believe it can be summarized as follows: Our education has produced an aggressive and watchful (advantageous) people, and in what we have tried or achieved in changing we do not constitute a critical mass yet.

Love, in the morning they gave me a bag of IDA [Institute for the Development of Antioquia] newspapers. The oldest is of March 29. There are also copies of some communications of the FARC-EP. I was very pleased thinking there would be notes for Gilberto and me, but that didn't happen.

The dictionaries and the medicine still have not arrived. I think the coffee is making me anxious. I'm surprised how I feel its effect now after my body has been "cleansed" of its accumulated effect.

Last night I stayed awake, but rather than get up, I stayed in bed thinking of you and the children. In these days, both Gilberto and I have been feeling a little sad. The arrival of the newspapers lets me see you again in various articles in the foreign newspapers. You look very beautiful and active, and I really liked your statements and the commentaries that the reporters made about your attitude.

I hope that the second package gets to you soon. I'm sure the chess will have mold. All you have to do is clean it.

Today the humanitarian accord takes center stage because of the anniversary of the kidnapped of the diplomats from the Valle; and in Congress, giving additional legal tools to President Álvaro Uribe to achieve an accord.

Love, we just finished lunch, and they also just delivered the messages of the officials and sub-officials, two gunny sacks full. I'm so happy for them, since for them as for us, to receive something is like again being in contact with you all. I love you.

Well, we've reviewed everything that arrived, and imagine our surprise when we discovered that it came with cookies, some Frunas, a hairbrush, and three supplements about nonviolence from April last year. I believe it is part of what you had sent to the Red Cross since the time of the kidnapping. They still haven't delivered the letters, so I think very soon they will make another delivery.

This has been enough to give us reason for joy and to forget the pain a bit. Now the boys are beginning to share candies, and each one is showing off his gifts to everyone. Nevertheless, they have not given letters to anyone, which is very strange. The commander has said that he will ask about that.

Here we have seen spiders that seem harmless, like those that in the beginning of our kidnapping made me and Gilberto so afraid.

**Saturday, April 12**: My love, good morning. Starting hours before dawn it has rained, so today seems a gray day. I hope that indicates good meteorological conditions for hearing the program tonight. Last night I heard that Congress will move (I have written that). I am sure that I have repeated many things in these letters. I'm not going crazy. Here all the days are almost the same. Time is flat and that confuses a little tracking what happens.

Today Speedy González was much more special than usual in the message you sent. I'm so happy that you could talk to Matthew and Daniel. You did not explain to me what the reason was for changing Daniel's school.

**Sunday, April 13**: My love, good morning. What a joy to listen to you twice last night, after having listened to you on Saturday morning. The good news about Frontino on the topic of the labor unions, the 113 rural houses, the semi-Olympic swimming pool, and the plans for reforestation please me.

In the second package I sent precise instructions about other topics. Particularly important is the urban development of the municipality toward the farm of the Morenos. I think that the department can buy these lands to carry through an ambitious project of urban development there. That will convert in surveying the development and is a key piece in its urban planning.

Regarding reforestation, I really liked the page that came out in the newspaper promoting the northeast nucleus and giving a well conceived explanation of the program. Congratulations to Serio [Trujillo], Gustavo [Rodríguez], and Gonzalo [Bernal], besides all that is involved in this topic.

I have returned to looking at the Gringo newspapers that you sent, and I really liked the interviews. Your photos are also beautiful, and with the others that you sent earlier I have a good selection which permits me to contemplate you every day.

Today Diana Uribe spoke about the history of oil. I'm happy to know that you will be with your parents in San Gil. I have continued with the reading of *El Mundo de Sofía (Sophia's World)* I think it is a book that you should suggest to your children. On my side, suggest it to Daniel, and I also will write him regarding it. Adelaida, Seth, Irene, and Duncan also enjoyed it, and I think you will too, if you can overcome your aversion for reading.

A few days ago you told me you had gotten a computer for the apartment. I ask myself if you are using it. I hope, my love, when we arrive you will be an Internet and e-mail expert, so that you can teach me all that I have to learn, since the little I did know now should be obsolete. I also think that you should encourage it with Papo, Mafer, Daniel, and Matthew. By the way, is it possible to think Daniel could get a good computer? I don't know if the salary will permit it, but we should make an effort to have a modern one. I remember the old useless one in Adelaida's house the last time I was there.

We just heard mass. What a pleasant surprise to hear you and Aníbal. The father maintains his line in mentioning nonviolence in his homilies. Readings, as well as your final word and those of Aníbal, fill us with joy.

Thinking about Frontino, I have an idea to write a letter to the people of Frontino. I'll think about this and I'll tell you later. A letter to Frontino which can assimilate much for the other key municipalities for regional development. It contains my actual and future vision of what can be done to better the future of the people.

**Monday, April 14**: My love, good morning. I'm going to begin the English class and then I'll write you. Kisses. Your message about the trip by the roads of Frontino and the memories of our childhood delighted me. You also have an excellent guide. It was like returning to childhood and traveling over each one of these landscapes with you, which are so full of experiences and magic for me.

As I have described to you here, I also review them frequently in my memory and dream that someday our children can enjoy these same climates in peace. I'm thinking of the possibility of developing an ashram[41] in La Nivel [farm in Frontino]. I also think of the area of the Mina del Cerro.

**Tuesday, April 15**: My love, good morning. Your message is the most precious information which we could receive about the communication of the FARC-EP. I suppose that on the basis of these developments, you have decided to stay a few more days.

After mid-day we heard the statements of President Álvaro Uribe. It seems to me that it is an aggressive, arrogant, and mistaken way to answer the position of the FARC-EP. I think it gives the idea that the president is not really prepared to put forth any effort for the humanitarian accord. In fact, I believe it was the moment to name negotiators, but rather, the president comes out with a disqualification of the FARC-EP. And from what I gather, closes the door to the humanitarian accord.

For me it is a desolate position. The president has maintained a prudent position in relation to the majority of the delicate topics, but this allowed his character to be betrayed. It is painful to admit it, but this attitude supports the FARC-EP in saying that the establishment does not listen except when they are spoken through arms. Rather than General Mora becoming infected by the prudence demonstrated by the president, the arrogant language of the military is adjusted. What a sad development.

On this topic of managing the language, I wrote a few days ago. Because of the previous, my love, you all should be prepared for this situation to be extended. As I have written you on various occasions, you can be sure that we will resist, and that even if the treatment that they give us hardens (something that I do not think will happen), your remembrance, your messages, and your love will make my life continue being beautiful and the sacrifices small.

Love, I continue being concerned about your father's accident that you mentioned. You have not mentioned what it was nor how serious it was, and I have the perception that at his age the most serious thing is the inactivity that goes with recuperation. Martha Inés's mother did not die from the fracture but what the doctor's call pneumonia position. So keep the batteries charged to keep moving and maintaining activity.

In other words, don't think about it too much. Or rather, think about it but don't let it "put you in bed." These circumstances bring to mind the illness of Ángela, wife of José Fernando Montoya, who I have included in my daily prayers. And the accident of a relative of Álvaro; a topic which worries me, and about which I don't have any information.

Well, mi vida, I hope that soon you will help me clear positively these unknowns.

**Wednesday, April 16**: Sweet princess, good morning. Today, besides your message, you gave very good statements about what President Álvaro Uribe said in Villavicencio. God has also given us a beautiful, sunny morning. The blue sky stands out from the foliage of the trees while the sun's clear rays penetrate and are projected on to the floor at the same time as coves shine against the moss-covered and humid stalks that drip.

Your words are measured and maintain the hope and the confidence in the aforementioned will of President Álvaro Uribe. Also, you have calmed me regarding the fall of your father, the injury to his leg; and it comforts me to know that he is surrounded by Ana Rosa, Juan José [Yolanda Pinto's siblings] and our Santanderian family.

The whole atmosphere there is infused with the spirit of Holy Week. Here it is not possible for me to live it. I will try to maintain it internally, but it is difficult isolated from the context.

The new statements of President Álvaro Uribe seek to alleviate the reaction of the families. But for me, they reaffirm his attitude of pretending that, more than a humanitarian accord, the FARC accept some terms of defeat. Lucho Garzón said some statements regarding La W[42] that I liked.

The English class was for two hours. They are translating the newspaper articles from Atlanta that you sent us. Last night I couldn't sleep and the same happened to Gilberto. I think the anxiety that the statements generated in us is brought on by the magnificent coffee that we have been enjoying these past few days. This time I got up and by candlelight I wrote until midnight the first draft of a letter to the people of Frontino.

In chess, although I have improved a lot, still they beat me frequently. Some nights I go to bed thinking of the mistaken moves or what I should have done, and I spend a good time going over the chessboard and the chessmen in my head.

For this letter, I'm going to have to have you insert the paragraphs that I wrote about what there is in the pilot rural workshops for housing and eventually on fish culture. The idea is for them to thoroughly correct it. They let my father see it, and if he considers it adequate, they publish it or make it known to the people of Frontino.

Last night your photos accompanied me in my sleeplessness. You were beautiful with your love and your happiness.

**Thursday, April 17**: My love, good morning. Today also is a beautiful day, with the radiant sun which helps diminish our sadness. Your message calms me about your father's accident and the sadness of the death of Ángela. I send to José Fernando a huge embrace of condolence, together with his daughter. Some days ago I wrote a letter to them, and now I'm going to prepare a note that expresses my pain for her death.

In the afternoon Gilberto and I were invited to play volleyball with the fighters. It was an entertaining afternoon, and with Gilberto's happiness and good humor, we all enjoyed ourselves for a good time.

Later the commander asked us to write a note for you, telling you that we received the merchandise. So, Gilberto and I did so, hoping that we can send letters again. When we went to give them, they did not authorize more letters. Instead, they invited us for some shots of brandy, then we ended up drinking moonshine. We spoke a little about nonviolence and about Manna. We could discuss in a peaceful way topics of social justice.

We are including a couple of petitions for you that the commander made for us in the course of the conversation. I hope you can take care of them. I want to send you letters soon, since in the previous opportunity, and now with this, we have to write as fast as we can, thus there are many letters and topics to send you.

**Friday, April 18 (Holy Friday)**: My love, good morning. I always wake up with a hangover. With alcohol, as well as strong coffee, after so much time of not tasting it, my body reacts with great sensitivity. To have the organism clean also permits me to clearly feel the damage that liquor does to me. Also in this area I want to introduce changes in my habits.

I hope we can send you something for Mother's Day. I'm beginning to feel real anxiety for Viellard and Martín, since the medicine for *leishmaniasis* still has not arrived. In the note last night I mentioned building a better system to get them here. I think that it is necessary that we here know when they were given to the FARC. I spoke to you about Uncle Leonel; that would be the way to know it.

Viellard's wound is above the right eyebrow, and I'm concerned since it continues to worsen and really bothers him. The blessed medicine should have arrived several days ago, since according to your information it was delivered that Tuesday (March 25) and that was almost a month ago.

Today I was listening to the sermon of the Seven Last Words of Jesus on Radio Caracol. Monsignor Augusto Trujillo, bishop of Tunja, delivered it with a lot of fervor and very full of the message of the love of Jesus. More and more I identify the message of Jesus with true nonviolence.

The bad news was the crime by bicycle in Arauca and the attack at Dolores, in Tolima, where the mayor reacted with great force. But her words leave in me more of a sensation of affront than of restful reflections. Again we react, and we do so with violence. Good night, mi vida.

**Saturday, April 19**: Significant date. Good morning, my love. Your message I received almost without waking up, and I'm glad to know that your father is getting better and that you could see La Cristalina.

I suppose that soon they will have the meeting that you mentioned last Saturday (related to the answer to the letter), and which Martha Ines also has said they are going to support, probably Monday.

The success of the youth symphony in its tour of Europe pleases me so much. I remember how we bound ourselves to take them to Urabá and that the insecurity of the roads prohibited it. Fortunately here the good weather continues. You also mentioned that you passed through Chiquinquirá to pray in the cathedral. I'm sure that at the same time we listened to the sermon of Monsignor Trujillo—me in Tunja, and you in Chiquinquirá. Pedro José Guarnizo is "married" to a girl from Chiquinquirá, Isabel. He tells me he would like you to pass by the house of his mother-in-law.

Today the commander leaves. We hope that with this absence news arrives about the medicine and eventually about the leaving of the second package as well as the delivery of the correspondence of the officials and sub-officials. I hope to hear news about Yolandita. Love, I will be very attentive to the messages tonight.

**Sunday, April 20**: Love, what a beautiful message, and what wonderful good news to hear you speak about your father and La Cristalina, including your words about the celebration in the morning and the presence of so many personalities, the same for the scheduled program.

We feel well known among the colleagues who will attend and other persons of national stature, but I insist that more important would be acts involving the marginalized, the poor, and the people without privileges in solidarity with us. The rural folk of Antioquia and good people of the rural areas would offer the best expressions of support that we could have in the circumstances that affect us.

Equally, I think it is more important that these occasions extend the message of nonviolence—and that on this rest the speeches and words of those who attend. Hopefully, thus will be registered in the media.

Lamentably, I lost the opportunity to send you the reflections about the secretary of nonviolence in the last shipment (April 17, 2003). I tell you we have been enjoying your snacks, above all the milk, the chocolate, the coffee, the sardines, the tuna, and the vegetables. We also have the good fortune to enjoy popcorn quite regularly thanks to my administering it with great rigor.

I continue being concerned about the *leishmaniasis* of Viellard. Yesterday we could speak about it with the fighter who cares for the wound, and we will try to make it more urgently felt that they administer medicine immediately, since I'm really afraid that he will lose his eye if it is permitted to worsen. According to what they tell us here, the PAS requires that they show proof of the illness of each person to deliver the medicine to them. (I imagine that it requires a blood test and a culture from the wounds.)

Nevertheless, my love, we should clarify and resolve this. It should not take so long for the medicine to arrive, and neither can I manage for long the uncertainty of its arriving in the hands of our captors or not. In summary, I should know when the medicine was delivered to the hands of our captors and how many doses were delivered. And you should know that I received this information.

It's very pleasing to know that the concert will be the responsibility of Piero and also that the Mass in Invias will be among the engineers and in the Basilica. How good to again know of Don Genaro.

Love, what a huge surprise that they would read Daniel's e-mail. The first, in which he announces that he will continue writing weekly, and he tells me about his girlfriend Katherine, and his progress in music and reading. What a great surprise and what pride to know that he is writing with such ownership and freedom. That's another reason to wait each week for this wonderful dawn.

Here for various days they brought chickens and rapidly the population is increasing. There are three roosters. It is interesting to see them care for their chickens and their rooster and the care with which they nurture their chicks. In the afternoon, we like to see when the roosters call them to perch, and the way each one covers up to ten or twelve chicks. It gives the impression they are talking. This breaks the monotony of life here.

During the last conversation with the commander, he mentioned that the FARC has received the dictionaries and that the books are on the way. I hope it will be all that I asked for about nonviolence. I continue my reading about philosophy with great enthusiasm.

The Nopikex has been a complete revelation. It is the best repellent and really is effective. It lets me remain in shorts without the gnats and mosquitoes bothering me. I am sure that it is a good defense that protects Gilberto and me from the insect that produces *leishmaniasis* so that you can be at peace; I am so "cowardly" that you cannot doubt that I will tell you of the least suspicion when one or the other of us is suffering. Remember that the key to speak of deliveries is with Uncle Leonel.

Well, mi vida, one day from completing a long year in captivity and separation, I can tell you that my love has not ceased to grow and be strengthened, and that without your understanding and tenderness surely I would have been lost. I miss you so much, and in like manner you fill all the emptiness that this captivity causes with your daily love. I have your photos and your letters and an infinite accumulation of happy memories that permit me to lessen the loneliness that oppresses us. Now I'm going to enjoy them again.

**Monday, April 21 (one year)**: My love, good morning. The day began with a strong dose of solidarity. All kinds of expressions, and the events programmed in Medellín and Antioquia, forcefully expressed the way the injustice that is committed aginst us and all the kidnapped ones is understood.

I'm pleased that in your speech, that of Governor Eugenio and those of Martha Inés, Lina and my mother spoke, without faltering, of all those kidnapped. To complain for us would be a question of advocating for rights.

Precisely, I think that the merit of our kidnapping is how it can generate what it is achieving. The resulting injustice touches the conscience in every town. The fact that all this solidarity is oriented against the kidnapping is the maximum achievement of our sacrifice. Nonviolence should precisely tend to unmasking the injustices, removing the veil that does not let us see the spiritual scars. I have spoken to you before about these scars on the soul

The message of my mother was very beautiful, and it is comforting to know that Daniel and the aunts are spreading our positions in their communities. The generosity and the solidarity of the friends of *How Medellín Woke Up,* and in general of Radio Caracol and other media that have recognized the importance of not letting this topic pass by, merit our gratitude.

The whole program today was filled with praises and reminiscing about our efforts for peace. The letter of Carrasco was very flattering, and as usual it's sharp and hits the mark. The words of the rector of the University of Antioquia, Alberto Uribe, and the tactician in soccer Juan José Peláez, as well as President Uribe and those of Ventura Díaz, encourages us, and I believe help push our search for nonviolence.

Lastly, I especially believe the permanent effort and the solidarity that we have always received in the church and with the bishops, the archbishop, priests, and the faithful. Particularly in me the diverse religious ceremonies that are offered daily for our health and liberty inspire great joy. The services today in the cathedral by Archbishop Alberto Giraldo and in the north by Bishop Flavio [Calle] have special significance for me.

In Frontino, the priest's generous mention in various services of nonviolence and the constant concern for our well-being also demands our gratitude. In Santander, Monsignor Darío Monsalve also demonstrated concern about our situation and his statements about the humanitarian accord had great visibility. Monsignor Alberto Giraldo has pointed out the gravity of "this kidnapping" and expressed his sadness at the lack of willingness by the FARC to open a channel of communication.

In short, a good balance now that we cannot do anything from here. We can only pray that all your efforts and the solidarity of support that you receive from so many people achieve drawing near to the humanitarian accord.

Thinking of the trainers-directors, I hope they can push sports in the municipalities. I ask myself if we continue training them what role they will be playing in our communities. Based on the success of the youth symphony and thinking of the capacity of music, I also think that sports could develop similar processes of social recovery.

The trainers-directors could try to respond to this effort in the metropolitan area and in the regions of Antioquia. To promote sports with the clear intention of offering spaces of personal growth to a population very closed off by violence and marginalization, a little like the style of the municipal schools of music, so that in the municipalities or among various ones there spring up schools of sports. Seed beds of sports where additionally there is emphasis on forming nonviolent human beings committed along with their families and the community.

In terms of solidarity and efforts to push the accord of humanitarian exchange, the day has been tremendous. Really, we have received an avalanche of will and support.

The impasse of the heavy shower in the discovery of the mural was pleasing and well compensated for by the great attendance in the march. I imagine that many people formed the human chain and that the concert by Piero and South America would have been very emotional. It turns out that an idol of Latin American youth is in charge of carrying the voice in these moments of our lives.

The words of former President López constitute, as I understand it, the most solid and clear support of all the efforts to make the humanitarian accord a reality. He has put the finger in the wound, and his position describes the pitfalls that exist. To achieve the exchange, the government should understand that it is not trying to inflict a "defeat" on its counterpart and vice-versa.

I also believe that all those persons who want to help, like Mayor Luis Pérez, for example, should abstain from launching new proposals, and in its place offer help to strengthen the strategy that you have been shaping with the help of Dr. López. Now all the effort should be on behalf of having the government name negotiators, hopefully Dr. López among them, or better heading them.

I was sleeping when they woke me to listen to *Hora 21* with Yolanda Ruiz and also Caicedo. An excellent program, love. I suggest that you get a copy. I was hoping that at any moment they would interview you.

Yesterday we listened to my mother a lot; in all her contributions she was really wonderful. In the afternoon I listened to a beautiful message of the Caicedan people in which they pointed out that they keep the nonviolence flame alive. How pleasing it was to know that they have not died despite stumbling blocks. Nonviolence triumphs when we are willing to overcome the defeats and persevere with love and confidence.

The balance of this commemoration is really surprising and, despite the sadness, they never abandoned us. I feel great joy in knowing that nonviolence has been abounding with our efforts and sacrifices and marches on its own power.

I congratulate you, love, since I know how much of this day is due to your careful attention and engagement and the attendance of the whole team of the government, with Eugenio Ruiz infused with nonviolence.

I was pleasantly impressed with the capacity of Yolanda Ruiz. I think that you should keep her in mind and pursue with Hector Rincon ensuring that they know the depth and seriousness that nonviolence signifies, the effort that Antioquia wants to make to promote the culture of nonviolence, and the way we believe that can help the country overcome all its violence.

It is important that these persons know that nonviolence involves not "religious fanaticisms" but "humanitarian and political science." It is important to disseminate unrest among them so that they explore and fall in love with nonviolence, or at least feel a loving predisposition, a product of its knowledge. It is something I propose to do in a systematic way when I return but which you can notably promote now.

I'm only missing news about what Daniel and the aunts have prepared in their communities. Well, mi vida, I think that it has been a wonderful and very intense day for you all. I send you my love and kisses. Good night.

**Tuesday, April 22**: Love, good morning. Very early today I listened to Ana Rosa [Pinto] and later I listened to you. Actually, we feel that the communication of President Uribe again expresses a willingness to advance toward a humanitarian accord. Nevertheless, I will only believe that it exists when negotiators are named and that depends on who the government chooses. Again, my love, I congratulate you for the session yesterday, and I extend congratulations to the whole team and to Martha Inés, Lina, and my mother.

Love, I think that today or tomorrow you will be receiving the news that we sent the seventeenth (they left in the early morning of the eighteenth). Today Daniel and Adelaida sent messages. Lamentably, I could not hear them since I had gone out to the outhouse immediately after your message, but Alejandro told me what he heard.

Daniel spoke about the basket and the piano, and he announced that he intended to tape a couple pieces for me. Everything indicates that it was a recording before Holy Week. I hope that this weekend, in his e-mail, Daniel tells me how it went in the march commemorating the first year of the kidnapping. Good night, my love.

**Wednesday, April 23**: My love, good morning. Your message indicates to me that you were in the Baho [place where the march arrived, situated between Santafé de Antioquia and Caicedo], trying to leave a commemorative plaque, and I thank God and the Virgin that nothing happened to you. For the way the news was produced it seems that finally it was able to be placed. I think that if it hadn't been placed, a very visible site in Medellín could have been chosen and installed it there with a clear explanation indicating that it should be in another place and the reasons why it was not possible to do so there. Another option could be in the plaza of Santafé de Antioquia or in the little plaza of Alpujarra.

Today is the meeting of President Álvaro Uribe and Hugo Chávez, and that will undoubtedly occupy the attention of the media. Nevertheless, in the morning we listened to the ambassador [Luis Guillermo] Giraldo speak about the contacts of the government and the FARC-EP, and his opinions about the humanitarian accord and the role of the United Nations. Then we listened to extensive declarations of Minister Londono about various themes.

From today, the thing that I liked most is your news about the Children's Camp of Nonviolence in Santafé de Antioquia. I had understood that about 2,000 would attend, of which 500 would be from the west. I would like to know if that is how it was or did it mean only a total of 500 children. As I have told you, it seems crucial to maintain this effort and also look for ways of having it continue after our government ends.

Additionally, I think that the creation of a secretary of nonviolence can imply finally a true commitment of our administration and have the needed critical mass to "think" and "prompt" the multiple transformations that are going to require the change of attitude toward the culture of nonviolence in Antioquia.

It will be necessary to promote changes in the public and the private sector. In the governmental institutions, this will require attention to the three levels—local, state, and national—in the same way that I consider a secretary of nonviolence in Antioquia necessary and desirable.

I think the country would benefit enormously from the creation of a minister of nonviolence, and it should be called that, not "of peace." To signify that it treats a specific task, "to produce the necessary changes to turn toward a culture of nonviolence." The private sector also should think in detail about nonviolent institutions, since that could constitute an enormous opportunity for generating employment. The job is to begin the process of institutional and management transformation toward a nonviolent society.

This transformation would require and demand a great many nonviolent "person hours," from the academics and trainers to the workers and technicians trained in all the disciplines, applying their creativity to look for products that promote nonviolence, rather than what we are accustomed to using and enjoying and which are instruments of violence or make a permanent reference to violence when they do not foment it—like arms toys, movies and computer games, war and suspense novels, etc. This transformation demands a creativity that can give way to forming specialized consulting firms dedicated to supporting the changes necessary to achieve a nonviolent culture.

Thus, as ecology presents a great opportunity to benefit, protect, and discover unexplored resources, so also does nonviolence open doors to processes that will demand human resources of every quality, specialty, and levels of expertise.

As in the private sector, in the public there are opportunities for whatever. A great initial effort should be made to identify all the spaces of violence, to measure and construct indicators, and to structure nonviolent solutions. It will be necessary to promote creation of all types of nonviolent institutions: academic, public and private, of production, of consultation, and of promotion or formation.

Finally, there is a field in which sooner or later, the government would have to involve itself. This has to do with the new role that the armed forces and the police should play in a nonviolent society along with transforming the approaches to punishment and rehabilitation that society presently uses.

The state, if it does not permanently take care to do so, runs the risk of being violent in many of its actions. An effort to detect these risks and transform its conduct can permit easy and very telling changes in its willingness to conciliate the change toward nonviolence. In short, to reflect on this a little could bear fruit in a very short time.

I insist to you in recommending that they look for Speedy González, in *How Medellín Woke Up*, to prepare some daily reflections for the people of the government. Hopefully they can do so quickly. Indeed, it has to be asked for so that it is done through the lens of nonviolence. What do we do that generates violence? What do we do that violates our "customers"/"users" / citizens? An undeclared problem is part of the landscape!

Love, remember Carlos Matus. Glenn Paige's book is really very good. He has truly made an effort to point a way toward a nonviolent/nonkilling world. His positions merit being studied well. I recommend his work to you and also to Eugenio.

I forgot to tell you that the statements of Luis Javier Botero on *Hora 21* I really liked; only I believe it is necessary to clarify a little of my uneasiness concerning nonviolence after the campaign discourse about the capital alternative of solidarity. In connection with all this, I ask myself: How is the campaign to disarm Antioquia going? Everything indicates to me that we are quiet. Have we left it in the hands of the mayor?

On this topic Alirio López, the father in Bogotá, can give us some light. Do you see why a secretary for all nonviolent topics is necessary?

Today two pieces of news filled the day, besides the meeting of the presidents: The first has to do with the announcements about the designation of Luis Carlos Restrepo to negotiate the humanitarian accord, and the second is the announcement about the pronouncement that we anticipate to be very favorable about our cause—that of the former presidents Lemos, Samper, López, and Turbay slated for next Monday.

We believe both events will help, since they permit that in a way you pressure the commissioned person for results. The statements of former President Samper also seem to me to be in the line of your efforts. In the end, we are passing through some good moments again: very ample communication with you and the children, possibilities for Yolandita, a very useful commemoration for the cause of nonviolence, and full of solidarity. And the humanitarian accord again is in the eye of the hurricane with good lawyers.

Among the concerns that we have in the first place: The health problems for the *leishmaniasis* infection of Viellard and Marín and the illness of Tapias, who for two days suffers with malaria (Tapias has been kidnapped for the most time: on May 28 he completed six years and with this one he has had malaria attacks nineteen times during his captivity). Despite our not receiving the medicine, the remedies we have been using have helped contain the infection in both, and the person in charge is confident they will be healed.

**Thursday, April 24**: Love, good morning. I heard your statements as well as the message. In both opportunities you look very good. Then we listened to the interview of President Álvaro Uribe, and I confess that it did not make me very excited. I don't see in him any real willingness to negotiate. His statements let one see the attitude of the government itself that "believes" it can militarily defeat its counterpart.

President Álvaro Uribe has not taken to heart that what is being talked about is a humanitarian accord, and he continues acting as though he was in a position to impose all kinds of conditions, fitting for a victorious army.

Two things stand out for me: to confirm what Vice-President Santos says in relation to an eventual division in the interior of the FARC-EP, and to let it be seen that the armed forces do not willingly accept the humanitarian accord, since frequently he refers to his obligation to maintain the morale of the troops.

Gilberto is more optimistic. The expectation of release for Gilberto drew our attention. It really made me emotional. Nothing would make me happier than to see him released, to know he is free and at the side of his family. Nevertheless, here nothing is perceived in that direction.

I ask myself how things are going in the Nonviolence Camp. Despite the fact that President Álvaro Uribe expresses reasons that seek to demonstrate his agreement, I think that what is fundamental is that a humanitarian accord be accepted that is only that—humanitarian—and not entail other motives or demand other justifications.

Love, tomorrow we finish various items in the provisions that you sent us, among them popcorn and milk. These are my preferences and my weakness. The popcorn has reached everyone, including the fighters. The milk I'm more stingy with. We still have good coffee and chocolate. This last type that we liked most was the milk chocolate. We have greatly enjoyed these snacks. Again, thanks, mi vida.

In the line of a nonviolent campaign, I believe that one we should face is the battle against centralism. Analyzed well, centralism is a form of oppression, especially if the central power is exercised under the influence of corruption or in a mediocre manner based on favors. Undoubtedly President Álvaro Uribe has elements to recognize the force of this argument and the enthusiasm to take historic corrections.

Equal to our complaints, it is necessary for the Antioquenian people and their directors to know that we want autonomy, that we seek it with them, and how we are going to organize ourselves and prepare the institutions so that this autonomy is translated into changes for the good of the community.

What administrative reforms will be introduced? What fiscal and economic reforms does Antioquia need? What changes in the political plan should we make? What effort will we need to translate in clear politics the new power of the recently "freed" Antioquia?

The answers to all these questions should be found, even preliminarily, in the interdisciplinary work that I have asked for in various opportunities. One area of work that I would convert into one of the principal responsibilities of the new secretary of nonviolence. The Nonviolent Campaign in Antioquia for the Regional Autonomy. I dream, mi vida.

Love, yesterday the families of six kidnapped ones in the Curillo received proofs and a video. Apparently they are of those who for almost two years had not had proofs. That is very good news, and everyone was filled with joy. Hopefully, they won't delay so long the proofs of all those in similar conditions will know.

**Friday, April 25**: My love, good morning. Your message and the little news you give me about the children are very pleasing. The statements of former President Samper and of Monsignor Castro also are encouraging.

With optimism we hope the meeting Monday and what was announced from the Chamber by Representative William Vélez for the fifteenth of the month. The commander has not returned. Tomorrow it will be a week. He should be attending some important event.

Tapias has been in bed for two days with malaria. Fortunately the tea that you sent is the only thing that enters.

**Saturday, April 26**: Mi vida, good morning. Your words full of confidence alleviate my sadness; I woke up today quite strengthened. In *How Medellín Woke Up* they put Mercedes Sosa singing *Como un Pájaro Libre* ( Like a Free Bird) and that beautiful song, which I really loved when I was young, filled me with melancholy. It is a beautiful way that Mercedes Sosa uses to express love for her son.

There are books and songs that when read or listened to are very difficult. Others, however, immediately leave a mark on our soul. It is like it was cast, with wax, the material that fits us. I think of this in relation to the words of Gandhi and many of the Andean protest songs.

In the music, the South American songs with Indian flavor stand out. Also without a doubt, those of the younger generation of Leonardo Favio y Piero and the tango, which easily melt the sentiments of my spirit. Mercedes Sosa, María Dolores Pradera, her voice and the unique force of her songs make my soul vibrate.

In the news they said something about the process in Cuba against the opponents of the Castro regime; some assassinated, others condemned to various thousands of years of prison. The charges: rebellion and kidnapping. The figures are not very precise in the generalizations of the media, but it talks about a penalty of about 1,700 and some years. That is several life sentences for something like twenty opponents/rebels, and the other fifty persons who participated, and the imposition of the death sentence (by shooting) of the three who were the leaders.

This is, in summary, the way that the "revolutionary" regime *par excellence* in Latin America treats those who kidnap and create a revolution/opposition to authority. It's been forty years since the revolution triumphed in Cuba. At this rate still they try to evade any questioning and silence it with a display of force.

Several reflections are aroused: Do the repressive attitudes of other government ideologies legitimize this attitude? What is the hope of a revolution that triumphed if after forty years it must still exercise force to maintain itself? What punishment would the Castro regime impose on our fighters for using kidnapping? What is the balance that Cuba could offer to the world after forty years of exercising exclusive power?

All of this inclines me even more toward nonviolence and the words of Gandhi: "Whatever might be the noblesse of a cause that must be defended, hatred and violence compromise the peace that is sought and duplicate this hatred and this violence."

Also I remember the words that I've known since childhood: "He who kills by iron, will be killed by iron" expressed by the woman who killed Attila (in the 8-mm. movies of our childhood) that really are the words of Jesus to the one who cut off the ear of a servant of the high priest who was arresting him: "Return your sword to its place, and all those who live by the sword will die by the sword" (Matt. 26:52).

Why are we humans so capable of doing what we condemn when others do it to someone else? For a long time Castro helped the Colombian fighters, who are among the principle kidnappers of the world, and today the need is seen to punish the kidnapped in their own land. What will happen to Cuba when Castro passes?

Here in Colombia, what country can we construct on the basis of exercising violence? It does not matter what kind of verbal juggling is used, he who uses a weapon is still using violent means, be it the state, the fighters, the AUC, or citizens. I desire that we unite to construct (the term *reconstruct* does not fit, since it did not exist previously) a more just and peaceful society. I believe that nonviolence can go teaching us the way to walk together, to reconcile ourselves and resolve with creativity our enormous problems that do not cease to be problems of any society in development and maturation.

In a conversation with the commander, when he spoke to me of the hunger that the people suffer and how this is the impulse for the war, I answered him showing him the MANÁ Antioquian and how it attends to a hundred thousand children of Sisbén 1 and 2 in Antioquia. His answer was immediate: And what about the rest?

Love, that is the answer that we should give. That is why I insist that the program should cover all the children of Sisbén 1 and 2 that need it. First up to five years of age, then extend it to fourteen years of age. Look! The effort that Antioquia makes, for no reason, should free the ICBF of its obligation to the children of Antioquia.

On the contrary, one has to achieve that the ICBF commit itself even more and for a long period. The fighters will always ask, And what about the others? Thus they do not know how many are "the others." That is the way to question us. For that the solutions for all must be constructed. Thus we begin with pilot projects. One has to contemplate the way to amplify the coverage and, especially, resolve how to get to the most isolated rural person.

Today they brought us seven avocados; we laughed about the special delivery. Love, today I finished Paige's book. I have continued with that of Gandhi, and I'm slowly advancing in *El Mundo de Sofía* (*Sophie's World*).

The commander has not returned. I hope that an event that has required so much of his time implies changes and advances about our release.

The sad news about the recovery of the body of the teacher of Cocorná, kidnapped and killed by the ELN, causes Gilberto and me great pain. Only a great desperation and loss of discernment could cause a fighter to act with such fierceness and cruelty.

Tonight, Lord willing, I will listen to you and hopefully also to Daniel. Good night, my love.

**Sunday, April 27**: Good morning, my love. With your words and your image I woke up today; a sleepless night, but content.

I don't believe they read any message from Daniel on the program. In the morning on Diana Uribe's program they only talked about the petroleum war and some news, among which drawing my attention was the comments about what was said by the writer Susan Sontag. I have given you my opinion about her. I think she is a courageous and valiant person.

Also, some comments about a rumor concerning the paternity of Bolívar in relation to Flora Tristán, taken in passing in the new historic novel of Mario Vargas Llosa. We here have done a good study, and we arrived at the conclusion that actually Bolívar had a relationship with the mother of Flora, in Madrid, during the time which would have coincided with the conception of Flora.

Our documents about Bolívar, which are not a few, do not leave any doubt about the possibilities, and some, like those of Juvenal Herrera, categorically affirm it. All of this would be equivalent to "Gauguin n'est pas Gauguin."[43] Flora, on her part, has her own very meritorious story in the battle against oppression, besides being the grandmother of the painter.

The day is gray and looks boring, which will allow me to devote myself completely to reading and reflection. For a couple weeks we have not done any other exercise besides volleyball.

The malaria of Tapias has improved and the *leishmaniasis* of Marín and Viellard are frozen, neither progressing nor curing, although I should recognize that the "surgery" that they did on Marín on the little wounds which had begun to grow seems to have extracted all the center of putrefaction.

My main concern is the wound above Viellard's right eye, which now is the size of an egg's oval. Aranguren, with his artistic ability, has begun to make baskets and hampers of wild *potré*.[44] There's no end to them, and he has promised to make hats for Gilberto and me.

Something, and we don't understand what, has delayed the last two letters that Gilberto and I sent. Soon you should receive them.

The general feel of the program was enormous optimism among the families regarding the imminence of the humanitarian accord. I am a little more skeptical, but even so I see very positive signs.

The most valuable is the serious, prudent, and expert gesture of Monsignor Augusto Castro and the firm support of former Presidents Samper and López, in the aspects that would be called external. The internal motor is without a doubt the efforts of the families, and your role there is notable and very wise. As you have said so many times, I do not see the hour when I can embrace you and we can share our lives. What joy awaits us and with the help of God the expectations of a daughter, our loving Yolandita, could be a reality. I'm concerned that time keeps moving on and they are not making a decision, which then affects this issue. I think that we are arriving at the limits, since the doctor spoke of having her this year. I hope that one of the decisions that the commander brings will be this, since otherwise I think we will have to forget it. Just thinking about it hurts and makes me sad. I should get these negative thoughts out of my mind and replace them with much optimism and faith in the will of God.

Today on Radio Caracol they presented a program about the humanitarian accord. All the positions were in favor, and those of Samper and Monsignor Castro very clear and impressive.

In the media surveys they asked what opinion the Colombians had about women entering the army. I, who do not believe in arms, think that it is a trap into which the women fall, looking for equality rather than progress in the struggle for their rights. They are, like the men, converting themselves into slaves of war and violence. For me it is worth seeking equality but it should be to better and not to brutalize themselves, giving their energies to violence. To aspire to be violent like the men is to move backward. Good night, love of my life.

**Monday, April 28**: My love, good morning. Your message arrived clearly, and with the news we understand your recent optimism . Today you spoke of efficiency, and it is clear that the topic is progressing. We are optimistic about the meeting of the former presidents, and the same with the communication of the FARC-EP. There is also news about the surrender of a FARC front commander.

Love, I read the information about *chonta* palm that you sent me. I have two comments. First, I think it is very little; and second, the *chonta* to which I refer is different. Its trunk does not have thorns, and it reaches a much greater height. Here there are many species, but we distinguish four: the *patona*, which has a cone of roots; these with prickly fruit, the *pipona* or big belly, which have an enlargement which give them the name, and I have seen them more than fifty meters; the *milpesos*, which give a fruit that is used to produce a juice somewhat chocolaty; and the other I don't remember. They produce very heavy wood, and this is what I want to investigate, but I'm more interested in these being evaluated and studied in depth there.

The former presidents' meeting had great appeal, especially the jokes about Minister Londoño. We hope things continue well.

Today I looked at your beautiful photo, taken on April 21, 2002, before leaving for Santafé de Antioquia, showing your characteristic outburst of laughter. Now it is near suppertime. Today it seems new provisions have arrived; we are waiting for what they will serve us.

Late in the night the commander arrived. Good night, my love.

# Part V
## LETTERS TO FAMILY AND FRIENDS

*Note: In the Spanish original, three drawings by the governor depicting scenes during his captivity were reproduced here. The drawings were not available for the English translation.*

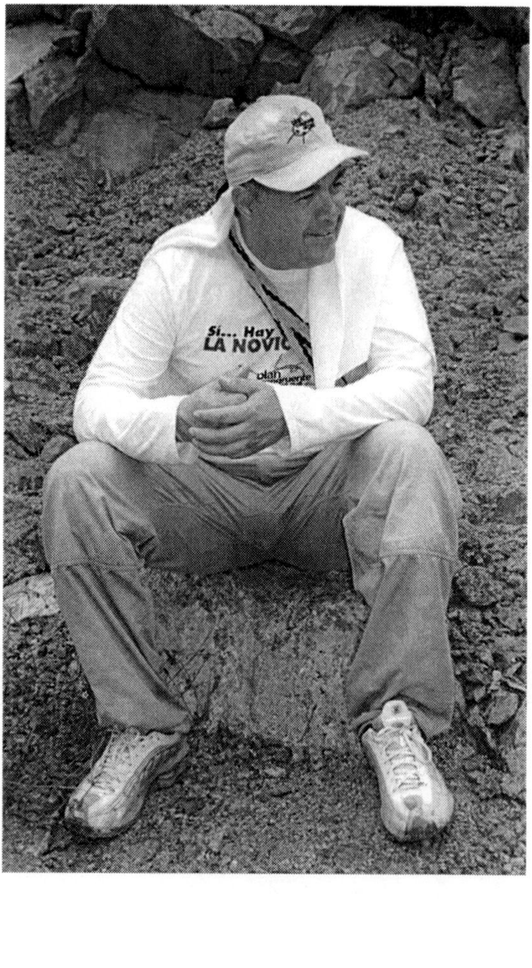
Si... Hay
LA NOVIC

## LETTERS FOR FAMILY AND FRIENDS

*(These letters corresponding to the months of May, June, August, October, and November 2002 were sent by the FARC together with the first part of the diary. They come by way of the Public Defender of the People of Antioquia on the twelfth of December 2002. Those dated January and March 2003 were given to Yolanda by an emissary.)*

**For Germán Andrés Tapias Pinto, "Papo"**
**From the Mountains in Colombia**
**December 13, 2002**

Dear Papo:

It is Christmas time and the end of the year, I write you this letter-Christmas card because I miss you so much and I miss trimming the tree with you, with Danny, with Mathew and with your mother, and the manger scene. And also, I would like to tell you all some wonderful stories that exist around this beautiful time in which we celebrate the birth of the God-Child in Bethlehem. Stories that have been passed down from generation to generation about the Wise Men, what they tell about the "star of Bethlehem" and the many problems of the parents of Jesus, Joseph, and Mary in their pilgrimage to Bethlehem, etc.

On the other hand, I hope that you are having a good time with Mafer in London and Paris. There it will be in the coldest part of winter, and I imagine you are "very well protected" when you go out on the frozen streets to enjoy the shopping centers full of people, and you will see some winter sports.

England became, in due time, the best empire of the Earth, and it has very beautiful cities that were built on the basis of the riches they collected from their conquests and with the efforts of their people for many centuries. We, on the other hand, received from the hand of God a very beautiful country with great natural riches, and we can say, compared with the European countries, that we are just beginning our history.

We have an enormous challenge before us: to construct a just and peaceful society so that you can live, organize a beautiful family, and enjoy this country. That is why one day your mother and I began a peaceful march of reconciliation toward Caicedo [a small municipality of Antioquia].

Our goal was to help the reconciliation, but our intentions were not understood nor shared, and that is why we are, still today, held captive in the jungle by the FARC-EP. I want to tell you that no other circumstance will stop us in the future from sharing with you and your mother these Christmas celebrations.

Papo, in these marches through the jungle, I have learned many little tricks that we can practice when we go camping or fishing later on. We have seen parrots, parakeets, sloths, all kind of snakes, congas (ants similar to the Santanderians but much more fierce, which cannot be eaten and their bite is worse than a scorpion), scorpions, condors, eagles, guaguas.

We also have fished lisos, shads, sea fish, and moncholos. Here in the camp a dog of the fighters had three puppies, and they spend the whole night under our camp making all kinds of noise some days, and then others they're very well behaved. I imagine you'd like them to keep company with Tino [Papo's Labrador dog]. There is also a companion who has two parrots (Cariaco and Cariaca). You'll probably see them if they take out the video we filmed in November.

Papo, your mother is a wonderful woman and she tells me that you are doing very well in school. There are many children in Colombia who do not have the possibility of studying in a good school like you, so I ask you to make good use of your time in school and learn a lot.

Soon you will realize that, as you grow, one of the best pleasures is to learn, and that as you study and learn, you'll grow as a person and it will help you enjoy every instant of life and make them happier and more interesting also for others.

Today the computers and Internet play an important role. You should learn to navigate through them and progress the most you can in the computer. You can also teach your mother and me a little of what you know when I return.

I'm sending you these horses, and I hope that some day very soon your mother and I can have a little farm to have some good horses for when you come to visit us. Your mother told me that you saw some horses in La Ceja. How did you like them? Do you like them or do you prefer to have domesticated ones?

Papo, when you have a moment, if you can, write me a little letter. I would be thrilled. I would be so happy to receive your news about how it's going in all your classes. In which one do you have problems? How is soccer practice going? I imagine that you are a *crack*. How goes horseback riding? Have other sports made you excited? How did the trip go to visit your sister? How are the girlfriends doing? Do you know how to dance as well as your mother?

I'd like to know everything that you want to tell me and also that you send me some of your photos so I can put them up, next to Danny and Matthew, in my camp, and that you can be a little company for me (ask your mother to laminate them).

Papo, in these days they have me captive against my will. It seems wonderful to me that you can be with your mother some weekends. Surely very soon you will know other Antioquenian boys and girls with whom you can have good friendships. Try to visit her frequently to make her happy in these lonely moments.

You have a very special and wonderful mother. We all love our mother and consider her the best, but you have a very special one among all the mothers, and I know how much she loves you and is so proud of you.

This year, your mother got more than 91,000 gifts and shared them with the poorest boys and girls of the towns of Antioquia. I don't know if you went with her, but next year we can go together, how would you like that?

Well, my dear Papo, you have always been a happy and generous young man. I've never known you to have a violent or aggressive attitude. That's why, lastly, I want to recommend nonviolence. That characteristic is a great blessing.

I would say, like Gandhi, that you are a "Natural Satyagrahi." I want you to read about Gandhi, about Martin Luther King, and about the nonviolence of Jesus. And when I regain my freedom, I hope you can help me convince the people of Antioquia to take this philosophy of life which, I am sure, can transform the cruel reality of the country.

I wish you a great 2003, full of joy and love; I hope to give you a big embrace very soon.

Your friend who loves and misses you.

Guillermo Gaviria Correa

**For Carlos Wolff**
**From the Mountains of Colombia**
**March 5, 2003**

Dear Carlos:

For several days I have wanted to write you and answer your letter. Today the news of the verdict of the attorney's office makes putting off this intention, despite my not knowing when these lines can be sent or if they will even arrive.

Your noble words and the excellent action that, with pride, you can offer the Antioquenian people as well as the innumerable and appreciative mentions of you that Yolanda says in her messages, make me feel like a very fortunate man.

I was right in choosing you for a mission which, from the first moments, brought out your enemies. And in each effort and achievement you have shown your honesty and commitment to Antioquia and a special affection for me and loyalty to my family which has no equal. You can be proud, and I'm sure that this Friday, in the budget reports, you can show our beloved Antioquenian people the irrefutable proofs of the honorability and capability of your actions.

I remember during the campaign the government was looked on with disdain by some directors, and various candidates structured their campaign on the basis of the failure of the department. Such was the situation, and in only two years your vigilance and your vision have been able to transform the department into a very distinct territorial entity, and you have given a direction that guides it toward a solid financial situation.

I ask God that you succeed in resisting all the hatred perceived in the legal actions of which they accuse you. I have made my decision—my conscience never is separated from the confidence I placed in you and has only grown amid the difficulties.

Like a captain who at times has to give rough steering to a beloved boat, thus I have acted on some occasions, carried by the conviction of the friendship and confidence that unite us and perhaps convinced by your strong temperament.

Nevertheless, your nobility makes this dark cloud of remorse that was born in those moments, and I appreciate it in you. You should know that the friendship and love that you mention are strongly and definitely matched.

Please, give a very special, loving embrace to Astrid and your children. For you, a special embrace and all my solidarity, from one who has been submitted to the same attacks and knows that "they only throw stones at the tree that gives fruits."

Courage, my loving friend. My prayers are with you. Receive my congratulations and gratitude for your actions and for accompanying Yolanda and my family.

A huge embrace,
Guillermo Gaviria Correa

**For Guillermo Ángel and María Mercedes Pérez**
**From the Mountains of Colombia**
**March 7, 2003**

Dear Guillo and María Mer:
Having news from you makes me very happy. The difficulties of national engineering, which should face the intellectual pride of a minister who, with the personal help of the president, also infused with a good dose of this bad advice, considers that nothing has been done before his action and believes that it is possible to reinvent everything concerning commerce and civil works.

They would be many, and I am sure will be very costly to the companies and the country. I found shelter in the hope that the complaints were made in Antioquia, for their past errors would have served to assume a less aggressive position. But besides your reports, I have listened to some of his interview giving statements which were later retracted, such as they were.

I continue thinking that the national engineering needs good spokesmen and sufferers in Congress and, eventually, entry into petitioning the national government, since it is there that unfortunately decisions are made. I hope your patience and prudence help you successfully sort out this period.

I'm glad for the news about your children, knowing that these moments in which I write are now old. I'm glad because I know how much love and joy they generate in you, and you can have the certainty that if I am free for the graduation of Juan Pablo [Ángel Pérez], I would be honored to attend.

The triumph of Medellín in soccer makes me so happy; like I was the most fanatic of its fans, like the last defeat with the Colo-Colo caused me such frustration. I hope they raise up their head and offer the people of Antioquia new motivation for joy.

I frequently remember your words, and I should say that rather than lose confidence or conviction in nonviolence, amid the reflections that permit these circumstances, my position now is much more solid.

To be on the margin of what is happening but not to follow day after day the happenings in the whole country, is beneficial and even a privilege, even through such an imperfect means as radio.

Later, here I heard the answers that the government gives to the acts and the statements of the subversion. The clamor of the citizens is felt by attacks on occasion by one or the other actors in the conflict. The sensibilities of other nations are sounded, and which we feel offer solidarity and which are permanently calculating their potential benefits before one or the other position. Also, one comes to have a type of *feeling* about what the counterpart thinks or feels. To see the newscasts on television in the few opportunities that we can do so is a martyrdom.

The picture of the country that we have from here shows a complex Dante-esque image of confusion and errors that end up "resolving themselves" by violent means. It is surprising the ease with which violence is used to treat minor differences.

For all this, I continue being convinced of the need to actuate a culture of nonviolence. To look for the society to achieve a change of attitude and to learn to evade this almost natural tendency that we have developed to resort to violence as the arbitrator or judge.

The sick community should be given the opportunity to apply to itself the remedy of nonviolence. The process should be understood as a long ascension by the stairs, rung by rung, step by step, the first of which should be a tremendous education and re-education effort, for the new generations as well as for older ones.

Subsequent steps (but concurrent, education for nonviolence should never slacken) can focus on resolving the defects of childhood malnutrition and hunger of many countrymen, the lack of housing and public services, access to employment, etc.

Now on the topic of malnutrition we are doing something. I do not doubt that you know and are always helping through your habitual generosity. I hope to be able to give much more energy to this program and consolidate it before my term ends, and the same with the other key topics that you know of: housing, reforestation, education reform, and the Consistent Peace Plan. In short, I prefer to conclude this long series telling you that if something good comes out of this kidnapping, it is being permitted to see what will happen with our death. That which seems hideous results in being practical, painful, but at the same time formative.

Of it all, the hardest and most grave is the pain to my loved ones, and what gives me the most pain is Yolanda.

She has behaved with exemplary valor and her integrity permits me to resist without weakening. Her messages, and the certainty that she gives me with her love, are like a rock on which I have planted myself, certain that I can resist all the weight of this devilish captivity and much more.

To know she is among true friends like you and María Mer gives me an indescribable calmness. I ask you not to abandon her for a moment. I know the therapeutic capacity of the outings to your farm, and if she can take Papo, all the better.

She has the strength of an oak, but friendship when it is pure and noble, like that of you both, is a balm for the tormented soul. Up to here are the halos that fill me with joyful gratitude.

"Friendship is preferable to glory," Bolivar said. Dear friends, I ask you to accompany my adorable Yolanda until I return. Receive all my love and friendship in a strong embrace from captivity.

Guillermo Gaviria Correa

**Para Carlos Villegas**
**From the Mountains of Colombia**
**March 7, 2003**

Dear Carlos and family:
How pleasing to receive news from good friends and their families. The budget report was just done, and we could not see or hear anything. Nevertheless we heard on *How Medellín Woke Up* some loose news and this, together with the third report of conduct, pleases me.

I also knew that the signing of the contract with the workers was achieved, and I'm pleased it was done without bad feelings and conflicts.

The progress that I perceive pleases me, and I'm only concerned about the lack of decision in "Plains of Cuivá-San José de la Montaña" and why I do not understand the definition of the topic of the tunnel of the East.

Also, I would like us to use more force to accelerate and increase allocations on the coast, especially in the Turbo-Necoclí section. Remember that it was the first priority of Urabá.

I'm glad to know that Andrés Uriel Gallego is helping. I know that you know how to work with the required intensity so that Antioquia gets the allocations necessary in public roadways, with resources principally from the nation.

I believe, Carlos, that the resources from the department should be used primarily in the other key programs and that the department should designate the minimum possible to infrastructure without abandoning its maintenance. Also we should concentrate on finishing what was begun.

I'm very pleased to know of the progress by Carlitos, to whom I ask you to give a huge embrace and a kiss from his friend *the Gov*. I also remember him with much love and your whole family, with whom we already unite in a long series of indestructible bonds.

I ask you to take care of my adored Yolanda. She needs more than ever for our good friends to help alleviate the pain this sad separation causes.

Here I think a lot about the business of the wood. Ask Yolanda to show you what I have written about the *chonta* palm [*macana*], the *abarco* and its magical bark, the *comino crepo* and other varieties that these jungles generously offer.

There is a sub-official here, Heriberto Aranguren, who is greatly skilled in construction and carpentry and is an untiring worker. I am encouraging him to become independent and set up a business in this area.

When I leave, I want to know the business of your family a little better since I believe that wood and its industries will receive a great boost with the reforestation program. The topic of the construction of prefabricated houses is constantly rolling around in my mind, and about this I also wrote some lines to Yolanda. Give your brother a huge embrace and for you all, all my love.

Adrianita, congratulations on your efforts and thanks for the information. I can see that the finances of Antioquia today have a very different face. Receive a strong embrace from captivity.

Your friend,
Guillermo Gaviria Correa

**For Aníbal Gaviria Correa**
**From the Mountains of Colombia**
**March 11, 2003**

Dear Aníbal, Claudia, and Emiliana:

How ungrateful I must seem you. I do not believe there is another person who merits more than you my gratitude and my words, yet yours are the last letters I answer.

I know that you stay awake for our cause and for the great companionship for Yolanda and also for many in the cabinet. I know the crucial role that you play in the nuclear family, and I feel very fortunate to count on a brother like you. From this captivity, and with time for reflection about so many topics, I believe that in my scattered life I have never met a person like you.

And if your professional merits and your intelligence are sufficiently superior to everything that surrounds us, in reality it is your spirituality and humanity and the solidarity implied in your actions which lend your person titanic dimensions.

I have been reading the Old Testament, and there is a book that I think you would like (Ben Sirach or Ecclesiasticus). Really there are many interesting things in the Bible.

It pains me so much to miss the first years of beautiful Emiliana, as much as if it were the daughter Yolanda and I want to have. I imagine the wonderful stories that you will have to tell me about her achievements, and also I really miss Claudia and news about you two.

Aníbal, please keep insisting to Yolanda and Eugenio so that our commitment to the church outside of Sopetrán [the temple of the patron saint of travelers] is not neglected.

Brother, your letters are full of wise and very helpful advice. Of course some of our efforts to communicate with our captors have been fruitless. This means that many things that could be achieved in captivity, and would without a doubt be beneficial for the progress of the country, and would offer less costly and painful solutions to the conflict, are not being achieved.

Many things that I could be learning (since I have the time) I am not able to learn because I do not have access to books on the topics that are portable. Such is the case with agriculture and forestry. With telling you that in the beginning, I thought that enjoying the orchids would be a great pastime, and I've only seen a few in all the distance traveled and the camps. I would like to learn everything about the *estevia*, corn, about some forest species like the *abarco*, which in addition to use of its wood for construction produces a bark whose properties seem to me to be magical. I believe that it could be used to produce clothing of an excellent quality.

In short, here I only can acquire the restlessness but, with difficulty, I can manage some advancement. Only reading produces in me the sensation of not wasting time. For that I need the literature on nonviolence that I asked for, and all the other topics that I can get. Your books have been excellent entertainment, although, because of being in the jungle I do not have the opportunity. . . [a line missing in the original].

All literature is welcomed, and I'm having the opportunity to review and go deeper into the topics of our history, which is very useful to clarify errors that our leaders have committed in every direction over the 200 years the Republic of Colombia has existed.

I know that things have been learned, but with difficulty could they be compared to a sabbatical leave for the accumulation of limitations that I omit. The most important reflections have to do with two topics: the family, and the management of the government, or our role in guiding society.

About the first, I clearly perceive the enormous error that we commit when we permit work to usurp the rights of the family or do not designate to family the careful attention and love that it requires and deserves. I say that with a calm remorse, since I believe that still should compensate my the lack of presence to my children.

I believe it is necessary to better these aspects, and I hope to be able to do so, hopefully with the dream Yolandita. In my case, also it is crucial to better the relationships with the children of Yolanda and to reassure and be established with the two youth [Papo and Mafer]. More time and better quality, more family plans and more conscious planning of [last line of the original missing].

Really, when I speak of family I'm not only referring to Yolanda and our children. I refer equally to you all and our brothers and sisters, their families and their in-laws, our Antioquenian family and the Santanderian family.

I think it is good to take more seriously the political bonds which are converted into "relatives" with the respective marriages. There is a huge task ahead, and I hope you can help me to establish it and begin the process.

The second topic which has to do with the government is a bit more simple. After thinking about it many times, I think that the Plan of Development which we present is really well conceived.

I continue convinced that the three areas of development and the Consistent Peace Plan are to be conceived under an integral human, physical, environmental, and productive development and institutional development. There we should concentrate our efforts to guide us toward a good government with a participating society, to accomplish educating and creating a nonviolent culture for equity and liberty, and to make Antioquia a competitive, vigorous, and sustainable department.

I continue being convinced of the six key programs: MANÁ, Reforestation, Housing, Educational Transformation, Consistent Peace Plan, and Culture of Nonviolence. To justly achieve consolidation of these six programs and have the population know, approve of, and participate in strengthening them would be an immense triumph and able to. . . [line missing in the original].

I believe we have made advances, but I do not deceive myself with respect to what is still lacking to enable them to be really consolidated in the conscience of the people. On this you will find much in the previous writings and the letters with instructions. I would add that we ought to make a great effort to open the possibilities of teaching occupations to our young people.

Today (March 11), on ITM[45] I listened to a program with the mayor of Medellín addressed to teaching occupations, which just graduated 1,500 young people. Bravo! This multiplied by ten is what our people need to recuperate the strength of long ago.

Gilberto's essay about education deals with this. He sent it in the second package that we gave to the commander more or less a month ago. This is the direction of the transformation that I want to activate in our system. I hope that they understand it in the secretariat and that they manage to give it a good run.

I am happy because I see that my efforts and diplomacy have achieved through the system of higher education a spirit of unity among the public institutions of the department. I have a lot of faith in the positive results that are going to be perceived and the synergy that the whole system acquires. Education in nonviolence and for nonviolence—there is another challenge. For that I consider it necessary to create the Global Center for Nonviolence in Antioquia. We have not given enough exposure to the topic, and it is going to require continuing efforts after the end of this present period.

I think a lot about nutrition, and I'm very pleased with Colanta and at the same time very proud of this company. There are few institutions that I know of that unite such desirable characteristics for a community.

Colanta is now firmly committed to the program of MANÁ and is secure in the imagination of the Antioquenian people. There is something profoundly connected to my soul in this business, and it pleases me to be able to determinedly continue in this program.

Finally, there is reforestation. This topic, as you well know, has the purpose of transforming the industrial vocation of Antioquia. We are planting for the future of the department and the country. RIA should be a reality, and it is going to need Gonzalo. Please do not let them cheat you in this. It cannot be a timid appendix. It should be the enterprise of the department.

These jungles and forgotten and useless lands are called to be reforested to produce information about its biodiversity and genetic material, and I know how much more. Also, there are large tracts with no other future but reforestation.

Read what I wrote about the *chonta* and *abarco,* and I am sure that there are many more examples and species of value and utility. As you have said well, this 2003 year will be historic, but only if we achieve the objective to consolidate RIA and reforest at least 20 to 30 thousand hectares. I feel I am repeating what you already well know and what I have previously written.

Dear brother, Claudia and Emiliana: I [here a line is missing] . . . my dear Yolanda, to my mother and to my father.

I miss you all more every day; eagerly I hope that God permits us soon to be together. Aníbal, give everyone a fraternal embrace and a kiss for each one of you from captivity.

Hugs and kisses,
Guillermo

**For Adela de Gaviria**
**From the Mountains of Colombia**
**March 26, 2003**

Adored Mother:
The letters and correspondence that I sent to Yolanda and which

she shared with all of you makes me feel less anxious for not writing to each one of you. In the beginning I harbored doubts if I could write letters to persons other than Yolanda, but after a long wait we could send them November 17, 2002, and you received them December 12.

Since then I have been writing with more liberty and to many more persons. The first will always be Yolanda and my children, then you and the Oak, then my brothers and sisters and their families, concluding with answering the letters of all the persons who write us, among them the members of the cabinet.

Up to today, Gilberto and I have sent three packages of correspondence. You still have not received the second, in which, besides the letters, are sent two chess sets: one Gilberto sent for Camila and the other I sent for Danny.

What I feared the most has passed satisfactorily, and it was that you would receive our news, that you would know that they treat us well and that we enjoy perfect health (physically, because mentally never have we enjoyed it!) and valor.

We want you to know that we listen to those wonderful messages which keep us optimistic and hopeful. I also wanted you to know that, compared with yours, this is a five-star voyage.

The books you sent us have contributed to make this captivity a "summer camp" of studies in philosophy, history, literature, and poetry. Concerning these last ones, I'll tell you that we have devoured the three that have arrived. Yours, on Latin American poets, actually has good things but I'm a little slow in tasting it. The one by Silva really doesn't contribute to raising my spirits due to his sour vision of life. The Neruda book, which Yolanda sent me, offers a lot since it's written during his romantic period. Several of us have latched onto this one.

Those most enthusiastic about poetry are Navarrete, Pedro J. Guarnizo, Ledesma, and me. Of course I envy the persons who have such a natural gift to learn entire poems, because my memory is not very strong, lamentably.

I enjoy hearing from you, which brings a lot of solidarity and which contributes to maintaining our faith. Here the great deception has been the orchids, since I have seen very few, and I do not believe I have lost the capacity to recognize them. Since the majority of the marches are at night, this prohibits our seeing them.

I think that Toné would enjoy a time in the mountains, and if he were here, I can imagine a million things that he would learn, and us with him. (Of course I prefer to remain ignorant!)

I have two frustrations. The first is that despite the fact that on various occasions I have tried to write something in the form of an essay, I have not achieved anything that satisfies me. One would think that with all this "free" time it would be easy, but the reality is that there's a lot of noise and I suppose too much tension in the spirit.

The second is painting. I have water colors, but even with them, I don't have the faintest idea of how to use them and I don't want to "waste" the few sheets of paper that I still have.

Mother, I have had time to remember my childhood, and in doing so I ask myself how you permitted us to do all that we did; ride horses, go into the woods, hunt, fish, swim, etc. A great freedom and an immense confidence that certainly was molding our lives.

Looking back, and comparing it with the realities of the country and the childhood of so many fellow citizens, I really feel fortunate. If I could I would like to return and have the same childhood and offer it to my children.

Yolanda would have told you about Yolandita. I hope that God opens the way for this desire of both of us. The news about Danny and Matthew that Adelaida sent is wonderful, for my remorse as an absent father (doubly absent, before and now) has been calmed.

I hope you can help, especially Matthew with his reading, and that he loses the television habit. In my readings here I learned that in Argentina a child on reaching ten years of age has seen more that 85 thousand images of violence. If that is in Argentina, imagine the number that the children here see.

Television is, without a doubt, one of the biggest enemies of the people of our time; this avalanche of violence comes to compete with all that our educational system has achieved to digest/assimilate. It considers a "valuable part of our history," and a model that intrudes, as a paradigm for our youth.

One of the most solid demonstrations of the pacifist nature of the human being is precisely that, despite the intense brainwashing to which we submit our families (television), education, and daily life, we all do not end up being full-time assassins.

Well, I also attribute merits to your love and permanent protective presence. The Oak that resisted all the battles of time, and against that which collided the threats and dangers of our life was you, my adored mother.

Receive kisses from your son,
Guillermo

## LETTERS FOR YOLANDA PINTO DE GAVIRIA
### May 3, 2002

Adored Yolanda:
Love: I think of you each moment. I miss you so much, but I'm comforted in listening to you so strong and full of optimism. Your messages are life not only for me but also for Gilberto, and those of his family also touch me.

This space is very short to be adequate to the large circumstances. Also I feel so much the absence of Matthew and Danny. Give them my kisses and a huge embrace. We are in the hands of the Lord; his will be done.

To my dear mother, a huge kiss; I want to tell her that I am sure that her retention was a thousand times harder than this. They treat us well amid what is signified by being deprived of liberty. I very well know that my father was never in agreement with me regarding this event, and I hope that he accepts finally my expressed will.

To your family and our friends, I appreciate with all my heart the many expressions of solidarity. We have listened to all your messages on Radio Caracol on *How Medellín Woke Up*. Like when one loses one of the senses, the others sharpen. That is what we have done in our captivity: gained the opportunity to think more calmly about personal matters and those of the government.

We have listened to you, and it pleases us that the guard concerning nonviolence has not been let down. I am more convinced than ever that nonviolence is the way and that we should continue trying to guide Antioquia in that direction. The actions and statements about us should be framed according to the criteria of nonviolence.

One has only to look to Sweden, to the countries that have an audience and the masses of society to express freely and without hate, their sovereign will.

Love, I ask that you speak with Monsignor Rivera and that you take on the labor of visits that we were having.

Mi vida, on all the topics I have complete confidence in your criteria, that of Eugenio and companions of the cabinet. Help Martha Inés and especially Mono. It is a debt that I owe Gilberto.

Love, I know these are hard times, but I am sure that upon returning we can regain the time lost. It is interesting, but despite the distance, I feel we are together all day. I think of you and I remember the embrace I gave you when I said good-bye, then I heard your voice when you recited the rosary. I tell you that I am reciting it here every day, and it strengthens me and has been a great help to me.

I have thought of Papo. He would like this place. I cannot describe it, but I am learning things every day that tomorrow I will teach them to him and Matthew.

The fighters here treat us well. I don't want to worry you about my health. In the spiritual as well as the physical, I am trying to care for myself well. One could say I live a life almost "Gandhian," like when he was a prisoner.

I love you so much and I miss you a lot; I hope that God permits us to be together very soon, and also I hope that this captivity allows our message of nonviolence to help avoid so many useless deaths that occur in our country.

Lean on Father Yépez. He has a great soul and is an excellent comfort. I would like to hear him every so often. We are in the hands of the Lord. On him depends our return.

My sweet love, God bless you. I love you. A big kiss to all.

**May 5, 2002**

Adored Yolanda:
With much difficulty this letter will arrive on time. I want it to

celebrate Mother's Day that is coming soon. I hope you spend it surrounded by your children and Mafer.

A good thing about this captivity is that we have a lot of time to think and to reflect about the priorities in my life. Without a doubt, you and my children are the principal reason for my existence.

My vocation to serve Colombia and Antioquia takes on their real dimensions here. I believe that what we have tackled and tried to do through the government of Antioquia concerning the philosophy of nonviolence as an alternative to solve conflicts is appropriate and justifies the enormous sacrifice of being separated from you.

The love I feel for you helps not to go crazy in these circumstances, since I know that sooner or later God will permit us to be together again and recover the time we have lost.

We listen a lot to the news on *The Voice of Antioquia*, Caracol, and RCN, and it fills me with pride and tranquility to hear your statements about the progress of the government affairs.

Lean a lot on Juan Diego Granados and on Father Yépez, and support my mother. In all ways she is very strong, and I know that together you can sort out this test of destiny. I have faith that the FARC will understand and know how to appraise the message of nonviolence and social transformation that we share with them and moves us in this process, full of risks and also possibly misunderstandings.

True transformations in a society can be achieved when its foundations can be shaken, and this is much more difficult if one tries to do so without resorting to violence.

While I listen to the seriousness of the newscasts, I console myself to think that Gilberto and I, accompanied by all of you, do not stand by with crossed arms. Rather, we act according to the mandate of our conscience and in a way that is in accord with the planning of the campaign and with what I have been addressing with the Antioquenian people during these months of government.

I confess, love, that I am concerned at not being in charge to push more rapidly for the priority of housing, nutrition, reforestation, educational reform, Consistent Peace Plan, etc. projects. But at the same time, I'm satisfied to hear you talk and to listen to the statements of the cabinet members.

In regard to prayer, I am following the suggestions of Father

Yépez, and I also have *The Four Gospels* that he gave me. The force of the words of Jesus is surprising, along with how greatly they coincide with the plan for implementing nonviolence.

Please do not let the regional council of mayors fall. I don't know how your children will receive the news, but I hope that all of this does not affect them.

Send hugs and kisses to Papo and Mafer, and greet for me Daniel Ernesto and Óscar Mauricio [Yolanda's children]. Also congratulate your mother on her day.

My sweet love, if this letter reaches you someday, I want you to know and be certain that I'm going to love you more each day that passes until my death. And if I die here, I will do so thinking of you and struggling so that Antioquia and Colombia have a different, more just and peaceful future.

We are waiting for and want to try to see the phenomenon of the conjunction of the five planets. If you get this letter, it will probably arrive with another; Gilberto and I have written two letters each and each one of one page.

Love, I also ask that you share this letter with my mother, to whom I want to say that all you have taught us with your wonderful example helps me bear this absence with valor and confidence in God. Mother, on your day I will be thinking of the wonderful life that you have given all your sons and your daughters. In some way this experience helps me value much more your tribulations and the difficulties that in your time, I am sure, were a thousand times more difficult.

They treat us well here. Do not worry. God will reunite us, hopefully very soon.

This intense contact with guerrilla life, their ideals and reasons, constitutes a "brutal" induction for a way to see the realities of Colombia with different eyes. It has been an enriching experience. I hope we can fulfill our commitment and return to you all.

Yolanda, my love, I adore you. Mother, thank you for your love and your understanding. Kisses for all.

Also, to my sisters and sisters-in-law I send a huge kiss and embrace. God bless each of you on your day. You can share this letter with Martha Inés.

**From the Mountains of Colombia**
**June 12, 2002**
**For Yolanda Pinto de Gaviria**
**First Lady of the State of Antioquia**

Adored wife and my sweet love:

When we married, I remember I told you that "with this ring as a symbol of the union you entered my life to remain forever together with me and in the future will be my strength and my refuge." These words, love, each day in reality are made stronger.

When I hear your voice in the early morning hours on *How Medellín Woke Up,* I not only receive your message, which brings your words, I also wrap myself in your sweetness. I am comforted by the strength revealed in the tone of your voice. I am filled with pride by your clarity, prudence, and the generosity of your actions.

It calms me to know that my destiny and my dreams are bound with the gestations guided by your criteria and your love. Your emotional intelligence permeates the atmosphere and erases all the hardness of our captivity.

Finally let me stress how nearly each day's innumerable and wonderful examples and proofs of it feeds my confidence in your love, and makes it grow, occupying the space where anxiety, pain, sadness, and fear otherwise risk, as the days pass, taking possession of our hopes.

You, mi vida, like a triumphant gladiator, are defeating all the shadows that threaten our limited horizon. It can never be explained to me what your messages produce in us. They are for me the air that I breathe and keeps me alive, the light that keeps hope alive. You are my love, mi vida, and my whole heart and my life are yours.

I miss news from Matthew and Danny. I don't know if they know, but I imagine that it is impossible that Matthew does not know. I think that for Danny it has to be explained very well. I am sending a letter for each of them (please read them, mi vida).

If it is possible, send photos of them, as well as ones of you; I would love to have them to see every day. (It is necessary to have them laminated to resist the humidity.) Better yet, if you can, send photos of Papo and Mafer. The recent happenings make me think that our captivity is going to be prolonged; your messages and the photos will make our life easier here.

Love, I well know that these circumstances are harder for you all who are there, waiting for us and overwhelmed with the uncertainty of our survival and sufferings. Meanwhile we in the end receive your wonderful messages frequently, although the separation and sufferings torment us as it does you.

To try to alleviate this absence I daily write a little summary that I'm sending to you with topics that are conveyed through the news, the reflections, and some scattered thoughts that I've had. They are not literary pieces but only fill a little the emptiness of our absence.

Also, I'm sending you a letter that I wrote you for Mother's Day. Mistakenly, we thought they would arrive. However, now they arrived a little late, but with all my love.

Your messages also comfort me and please Gilberto, as do those of Martha Inés, Lina, Camila, and their children and daughters-in-law. They generate great optimism and courage in me. Please tell them of my enormous gratitude.

Love, if it is possible, I would be thrilled, it would be the best gift of my life, on returning, if you could have the recording of your messages, since they are my biggest treasure.

Love, I have thought of the economic difficulties that you could be suffering. If you have not done so, ask Ruth to give you the card and the code. I don't know what the situation is with my salary, but if they are consigning it, you can arrange for it with all freedom.

I don't know if it is possible, but it would be good if the bank would authorize your signature. If it is not possible, the card will allow you to manage the account. You can also sell the motorcycle and get rid of the lot in Guane.

My love, I'm sorry our inheritance is so scanty. You know that my goal never has been to accumulate riches. Now I lament that the economic situation is so precarious, and I have decided that, once I return, we will stop deceiving ourselves and secure an inheritance that will guarantee us a minimum of stability.

Princess, both Gilberto and I need you to send us some medicine. I include a list for you, and I believe it is necessary that they be packaged separately. I know that you sent a package but it has not arrived yet, so I don't know what it contains (a later note: now each one of us has received two packages).

My love, your actions regarding our captivity have been excellent. It seems to me to be wise to seek the help of the United Nations, and that the instructions Mary Robinson gave Anders Kompass are a good accomplishment. We also we appreciate so much the good will and efforts of the archbishop.

I think I should also thank those offering the multiple and massive expressions of solidarity. I imagine you are very active, and I'm pleased to think of you and know that you are heading it.

Please, have Mayor Luis Pérez receive our congratulations and thankfulness for the initiative and the results of the huge signing. I don't understand why it did not have more publicity.

I trust completely your criteria, my love, and the will of God. I continue convinced of the power of nonviolence. We cannot ask for or wait for miracles, but in the measure that the Antioquenian people begin to apply nonviolence in their lives, I know the way of peace will open and the social transformations will be rapid.

The mobilization of the real people, the marginalized people, who suffer the structural violence in the rural areas and the cities, can be explored. Social sectors and camps can constitute one very powerful voice (they are the real voice).

My love, I heard your message about Yolandita. I remain firm in my desire that we have a son or a daughter. If you are too, I think that you should take the necessary measures so that when I arrive, we will only have to take the "final step." It made me so happy to hear you say so; I hope that it is not only a phrase to alleviate the sadness of my captivity.

My love, please give a very big and strong embrace for me to Papo and Mafer and very special greetings to your children. To Papo, when I leave here, I have many things to teach him to go camping. You can imagine all that one learns living in the jungle.

I remember both of them every day. You should send me news about them, and I insist on photos. Mi vida, I do not want you to worry, really; they treat us well and the officials and sub-officials are really interested in caring for us well. There's all the more reason for you to be calm.

The medicine that we asked for is preventative and because it is not easy to get here. Concerning my spirit, your messages keep me in good form. And with the good humor of Gilberto, which never ends, the readings and prayers and the grace of God, I am very well and I can fight this adversity.

My love, finally, I ask you to give my mother an enormous kiss, and the certainty that this captivity is nothing compared to what she has suffered; that she be calm and not worry. Mother, receive a kiss and a huge hug from your son who loves you.

My love, please greet and send kisses and embraces to your mother and father, to your brothers and sisters, and to Liz, of whom you tell me nothing. I hope she accompanies you frequently in the apartment.

Mi vida, I love you with my whole heart and with all my strength. Soon we will see each other with the Lord's help. You are on my mind every minute. I adore you.

Guillermo Gaviria Correa

**ADDITIONAL SHEET FOR THE LETTER TO YOLANDA**
LIST OF MEDICINE AND OTHER NECESSITIES

My love, these are the medicines and requests. Please coordinate with Martha Inés so that, with specifications from Gilberto, you make two compact packages to help bringing them. Also, it is important that you send the instructions on using them. What affects me the most is the fungus (on feet, groin, and around the foreskin) and skin irritations.

**MEDICINE FOR BOTH OF US**
- Micofix (lotion)
- Canesten (powder and cream)—Quadriderm (cream)
- Strong antibiotics (to take)
- Vitamins (Centrum and Centrum Senior)
- Oral Serum (envelopes)
- Repellent (I understand that injections of B-Complex also serve)
- Camphor (to get rid of the snakes)
- Curarina (Martha Inés knows it. For ticks)

- Menticol/Alcohol antiseptic
- Creams for irritation and itching of the skin
- Antiofidic serum
- Glucantine (doses for one of us. Talk with Juan Gonzalo Lopez)

**MEDICINE FOR GILBERTO**
(Martha Inés also received instructions from Gilberto)
- Sun block (his tendency for cancer)
- Medicine for the prostate (consult his doctor)
- Medicine for gastritis

**SOME OTHER REQUESTS FOR ME**
- Photos (remember I said they should be laminated) yours and of Matthew and Danny and Papo and Mafer.
- Two pair of large, strong socks for boots (like for soccer, hopefully of cotton). Two or three underpants (my white ones, used, those for boots).
- Two long sleeved shirts (can be brown or green, strong). Okay with the one you already sent.
- Fish hooks, nylon, sinkers (I hope they let me fish). The fishing gear—remember? That which we bought for fishing, or something similar. I'm using size 42.

Mi vida, there are two additional things I want to include:

**1. Plan.** With Gilberto we began the constitution of a team between the government, the mayor of Medellín, and the private sector. Their responsibility is to select projects strategic for Antioquia and begin their structuring and execution. This task should not be suspended. The support of Luis Pérez is vital. Dr. Beatriz Restrepo de Gallego knows very well the needs and should move the topic. Please, make sure that those responsible for the state take up this topic with the necessary rigor and diligence.

**2. Visits to the Marginalized zones Fridays and Saturdays**: Love, as you know, they were being done by Monsignor Rivera. It seems to me important that you continue them. Please converse with the monsignor so that they are done with much care. The idea that I had was to program visits and assume small commitments; nutrition, educational support and topics of health, commitment to begin to exercise immediately.

Also, much can be done in improving housing. In short, I am sure that your sensibility and executive ability will greatly help. Also, I think about channeling help through the system of the Archdiocesan Food Bank.

The communication media have been very good. Please, send our gratefulness to the RCN, Radio Caracol, and Radio Todelar, and very specially to María Victoria Jaramillo, Oswaldo González, and Édgar Gallego O. for *How Medellín Woke Up*.

My love, today (June 13) I just heard your interview with Darío Arizmendi. Mi vida, you were wonderful. Here everyone congratulated me for having a wife so capable and loving. I adore you. Continue with this intelligent and sincere discretion.

Love, the officials and sub-officials have had the solidarity gesture of sending you a greeting and their voices of encouragement. It would be very desirable if you send them a response if it is possible.

**New:** For messages by radio you can continue with *How Medellín Woke Up*, hopefully after 7:00 a.m. since before that the signal is very weak. Also it would be very beautiful to hear you and the family and members of the cabinet, on *The Voices of the Kidnapping*, by Herbin Hoyos. Also on RCN, on the program *The Railroad Tracks* at 5 a.m. (from Cali).

**Mountains of Colombia**
**August 29, 2002**

Adored Yolanda:
Love, today we were informed that finally we can send correspondence. Since before making the video that you all know, I had prepared some letters that I will try to send, and I prepared these additional ones for Matthew and Danny.

The first thing I want you to know and that you keep in mind is that I love you immensely and that your love is a balm that cures all my anxieties and fills all the desires of my soul. Your messages each time calm me more, and the best gift is when I can see you, in the few opportunities that we have to see the newscasts on television.

Love, Gilberto and I are in very good health. You shouldn't worry about that. They treat us well, and in relation to food, lodging, and basic necessities of hygiene and exercise we are adequately taken care of. Despite the limitations characteristic of the circumstances, I would say we are doing "post-graduate" work in the simple life, austere nutrition, cohabitation with nature, and especially nonviolence.

Sincerely, I hope that you all are not worried about us. The love and solidarity that we have received from you and the families, as well as all the Antioquenian people, fill us with satisfaction. This makes us think that nonviolence can be converted into a valid alternative for building solutions to our social problems.

Love, we received two shipments (four packages). The first two arrived June 23 and the second two on July 17. It was wonderful to receive your letters, those of Aníbal, Irene, my mother, and those of Father Yépez; and equally those of Martha Inés. The books have helped us a great deal. I have especially enjoyed those of nonviolence, and I insist that you send me more, hopefully selected with the help of Mario López Martínez [University of Granada], about Danilo Dolci and his "Pedagogy of the Marginalized" and all that he can about "The Spring of Praga."

Nonviolence is not usually practiced by the government, so all that can enlighten us in that respect interests me. There is also an inclusive debate between Marxism and nonviolence which I would like to study more fully. In short I know that it is not an easy task, but I recommend to you texts along this line.

The video that you sent us is an excellent summary. I congratulate you all. According to the explanation the commander gave me, after we saw it, it was sent to the FARC secretariat.

To my mother, please do not suffer for us. We are fine, and like you say in your letter, "enjoying the walks." I would like to hear the children and my brothers and sisters once in a while, especially when you cannot send the messages.

Love, I tell you that the message that you sent Sunday, August 25, was wonderful, and we enjoyed it a lot. I also enjoyed, although they were very short and have not continued, the messages of the cabinet. I would like them to redo the messages and use them to inform the people and the governor.

To Father Yépez, a thousand thanks for his letters. I would like to know how to tune them in by radio and what days. We listen to mass from Frontino or from Urrao, but I would love to hear his sermons. Also, when he wants to, his messages can be made on the three radio channels: 1) *How Medellín Woke Up*; 2) *The Voices of the Kidnapping* (Radio Caracol); 3) *The Railroad Tracts* at 5:00 a.m. (RCN). Please, tell Archbishop [Alberto] Giraldo of our immense gratitude for all his good will and efforts.

I forgot; those texts on nonviolence must be photocopied and should be available to the cabinet. They can send us the photocopies.

I'm very happy to hear from you that they have fulfilled many contacts with people of nonviolence in the world. It is good that they continue and strengthen this task, love, since I propose to make an ambitious effort at the international level. So I hope they are thinking of an agenda for when I get out, and that they permit us at a national and later international level to arm a great team to strengthen and accompany our efforts and in particular that of creating a Latin American Center of Global Nonviolence.

Along this line, I have an idea rolling around in my head that has to do with the two projects for the Bellavista jail: the building of a farm, Liberty, and a new jail for the population of Antioquenian inmates conceived as a prison of nonviolence. In this sense instructions were given to Carlos Villegas, Luis Javier Botero, and Carlos Wolff to get land near the actual jail of the old farm of Tulio Ospina. I hope that this agenda is being acted upon. Better yet, designs and works should already be working very closely with the "work table" of the jail.

Recreation grounds, workshops, and classrooms for education, especially in occupations and decent lodging, are what I conceive as minimal elements for a jail that can house the inmates of Antioquia with dignity.

I propose, when I return, to spend a week "interned" in the jail, since I believe that this experience as a prisoner should signify an opportunity to evaluate and to better the conditions of those persons society punishes by taking away their liberty.

Love, the proposition of the government that we made to the

Antioquian people is very solid. Here, with the time I have had to think, I'm more and more convinced of this. I listened to the interview that María Victoria Jaramillo made to Eugenio [Prieto]. I see that my request is excellent; I have no problems, only recognition and satisfaction around the way you have been doing it. Please transmit to the team my gratitude for their work and for all the solidarity that we and our families have received.

My love, I hope that finally these letters can reach you, and you know that I listen to you each time you send messages; that through the news I follow all your actions and am pleased with your activity. I listened when you went to Bogotá, your interview on Radio Caracol, and I was so pleased with the way you conducted yourself and the way they treated you.

The sessions of solidarity activities, such as the great Liberty Chair, the mural and its record conformation, involved the participation of more than twenty thousand Antioquenians. I should recognize that these means of communication have been exceptionally solid. Please, I ask you to thank them for us.

The workday of July 11, when all the networks united to hear the testimonies of the families, and also the radio announcers of Antenna II during the Colombian Bicycle Race, we experienced as especially generous. By way of Baltasar [Medina], our thanks.

Love, if it is possible for you and Martha Inés, ask *How Medellín Woke Up* if they can pass messages around 7:00 a.m. or later, since we have difficulties hearing earlier because the station is hindered by Huila and Valle del Cauca. Only after 7:00 a.m. is the signal better.

It is possible that I will not send you the daily relating of the activities that I mention in the first letter. If you don't get it, don't worry. By the way, I suggest you review the spelling of the letters. You are missing some standards. I tell you that here, with the help of a dictionary, we are reviewing, and I'm going to return very sharp.

I love and miss you so much. Each day my last thoughts and my first thoughts the next day are of you. Don't cut short the messages. They give us life and hope. I would like to send you something daily. That is why I write to take them to you when I return.

Please get a little closer to Matthew and Danny. I sent a couple of letters to each one. You read them and give them a big kiss for them from me. For Papo, a huge hug and a kiss. (Now I remember, I want to bring them a gift—what do you suggest?) Also for Mafer, who I hope is doing well studying English. And please, send me news of them and all your family. I love you, mi vida.

Guillermo Gaviria Correa

**The Mountains of Colombia**
**August 29, 2002**

Adored Yolanda:
Love, I continue this letter inasmuch as I just finished listening to the program *The News of Antioquia*. They made very interesting announcements that I want to recognize; at the same time I would like them to inform more clearly and forcefully.

It has to do with Manna, Reforestation, and Housing. About MANÁ, I got that they have already begun with 47 thousand children in twenty-seven municipalities, and with the private participation of forty-eight percent, which removes a huge weight from me regarding how to avoid corruption and carefully measure and process the results.

It doesn't have to be said that the goal that we want to reach is all!—all the children of Sisben[46] 1 and 2. Congratulations to those responsible. I feel great joy at knowing that this dream is being realized. Please, don't forget to inform Antioquia about this; thus I will be informed and can follow the progress from here.

About reforestation, it was mentioned that we have allocated 1.7 million in forestry supplies, and that before the year ends we will be reforesting 5,000 hectares. Also excellent news.

Congratulations to Sergio, Gustavo, and Gonzalo, and to all those who are making this possible; please begin to study what I proposed about *chonta (macana)* palm. I also want them to inform me more frequently and in more detail about the advancement of the constitution for RIA.

Finally, on the topic of housing that was mentioned, sadly in such a brief way, that they advance allocations or projects for more than 9.0 billion. It is not clear to me if construction has begun and in which municipalities. How is the "housing value" going?

In short, I'm consumed with the desire to know in detail about the efforts and progress even as a doubt pierces me: Are we bettering housing in the Regional Council of Mayors of the North? Please, don't let these expectations be frustrated.

Love, in my first visit with Monsignor Rivera to the Carambolo and other neighborhoods, I wanted to highlight a school. Hopefully that will not be delayed. Please, speak with the monsignor, Eugenio, and José Fernando so that the work goes ahead.

Also, today I heard Dr. Iván Correa Calderón speak with much conviction about the program of "Universalizing the Internet." He did not mention the state and its decided and crucial support for the success of the program, but even so we have to get moving. I want to do so in San Pedro de Urabá and Pueblo Rico. The pledge is already so old, so please push it forward.

In short, these announcements have pleased me very much and made my day. I hope that this radio program will be stronger and will improve. Use it to tell them that the recordings are heard very poorly, and that for some reason, the programs are on some Saturdays and not others. It's a good effort, but it needs to be well done and better.

Mi vida, Gilberto and I miss news about the Consistent Peace Plan and in general about topics of the administration. Since there are so many channels it seems that they could ask the two secretaries to pay attention.

Love, today is Monday, September 2. For almost a week I have not heard your voice, and I have a deep sense of sadness and abandonment. I know I cannot let it advance, but it is beyond my strength. I hope that nothing bad is happening to anyone in your family.

I hope that you do not have problems. I beg you to not abandon your messages; I need to hear your voice. Perhaps you think I should not receive bad news, but you are mistaken. I am capable of resisting everything except silence and the false appearance of normality. Please, do not evade bad news by being silent. I prefer that you talk to me as you know how to do: with valor, strength, sincerity, and love.

Here one learns to look at the tragedies with more tranquility, and even coldly. But mi vida, I seek through the way of nonviolence to remain faithful to the truth and to be coherent in my life.

You, who are my soul, cannot function in a different manner. I love you and cannot live without your words. Here, every day I write you a little summary of what I do, think, or feel, so that on returning you can fill this emptiness that opens within me against my will. I cannot fill it with my voice or my presence.

I know it is not easy for you, but if you ask me to be strong, you should know that I will be that. But I need you to be strong and enduring. I dream of the moments we will live when we are reunited, and I think that later we will look at this voyage as an experience that taught us much about ourselves and strengthened our love.

I invite you, if you still want to, to take action on the matter of becoming pregnant. So when I return we can give the final step toward having our Yolandita.

You looked very beautiful the last time on television (Wednesday, August 28). Imagine my joy! I applauded, and everyone who was watching television (fighters) looked at me strangely. I was so happy to see you. Before I had seen you again, beautiful, in the video which they sent us, but that was a long time ago.

Mi vida, be certain that there is not a day that I do not think of you and the sensation of knowing that you are well. That I can count on you is what pushes me and encourages me to live.

You should know also that my love for you grows every day. I reread you letters frequently, and with the exception of the spelling, they are wonderful. I never tire of seeing them and reading them again and again. How it hurts me that I cannot make you know that I always listen to you. Even now, while I write, I have my doubts whether you will receive these letters.

I think that when the families who helped make the video receive correspondence of them, they will communicate it with you and will give you more tranquility, since they maintain their communication by radio. In short, I ask God to permit them to get to you quickly, because I know how anxious and uneasy you will be on not being sure that we hear you and that we are in good health.

Love, let me tell you that I am doing exercises almost every day, and I have lost a little weight. I still lack a lot, but it is not easy to get rid of the spare tires and big belly I have. Nevertheless, I hope to give you a big surprise when I return. Hasn't the treadmill that we asked

Duncan for arrived? I think that exercises also will make you better and pass the time.

I recommend that you read. You are not going to believe it, but I think I have completely overcome the vice of television. Now I know that we must take this horrible intrusion from our bedroom. What I have noticed here is my weakness for the different ways to eat corn. Here they know that when they give me an *arepa* (corn griddle cake), they bring me a double portion. I can imagine what popcorn would be like here. In short, it seems that the harvest is finishing, and I'm really going to miss arepas.

Love, I really felt the death of Hildebrando. Please give them my word of condolences.

Love, we have made efforts that they listen to our proposal to apply nonviolence in Antioquia, but, until now, we have not heard anything. I hope that the letter we sent to the commander of the block and the secretariat permit them to open the way for our offer to support a new attitude.

Nevertheless, I think of the immense inertia of the decisions by the FARC which makes it very hard to analyze and recognize the potential to transform the social aspect that we believe it has.

I am not going to die, but I think we will continue as political prisoners for an exchange of prisoners of the state.

In the news a great interest in public opinion is perceived, but I see little possibilities if a humanitarian accord is added on to the process of negotiations and peace.

We are in God's hands. His will be done, and my soul hopes that it's in his plan that we be reunited soon, mi vida. I love you and miss you very, very much.

Kisses

My sweet love, I want you to convince my mother to have her send radio messages with some frequency. I think this is a way of assuring her that I am well and that I hear her. Tell her that it is important that they are seen as content and strong, without hatred or resentments.

Have her tell me news of the family and things along that line, every two or three weeks, I believe this is a way to avoid her becoming too anxious over me.

Well, now I will end this letter, my princess; I send you my kisses, my love, my heart. My whole life is yours, loving Yolanda.

**Mountains of Colombia
October 11, 2002**

Adored Yolanda
My sweet love:
Yesterday I heard your last message in which you tell me of your time in Bogotá, and you speak of the need to prolong your stay to finish the gestations, and also you ask that we insist on sending our news.

As a divine work, the commander finally conceded our requests and told us that the departure of our letters had been authorized. The only thing lacking is to establish which channel, which we will know today or tomorrow.

I have reviewed what I wrote and I am sending the following:

LOT 1: Two letters for you for the celebration of Mother's Day and some requests, dated May 3 and 5, 2002.

LOT 2: A letter for you dated June 12.

LOT 3: A letter for you dated August 29.

LOT 4: Two letters for Danny also of June 12 and August 29. Two letters for Matthew, also of June 12 and August 29

LOT 5: The "diary" that I wrote, which goes from April 22 to August 29. I avoid including the last days, between August 30 and today, so that they don't run the risk of censoring the shipment. I continue writing it and will get it to you later.

LOT 6: Letters of greeting for you which the officials and sub-officials wrote, when we met for the video between June 12 and 13.

Love, I include a last letter of two pages on November 10. Proofs of survival.

Love, your messages on *How Medellín Woke Up* are wonderful. The same for what we hear Sundays on *The Voices of the Kidnapping* on the program *Waking Up In America*.

In the last few days I have noted your anxiety, and I want to reiterate that we are fine. You should continue with the strength and dynamism that are seen in your actions.

Congratulations, you fill me with pride. We heard the announcement about Nelson Mandela and also the news about the willingness of Archbishop Desmond Tutu to offer his services.

I dream of embracing you, hearing your free laughter and sharing my life with my wonderful Yolanda, and our Yolandita, and the boys.

In short, your love produces in me the necessary strength to resist and overcome whatever difficulty that could arise. If you happen to have the opportunity to send something, here's a list of additional things:

**BOOKS**
- About nonviolence: consult with Mario López Martínez (University of Granada), and Sofía (Guillermo's sister) can send them.
- Reports on the key programs (also the secretaries should try to send them by radio.

**MEDICINES**
- Vaccine against influenza (pills)
- Calcium supplements (very necessary; we don't eat anything that has calcium)

**CLOTHING**
I'm fine, although sometimes I am cold. Maybe a jacket from those that I have; used sweat suits (not bright colors). Socks to use with boots.

**ARTICLES**
- A good razor (jackknife) {to carve wood], although it could also be a good dagger. If possible a pocket saw (or if the jack knife has a saw). The jackknife should be large, but I'm not interested because it has many uses. It is to carve and it is important that they are two knives.
- Ropes. These are used a lot and are very scarce. The best are nylon cords, like those used on the canvas tents.
- Fine threads. White and black to mend clothes.

- Small batteries. For the radio you sent me.

**SNACKS**
- Candy (coconut), chocolates, sweets from Urrao (talk with Sergio Trujillo), arequipes (candy), (Colanta). Hopefully small and well packed in plastic bags.
- Cheese. Yellow cheeses, well cured, and that will make the trip (my weakness).
- Popcorn (to fry). What you sent was very little.
- Well, my love, I hope that soon we will be able to be together again. I love you, and only hope that God permits us, very soon, to be together again. Greetings to my parents and yours and to the families and all the children. Kisses to you and all my love.

P.S. Love, today it is already Sunday. I woke up listening to *The Voices of the Kidnapping*. I feel that you are very sad.

Send an embrace of congratulations to Papo; also send greetings to Antonio (Vargas), to Guillermo (Ángel), to Ana Rosa, and to Mercedes (Pinto). I love you and miss you so much. I enjoy your words so much. Good luck in the musical contest.

Guillermo Gaviria Correa

**Mountains of Colombia**
**November 10, 2002**

Adored Yolanda, my sweet love:

Princess, I am writing you a third letter in the hope that this time it gets to you. They have told us that the correspondence can finally leave, together with the video that contains the proof of survival (it is the second).

My love, I tell you that here there is a very positive spirit with respect to the interchange accord. They, as well as we, have the impression that it will bring positive results.

I do not want to appear a wet blanket, but I also want you to know that as long as I receive your messages and the love that you send in them, I can resist these afflictions and the sadness that I have in being separated from you and my children. If for some reason the accord ends up being defeated, we are prepared to endure it.

At any rate, among the fighters there is the conviction that these will be the last tests, and that before the end of the year we can regain our liberty.

In the early morning we could hear your beautiful message, and agree that the negotiations only have to be drawn up by both sides and the place has to be set for a process that, basically, consists of being in agreement as to how many and which prisoners should be freed.

In general, the messages of all the relatives reflect the same optimism and clarity concerning the real possibilities of the humanitarian accord.

Your messages, early Sunday mornings, are wonderful, and I love it that you do not let down your guard with them. All their information is very valuable for us and all the love and sweetness makes me bear this sad captivity.

The messages that I hear on *How Medellín Woke Up* also make me happy. Tuesdays and Wednesdays (which are the most repeated) I insist on messages from my brothers and sisters and more precise information from the members of the cabinet. I think they should, at least, give reports that they rotate among the secretaries and management in two months. These reports should be made with precision and in detailed form to permit me to be informed and up to date and at the same time inform the people of Antioquia.

Love, you insist that we try to talk with the secretariat. We have tried, not once, but many times, and it has been unsuccessful. Neither the service that we can give the national government nor our proposals for nonviolence and the openness and equanimity that we have maintained have interested the FARC. Their interest is in our value as prisoners of a political character and the possibility of exchanging us for some of their prisoners.

If you coordinate it with the families of the officials and sub-officials who are with us, it is possible that you can send some things through the Red Cross. It is a channel that has functioned for them in various occasions.

Love, I want to tell you how much I love you and miss you and how valuable your messages are—to hear your voice, to know that you continue active as usual, and that in every moment you are looking for ways to progress toward our liberation. It fills me with great pride and a peacefulness that makes this captivity bearable.

A few days ago I listened to your interview on Radio Caracol with Darío Arizmendi and María Lucía Fernández and it seems excellent to me. I love your spirit and the way they both treated you was really wonderful. At the end, the commentaries hit the mark about your beauty and the broach and the belt on the wrist with the Colombian flag. The way you expressed your sentiments around these simple but symbolic "adornments" was very beautiful.

Love, I want you to know that we are in good health. I would say astonishingly well. I do exercises daily, and I even bother some of the sub-officials, who in the beginning were enthusiastic about the exercise routine but later, one by one, dropped out. Gilberto also does exercises to keep in shape (but not so intensely).

One can say the food provides the nutritional requirements very well, but I think that it has a lot of flour and also a lot of grease (when there is meat). What I think is really missing is vegetables and calcium (milk and cheese).

At any rate, they treat us with respect, and now we pass moments of distress. There is good harmony, which only is interrupted sporadically, and this is understandable, given the stress that such intense, close, and obligatory living conditions generate.

You should not worry because of our health, which is excellent. The vigor you, Martha Inés, Lina, and the families of all those kidnapped give us is essential to our spirits. Your love makes me capable of overcoming any test.

I love you and hope to embrace you and share our daily lives soon. Tell me a little more about your children, your mother and father, your brothers and sisters, and of my family also.

I have noted the loyal way Eugenio has respected my confidence. You should let him know of my sincere and grateful recognition.

You should think a little about going forward with the necessary steps to become pregnant with our Yolandita. I would love to see you with a big stomach, caring for your whims and later taking care of our daughter and enjoying her growth and formation. So have the necessary consultations and make the decision as soon as possible, because we cannot postpone it beyond my return before this end of the year.

Love, I would also like you to think about what we will do on vacations. I would like us to take a few days for us to be together as a family, with our children, and that we do so in some pleasant place here in Colombia.

I received a recent letter in which you mention that you have had trouble sending it and tried five times. In it you tell me that the salary is coming in and you have been able to use it to take care of the most important commitments. I am glad. That is a relief since from the beginning it was a concern of mine.

I have decided not to send the "diary." I am going to wait and take it with me, since it is very long, and I write in very small letters, and I do not want to risk its not arriving due to difficulties in sending it.

Love, while we were waiting for the recording of the video to close the correspondence, the bishop of Zipaquirá was kidnapped. We are concerned, but we continue trusting God. I will continue writing you this letter until the video is filmed and we can send it to you.

Mi vida, today, November 15 (Friday) I listened to your message in which you tell me about the visits to Cáceres, Caucasia, El Bagre, and Zaragoza to check on the MANÁ program. I'm so pleased that we went ahead with this, and I hope we can reach the goal of the 100 thousand children for this year. Uniting our efforts, we should commit ICBF so that we achieve total coverage (if I'm not mistaken, 250,000).

In regard to the humanitarian accord, we remain optimistic, and we are supported in: 1) The attitude of the president, Álvaro Uribe; 2) The discretion of the UN (Lemoyne); and 3) The feeling in which we live through the radio and here itself.

I think a lot about Papo and about Matthew. I imagine how they will have grown when I arrive. It will be wonderful to again embrace and play with them. I have decided that I am going to take the chess set to them, but don't tell them anything, I want it to be a surprise.

In the beginning I began to carve you a gift, but the lack of tools and the hardness of the wood made me stop the work. I'm looking for a new piece to continue it for you.

I hope that very soon we can send you the video and these letters. It would be the best birthday gift the FARC could give me.

I love you immensely, and I miss you the most in all the world. Also, forget about the photo camera, it's not possible to use it here. Give all my love to my children and to yours. Greetings and kisses to my parents, brothers and sisters, brothers-in-law and sisters-in-law. Greetings and give a kiss to your mother, and embrace your brothers and sisters. A very special greeting for the whole cabinet and the nonviolence team. God bless them all.

Until soon, mi vida; my spirit, my soul, my heart goes with these short words that cannot express the beautiful love that I feel for you and the strength that your love gives me.

God keep you, mi vida. Kisses to Danny, Matthew, and Papo.
Guillermo Gaviria Correa

**Mountains of Colombia**
**January 17, 2003**

Adored wife, my sweet love:
First, I should clarify some "complaints" that I made in the earlier letter about the messages of our Antioquenian family. Now I began to listen to *The Voices of the Kidnapping*, and I believe that they will continue doing so. Including, according to what I listened to from Irene, they will try with Danny from Adelaida.

Also, about some reports like that of Carlos Wolff, who I reiterate my joy for his letter. By the way, we heard about his difficulties with the attorney general's office, and I want to express my confidence that it will turn out well. I, better than anyone else, can testify of the sensational and even revengeful spirit of some in these investigations.

I am tranquil and my confidence in Carlos has not suffered the most minimal variation because of this. If eventually the attorney general insists, I want him to know that my friendship and faith in the correctness with which Carlos worked is maintained.

About the letters that I received, love. Again, please thank those who sent them and tell them that little by little I will be answering them in the next remissions. Love, the readings and recent happenings suggest to me new topics that I include for you as follows:

Nonviolence: In the documents they sent me, the majority of the V Conference, many institutions are mentioned that in times past have been working more or less along our same lines. I believe it is necessary that Luis Javier Botero make an effort to "inventory" all these and other institutions and persons who work at reducing violence. This network has to be documented and strategic contact with which to strengthen the work needs to be established so as to make more powerful the valuable efforts of many people who share nonviolent ideals.

It doesn't have to be said that "all that glitters is not gold." One has to be careful, but I know that we can, with patience, begin to build a great team. One has to do what is correct in the broader context.

Aníbal and Sofía can help, and I suppose that Irene and Adelaida also, given the closeness of the people of the Martin Luther King Foundation. The coordination and diffusion of these efforts can permit us to play a key and valuable role to empower these and other efforts in favor of nonviolence.

Another topic that I think is forgotten is that of Bellavista and the Liberty Farm. I have a lot of expectations regarding the success of our project to better the circumstances of the prisoners and enhance their circumstances through nonviolence.

Two topics are what compose this project: 1) building a new jail, having in mind all that we talked about of recreation, education, and sports and work; 2) buying land (Guarne) and building the Liberty Nonviolence Farm.

I consider this less difficult than achieving the commitments allowing transfer of prisoners who are really converted at the end of their sentence. This is a process of change and growth that permits them to reincorporate themselves in a productive and decent way into the life of the community. Luis Javier (Botero) and Juan Manuel (Restrepo) can achieve this proposal if it is proposed; it would be a good first nonviolence project.

Love, for quite a while the idea has been rolling around in my head that the Christmas gifts (balloons) be complemented with bicycles. I understand that in Bellavista they are being built. What I thought is that they can be combined in the following way: Antioquia has 7,000 schools. If fifteen thousand bicycles can be financed, we can give them to the best male and the best female students.

They should be from the first or second stratum, and for the basic primary courses, about under ten years of age. The numbers can vary, but I think we can aspire to distribute between ten and fifteen thousand bicycles. That's easy to say from here, since I have nothing else to do!

I love you. Love, I also send you a couple pages of the book by Gene Sharp that José Ricardo Villadiego sent me. I marked with an X the books by the same author that I am interested in. If it is possible, get them to me, together with the second and third parts of the same book. Hopefully in the Spanish version, if that is possible.

EDUCATION: In the magazine *Semana* of December 9, on page 154, entitled "Weaver of the Future," the Santo Domingo School of Art and Vocations directed by María Isabel Restrepo is presented. It really caught my attention, since the occupations are the central topic of our transformation of the educational system, and also it is clearly indicated in the essay on education that Gilberto is sending.

In this school, where they offer four occupations, 700 students study. We can imagine what Antioquia could do through the Poly[47] and the technology with the help of Sena[48] and the ITM, that I heard today can offer free job training.

If we could offer something like twenty occupations we could easily open them to productive options for about 5,000 young people who most desperately need to escape from otherwise tragic destinies. Gilberto mentions that there are more than 800 jobs from which they can choose. But, please, don't make future plans. The plan has to be made, then get to work.

Around the topic of jobs, and another that goes along with it, the dignification of work, I would like to ask Eugenio to try to change the mediocre and confusing custom that is very rooted among the public officials to call everyone "Doctor."

It can be insisted that all the secretaries communicate according to title, such as engineer, lawyer, physician, etc, instead of "Doctor." This should be reserved for those who have actually completed the requirements of study, besides an undergraduate degree, including the respective postgraduate degree and completing a doctoral thesis or a PhD. It can seem trivial, but thus we will begin to undo the hypocrisy that has us calling things by mistaken superlatives.

Regarding free education and taking advantage: There are various "surprises" in which the governors of some states and the mayor of Medellín announce their offer of "free education," and in certain cases obligatory, as recent developments and achievements without equal in history.

I just found two pearls: 1) Data of the efforts of the radicals for education. In 1870 the president, Eustorgio Salgar, decreed the "free obligatory primary education in all national territory as well as giving it a character of religious neutrality." How would Colombia be if the things which were decreed by its leaders were fulfilled?

2) Love, imagine the first efforts to make equality of sexes in the classroom a reality in the continent. Guess where? In Vélez, Santander, in 1853 the provincial legislature Constitution of 1853 voted to extend the suffrage to women, because the masculine universal suffrage was just approved in the new Constitution of 1853.

That was sixteen years before it was achieved in the United States, in the first state that accepted it. Would that have something to do with the fame of the Santanderians? Too bad the Supreme Court killed this initiative.

The culture and all that we do for it, to promote the cultural flourishing, to make us more conscious of our roots, and the potential of our territory and our people, our artists, and thinkers.

Guillermo Gaviria Correa

**Mountains of Colombia**
**March 15, 2003**

Adored Yolanda and my sweet love:
Princess, I write you this letter to try, with urgency, to take care of the shipment of Glucantine (medicine for skin disease).

You can be relaxed concerning me, and tell the same to Martha

Inés. But some of our officers and sub-officers are suffering, and it is necessary that the drug be obtained, since the remedies they are applying are only generating very partial results.

This petition has been authorized by the FARC-EP, and thanks to that we can attend our companions. Love, I reiterate that neither of us has been affected, but our companions have been suffering for about two weeks. Of course we are carefully caring for ourselves, but it is really desirable to have the possibility of receiving treatment the moment in which we might be infected. It would also be good if you could send technical literature about this illness to see if we can avoid it or at least minimize its risks.

We need doses for six adults about seventy kilos each. The most practical way for the shipment is through the attorney general of Antioquia (Dr. Girlesa), and with the help of PAS (Air Program of Health), I refer to the helicopter. She will receive instructions and based on these instructions will make the shipment, helped by the helicopter and the team of PAS.

This topic should not extend to public opinion. You should do so with all discretion. I think you can get it from PAS itself, or the secretary of health (in reality, they are both the same). I trust you.

Availing myself of the opportunity for us to communicate, I ask you to send us the following:

1) Spanish dictionary. That of the *Real Academia de la Lengua* that Gilberto gave me. Two small volumes, which I have in the office.

If you can, with it send some notes on reading and writing, since we have obtained authorization by the commanders to give Spanish classes (reading and writing) to the fighters.

2) English dictionary. A good English dictionary with explanations in Spanish. Let me explain: words in English and their description in Spanish. I'm thinking of the weight to send them, but look for the best. Hopefully that has standards and all that pertains to the language.

3) A good course in English. Above all, the texts. Videos and cassettes or records do not help us. I'm interested in the texts to guide in teaching.

4) Antiophidian serum. In the previous shipment (December)

they sent some and it has saved a life. I ask you to send the three decanters we have used. If you can send more, it will be beneficial.

My love, I am sending you the last pages of the diary, by the generous authorization of the commander. I tell you that today the same commander gave us the last shipment, with your letters and candies. I still haven't finished reading them, but the topic is so urgent that it cannot wait.

Tonight we will be listening to your message. The last two days have been wonderful. Your received the tests, and now we can send you this new communication about the urgency of the medicine.

Love, keep in mind that other letters are on the way, and the second part of the diary as well as the chess set for Danny.

Tell my mother that I adore and miss her, to have faith, and that in the next shipment I will write her with special love. In the second package is a letter for the Oak which she demands.

Love, the cheese and (edible) ants are a sensational surprise. The problem is that these ants—I don't want to share them, since in each one of them I feel that I am eating it at your side.

The news of Danny and Matthew fills me with happiness. The "letter" of Matthew (with the help of Adelaida) made me bawl like a baby. The letters of Dr. Glenn Paige fill me with valor and pride because I think that the mere consideration of a person like him and what he wrote about us are an enormous recompense. I hope that both are taken care of by their consignees, not in consideration of us but of the stature of the one who wrote them.

Love, the officials and sub-officials send you greetings. They excuse themselves for not sending you notes. You will know how to understand the haste. I ask you not to worry the families. If the medicine arrives soon, no major thing will happen and everything will be controlled.

Mi vida, greet all our relatives (Antioquenians and Santanderians) the friends and the cabinet.

Love, I quickly read your letter, and I'll pass on some thoughts that are rolling around in my mind.

In the first place, get sadness out of your mind. Every day my love is stronger, and to think of you gives me all the hope in the world. You should know that in each moment of the day I have you in my mind and my heart.

I trust your words, and I know that you will know how to overcome these difficult moments that come full of nostalgia and in those that seem that life is not worth living. I promise you that you can be tranquil, since neither will my love change nor will strength suffer a notch until we can embrace each other again.

The reading, the classes that we could begin, Gilberto, the officials and sub-officials, the army, the good progress of the government, and the health of all of you fill me with resilience and I think can alleviate any pain.

Additionally, nonviolence under your leadership continues spreading and growing among the Antioquenians and Colombians. All this adds to our well-being until we are together and share true happiness.

I trust in your words. You know and I know that each word that you send, above all on Saturdays, is full of content and chosen with care to describe with precision. I fully trust your criteria and actions and the wise support of Eugenio, Aníbal, and Guillermo Gaviria Echeverri. The humanitarian accord can be achieved and the appropriate way is through the Facilitating Commission.

I trust in Monsignor Castro as the person most adequate and capable, and his two companions also are very trustworthy. I have faith and patience. They will persevere.

Love, I have stopped smoking, and I congratulate you that you have done so. My silence was that I only learned of it in December. I love you and I feel proud of you. Cigars are another story. One every so often. I received the first shipment (December).

Edith Cecilia is wonderful. Antioquia and EPM are fortunate that she is the new director. I feel pleased that she assumes this responsibility, and I believe completely in her ability and her advantages over any other director. (Certainly I admire the ability of Iván and I consider that he has done well.)

Concerning the march to Caicedo, you will find arguments in the newspaper. My only observation is the following: Before it takes place, you should be certain that the FARC-EP does not see it as a slap in the face or a retaliation or challenge.

This can only be achieved if they talk with the command of the

José María Córdova block. If you don't manage that, my thinking goes against the commemorative march. If you achieve it, I am with you and in favor (correction: I will always be with you, mi vida.). It is important to understand it like that, not for fear, but because nonviolence still has a lot of steps to climb before touching the doors of subversion.

Finally, my love, I would like Juan Fernando Mesa to remain in the FLA.[49] I think it is not the time for changes, and he has to be able to finish his task. I'm inclined toward Pedro Juan González for Finances, and I'm strongly attracted to Federico Arango for Secretary of Commerce.

At any rate, I trust in the criteria of you all and of Eugenio. I believe that Wolff can help in this selection. It is necessary to resolve that of the Beneficence of Antioquia. At any rate, the Secretary of Finances should be someone who understands what needs to be done and the priority of the key programs. They should reread the comments that I sent earlier.

Love, I should end. I am running out of time. I love you and miss you. Only the certainty of your love keeps me alive. Receive all my love. Hugs and kisses from the depth of my soul.

Guillermo Gaviria Correa

## LETTER TO FATHER

Dearest Father:

I remember in the beginning, when I began to think of the march to Caicedo, conscientiously I avoided talking with you about the topic, since I knew that you would not agree with my proposal.

The whole process of preparation and promotion was taking place, but I preferred to keep you on the margin. I think that is how you understood it, and with resignation you respected my decision, not without seeing that you thought it was dangerous and useless, or of little use. You were right; I always knew that.

You were also right regarding my well-being and that of our family and loved ones; in what has to do with the ability to continue with my responsibilities of governing, giving me strength to correct the direction of Antioquia and fulfill the proposals given by the people of Antioquia; in the small possibilities that you expected the FARC-

EP to understand the great opportunity that this march of nonviolent reconciliation offered them.

The FARC-EP decided to not listen to the clamor for nonviolence that Antioquia was beginning to feel. They preferred to take us hostage, taken away our liberty, along with the possibility of continuing to work for the building of a good, honest government committed to the most needy.

Despite the limitations that this captivity imposes, I believe, nevertheless, that some of my initial proposal has been preserved, and, if so, passes my own expectations. It has to do with the diffusion of the philosophy of nonviolence among the Antioquenian people. Usually we want to achieve social transformations in a matter of months, when these transformations require generations and also a little or a lot of luck.

I'm conscious, father, that to sow and promote such a demanding way to understand our role in society constitutes a challenge that will require a life commitment; and I also know that in Colombia there are many people, among our own leaders, who believe that we are too violent to achieve our way of thinking the ideas that have moved people like Gandhi, Martin Luther King, and Jesus Christ himself, which would allow us to modify our way of acting, of facing injustices, problems, and violence itself.

Call it stubbornness. I prefer to think of it as perseverance. I continue thinking that, sooner or later, the Antioquenian people, and why not all Colombia, will look for the support that only nonviolence offers.

Amid captivity, it is comforting to me, the perception of having contributed to making nonviolence an alternative route, or even a complementary path, that would make our people think about the urgent need for a change in attitude.

It comforts me that our captivity has served to shake and maintain interested the national opinion about the fate of the thousands of kidnapped persons, especially those of the military, who as they themselves claim: "Never before have they been interested, not even the FFAA (Armada Forces) not the Colombian people, for which they struggle."

I am conscious that my actions have consequences that affect others; these consequences are very hard and sad for you, my mother, and all the family; for my wife; and very much so for Matthew and Danny.

Perhaps this is the true reason that I really felt hindered in writing you earlier—the deep feeling of guilt that intimidated me overwhelms my soul; I know that because of me you all are suffering and constantly worried.

I would like to ask your pardon for not taking you into consideration and for making you pass such terrible moments; indeed I believe I should ask forgiveness of everyone else.

On the other hand, what then is the correct action of a leader in Colombia if his convictions incline him toward nonviolence? Should he always avoid the danger in order to safeguard the family from suffering and pain? How does one arrive at a healthy equilibrium between security and the risk that involves the tasks of the leader of today in Colombia?

Is it possible to govern on the basis of nonviolence, without running the risk or mixing with violence that, in diverse forms, grows in our territory? How to face the injustices, to unmask them and overcome them, if we are permanently and principally worried that they don't touch us, that we be safe?

Isn't it precisely this small fortress that we have built around each government official to guarantee his/her security that impedes him/her from seeing the reality that the rest of those governed live daily? In short, I have asked myself many questions, and I lament that I have to say that I do not have all the answers; only some, and I fear that they are not very encouraging in the short run.

My conviction about the convenience of spreading and promoting nonviolence in Antioquia has been consolidating, and I can say it is growing stronger. It is not in converting nonviolence as a tool to transform the attitude of the FARC-EP.

Before aspiring to achieve that, it is necessary for the people of Antioquia to recognize and receive it, at least in an imperfect way. Really, we as a society need to overcome our faults and transform the reality that overwhelms so many people in Antioquia.

Here I have meditated on the leadership that I could exercise over my fellow citizens. The message that I can and want to give them is that of the transforming force of nonviolence, its capacity to make flower the best in human beings even in the worst of circumstances, and that we begin to create a conscience and commitment to work for a more inclusive and just country without the need to resort to violent actions.

There is too much violence in our customs and even more in the ignorance that even the Antioquenians who have the opportunity to go to school are subject to. Our traditional leaders and government officials have achieved in teaching us to make hypocrisy a strategy for success.

I feel that today the politics that predominate in our times seem to have as a standard the motto "The end justifies the means." And for me this maxim is neither valid nor acceptable. If we want a noble end and we desire to consolidate it and have a true social transformation endure, we who assume the responsibility to govern and direct must "watch our means" even more.

Our task, then, if we want a New Antioquia, is to open the door to the possibilities that nonviolence offers in all areas of life in the community: family life; education; relationships between people, the community, and the nations; the struggle against poverty; the inequality and the building of the progress of our people with human criteria.

I believe in the capacity of nonviolence to transform behaviors and attitudes. This can help us to generate other forms of doing politics and new models for social solutions. I feel we cannot continue accepting the "inevitability" of violence, nor the "spontaneity" with which we resort to it. Nonviolence, as Mario López says, allows us "to think of the human being as capacitated and not limited in nature."

"Capable to pursue the most elevated ideals and the best solutions." These words almost replicate that which I proposed in my campaign for governor. Now I have to share them with the people by being an example, and that is what I have done in suffering in my flesh the unjust torture that the Colombian people suffer: the kidnapping.

Well, dear father, these are some of my reasons, those I could not leave unwritten. I hope you forgive me the melodrama that could have remained and let me pass on to other topics.

I have heard about the advances in VIVA, and it seems to me that the hour has arrived for your proposal for housing to be converted into the real economic accelerator that the country so desperately needs. It is hard for Antioquia that Josué is leaving us for Bogotá, but if he leaves with the purpose of making the "Plan Gaviria" a reality, it seems to me that the sacrifice is completely justified and also can help to consolidate our pilot project with VIVA.

I would like to know how you see these advances in the state about housing and how you see these new developments.

I know the law still has not come out, but I trust that it now will be a reality. The urgent need to generate employment also will be an inducement for the national government to give the necessary support. I hope that all these circumstances finally, after forty years of being conceived by you, permit this "Plan Gaviria" to become a reality.

I consider it three reforms in one: The social, since it will attend the needs of housing and employment for about five million families; the economic, since it creates a new structure and give a serious push to economic growth; the urban, since it permits planning for the growth of our cities and rural areas.

The topic of food security: Our program already attends more than 55,000 boys and girls in strata 1 and 2 who did not participate in any other program. I had hoped that in 2002 we could reach 100 thousand, but we are only starting, and the program has a structure a little more complicated than what you propose for the milk program.

Where your help is clearly felt is in the participation of Colanta. I feel very pleased and content because I believe that this helps to consolidate the social balance of Colanta, converting it into a valuable ally of the social progress of the Antioquenian people, transcending the environment of the milk-producing communities to cover all the state territory.

A thousand thanks, in the name of the Antioquenian people, to you, to the Directive Council, and to Genaro for this contribution, which I am sure will continue growing with the program.

In summary, I feel very pleased because, despite my absence, the key programs are going ahead and particularly these two, which signified my greatest desires, since the third has another sorrow which makes me feel very tranquil: Aníbal.

Being here, amid simplicity and routine, can teach a lot to a human being as long as he/she is willing to learn. Jokingly, we talk about ourselves doing various post-graduate programs: that of tolerance and adaptability, in a supremely ascetic way of life; another about nutrition, since we have been able to prove how much the diet can be reduced without the body failing—and I have thought a lot about how much you like rice, here I have learned to value it, and I consider it a true dish.

When they give us rice, I do not eat all of it. I keep a little for the next meal, the same as I do with *arepas* (grill cakes); that way they are kept for several days. One could do an extended study about flora and fauna, but for that one would need a great teacher like Toné.

In the meantime I have learned and enjoyed the flora little, since I haven't even seen orchids. So I could speak of other infinity of small post-grads, with such luck that I am not totally wasting my time here. Also I teach English to the officials and sub-officials, and with much stumbling and with the help of a little dictionary, I try to improve my spelling (as you see, with little success).

Dear father: I would be very pleased to hear you as opportunity permits, or if that's not workable, to receive news from you. There are some radio programs *The Railroad Tracks* at 5 a.m., RCN and *The Voices of the Kidnapping* on Caracol where they receive written messages, whether faxes or e-mail and they transmit them to the kidnapped persons.

I do not expect you do so frequently, but it would make me very happy to hear you every so often; if it is not possible for you, I will understand. In that case, Yolanda can pass on to me some words about how things are going in your battles.

Yolanda told me that she shared the diary with you. I hope that you are forbearing, since my interest was not in producing a literary work but filling the space of our separation. I hope it helps you to know how our life goes on here and that it calms you concerning the risks that affect us.

Father, I have tried to produce writings that can serve as articles, but I have not achieved anything that satisfies me. I'm going to continue the effort but don't have any illusions.

For obvious reasons I have not gone deeply, in earlier letters, into my appreciations and positions on current topics and controversies. Now I think that the conditions are a little more favorable and I can write with less apprehension.

In the newspapers that have arrived and I have been able to read, it comforts me to see that your strength continues intact. Also I am informed about the trip of Aníbal and his inexhaustible agenda of efforts about my captivity. I am certain that this tiring work is bearing fruit and will certainly be the beginning of interesting projects. My gratitude is great, since I am sure that your support has in a large way made it possible.

The FARC-EP do things much more slowly than we citizens and rulers do. It is probable that our captivity will be prolonged, and I don't want you all to become desperate.

It is better, then, to be prepared in advance for a much longer separation. While the conditions you all, Gilberto, and I enjoy permit us a fluid communication, circumstances are also difficult, and I have seen little to suggest they will easily change.

At any rate, dear father, I wanted to express to you in this letter that everything I have been able to become in life so far owes much to trying to meet the high standard of the teachings that I received from you and from my mother; if on the way I have committed errors, these are my fault.

I love you and daily remember you with tenderness. I miss you enormously, and it deeply hurts me, this pain I cause you all. I hope you all know, through this letter, that I am fine and will resist everything to embrace you again.

Receive a strong embrace from your son who loves and remembers you.

Guillermo

# NOTES

1. *Trans. notes*: Alexander von Humbolt was a German naturalist who traveled in Latin America between 1799 and 1804.
2. Governor Gaviria is playing with words: Antiochian (from Antioch, Syria, in the New Testament) and Antioquenian (from Antioquia, Colombia).
3. Colombian novelist, essayist, and politician.
4. *Bandera* (flag) projects is an effort to train children as young entrepreneurs, leaders capable of creating their own businesses after leaving the school year.
5. *Marquetalia Republic* was a small rural socialist society, an area of 300 square miles in the state of Caldas, Colombia, between 1959 and 1964, held by the fighters. It was destroyed in 1964 by the Colombian army with participation of the USA in the Plan Laso (Latin American Security Operation).
6. *Paisano* is a native from the states of Antioquia, Caldas, Risaralda, and Quindio. The term is used for countryman, a friend from Colombia.
7. An armed group of the FARC.
8. A popular folk music from the Colombian Caribbean region.
9. Folk music from the mountains of Colombia.
10. Dairy Cooperative of Antioquia.
11. It is committed to advocate drama pedagogies and theater education to establish arts-based pedagogies and artistic education throughout every level of education.
12. United States Ambassador to Colombia from 2000 to 2003.
13. Housing Authority of Antioquia.
14. National Administrative Department of Statistics.
15. National Association of Financial Institutions.
16. Colombian Family Welfare Institute.
17. Macana palm or *Weltinia Kalbreyeri*.
18. Capital of the State of Huila.
19. Second city of the state of North Santander.
20. Sectional Health Service of Antioquia.
21. State Alimentary and Nutritional Improvement Plan. MANÁ means *manna*.
22. Carlos Castaño was founder of the Peasant Self-Defense Forces, an extreme right paramilitary organization that later became the AUC (United Self-Defense Forces of Colombia).
23. *Leishmaniasis* or Black Fever, a serious skin infection produced by a sand fly.
24. National Institute of Roads.
25. National Radio Network.

26. Colombian national instrument like small guitar with twelve strings.
27. International Monetary Fund.
28. Project Counseling Service.
29. Public Enterprises Medellín.
30. Many historians agree that "*La Violencia*" was the most brutal and bloody period of Colombia's modern history. The assassination of the liberal presidencial candidate Jorge Eliézer Gaitán (April 9, 1948) marks the beginning of "La Violencia." It was some twenty years of partisan conflict, especially among the peasants, and the beginning of guerrilla groups.
31. Chontaduro, fruit of the palm *Batris gasipaes*. In Costa Rica it is known as *pejibaye*, *pijiguao* in Venezuela, and *chonta* in Bolivia.
32. The plan deals with the attention of "every day" of the conflict, secondly with the pedagogy of nonviolence, and thirdly with the construction of the Social Pact for coexistence and development for peace.
33. Industrial Reforesters of Antioquia.
34. Air Program of Health (*Programa Aéreo de Salud*).
35. Capital of the state of Atlántico, the largest port in the Caribbean region of Colombia.
36. Secretariat of Education for the Culture of Antioquia.
37. Published by Xlibris, 2002, available online at www.nonkilling.org.
38. Pedro Antonio Marín, known as Manuel Marulanda and for his nickname "Tirofijo" (Sureshot) one of the founders and main leaders of the FARC. In 2006 the U.S. State Department placed $5 million dollars reward on his head or information for his capture.
39. Liquor control in Antioquia.
40. Capital of the state of Meta, southeast of the country.
41. Community of reflection after Gandhi.
42. Radio of Colombia with international music.
43. French: *Gauguin is not Gauguin*.
44. Wild plant.
45. Metropolitan Technological Institute.
46. System for Social Programs in Colombia.
47. The Polytechnic, public university institution.
48. National Training Service.
49. Factory Liquors and Spirits of Antioquia.

# THE EDITOR

James F. S. Amstutz (D.Min.) is Pastor, Akron Mennonite Church, Akron, Pennsylvania. He serves as the Missional Church Development Coordinator for the Atlantic Coast Conference and chairs the Homes of Hope-Ephrata district committee, a transitional housing ministry for homeless persons.

Jim and his wife Lorraine Stutzman Amstutz (Co-Director of the Mennonite Central Committee US Office on Justice and Peacebuilding) had the privilege of attending the First Global Nonkilling Leadership Forum in Honolulu, Hawaii, November 1-4, 2007. At this historic event, forty people from twenty countries gathered around the central conviction that a nonkilling society is possible. One of the honored guests was Colombian Senator Yolanda Pinto de Gaviria. In conversation with Yolanda and former Nonviolence Director for the state of Antioquia, Luis Javier Botero, Jim learned of Yolanda's desire to bring her late husband's story to an English audience. This set in motion the collaborative effort that has produced this work.

Jim is the author of *Threatened with Resurrection: Self-Preservation and Christ's Way of Peace* (Herald Press, 2002). He and Lorraine co-authored a chapter in *Making Peace with Conflict: Practical Skills for Conflict Transformation* (ed. Schrock-Shenk and Ressler, Herald Press, 1999). His doctoral dissertation focused on the interaction between leadership, ecclesiology, and community to bring about missional transformation at the congregational level. Jim and Lorraine have three young adult children and make their home in Lancaster County, Pennsylvania.

# THE AUTHOR

Guillermo Gaviria Correa was born on November 27, 1962, the son of a prominent Colombian family. Trained as an engineer at the Colorado School of Mines, he served as General Director of the National Institute of Roads (INVIAS) in Colombia. Running as the Liberal Party candidate, Gaviria was elected governor of Antioquia by an unprecedented majority on October 28, 2000.

He married attorney Dr. Yolanda Pinto Afanador on August 11, 2000, Antioquia's Independence Day. She was a campaign colleague and former General Secretary of INVIAS. It was the second marriage for both.

In 2001, convinced of good government's responsibility to meet people's basic needs, the governor diagnosed the cause of Colombia's violence as socioeconomic injustice. Inspired by his Christian Catholic faith, he began to study Kingian and Gandhian methods for nonviolent social change. Dr. Bernard LaFayette Jr., a close associate of King's, became an important consultant and mentor.

From April 17 to 21, 2002, accompanied by First Lady Yolanda, Governor Gaviria led a sixty-five mile people's march with one thousand participants from Antioquia's capital of Medellín to Caicedo, a mountain town harassed by FARC guerrillas. This unarmed march intended to show solidarity with the people of Caicedo and to engage the FARC in nonviolent dialogue. It was reminiscent of King's Selma March and Gandhi's Salt March.

On April 21 Governor Gaviria was kidnapped by the FARC along with Peace Commissioner Gilberto Echeverri Mejia, a former minister of defense and governor of Antioquia. Also captured were Dr. LaFayette and Catholic priest Father Carlos Yépez, but both were released soon after.

After over a year of captivity in the jungles of Colombia, the administration of President Álvaro Uribe launched a rescue attempt on May 5, 2003. Governor Gaviria and Gilberto Echeverri were killed by the FARC along with eight other prisoners. This book is the diary and collected letters written by the governor during his kidnapping.

Breinigsville, PA USA
29 March 2010
235143BV00001B/15/P